60 SUPER BOWLS

CHAMPIONS

THE GREATEST MOMENTS
OF THE BIGGEST GAME IN SPORTS

60 SUPER BOWLS

ALLAN MAKI &
DAVE NAYLOR

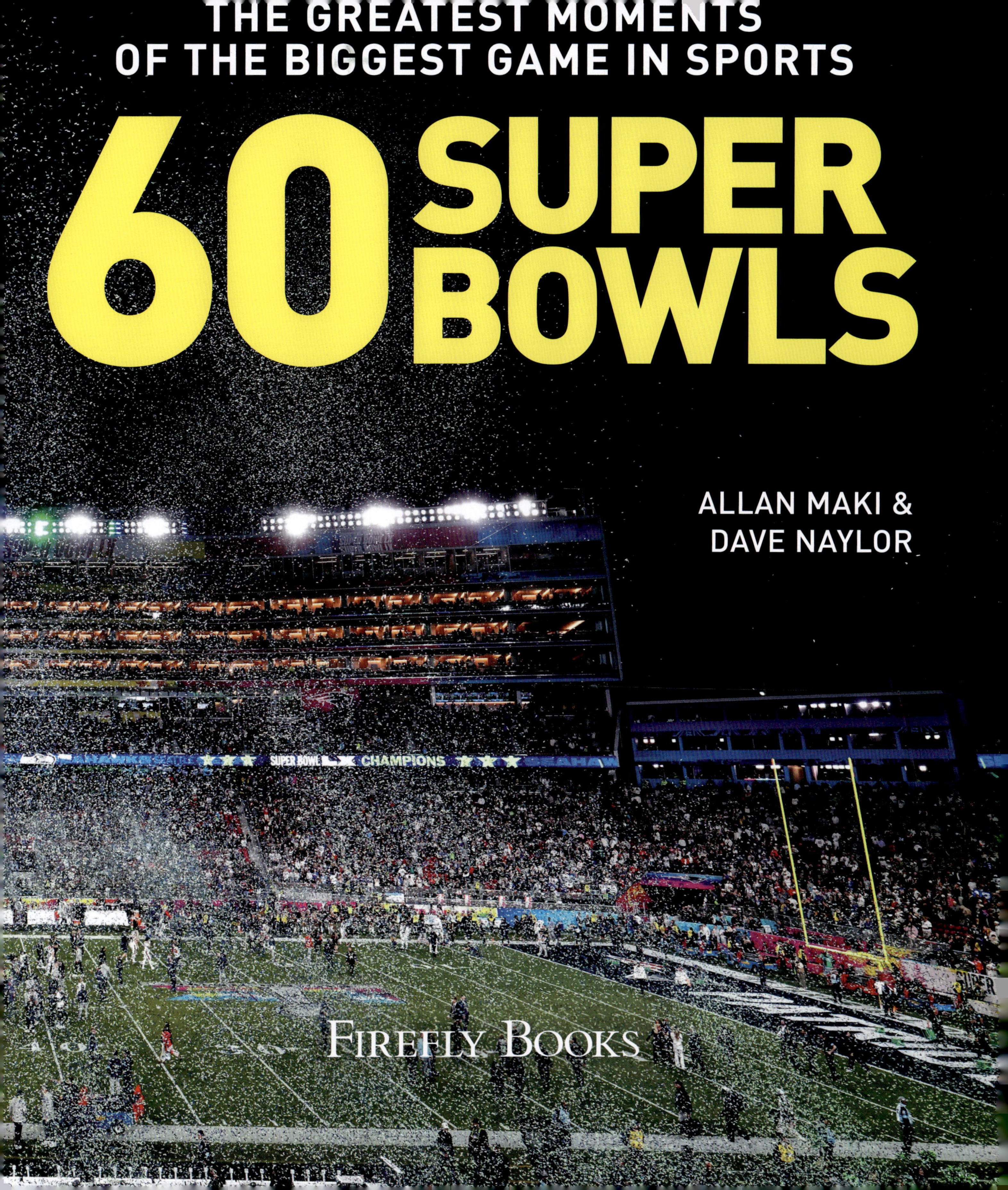

FIREFLY BOOKS

A FIREFLY BOOK

Published by Firefly Books Ltd. 2026

First printing

Library of Congress Control Number: 2026938107

Library and Archives Canada Cataloguing in Publication
Title: 60 Super Bowls : the greatest moments of the biggest game in sports / Allan Maki and Dave Naylor.
Other titles: 50 Super Bowls | Sixty Super Bowls
Names: Maki, Allan, author. | Naylor, Dave, 1967- author.
Description: Previous edition published under title: 50 Super Bowls. | Includes index.
Identifiers: Canadiana 20260175633 | ISBN 9780228106357 (softcover)
Subjects: LCSH: Super Bowl—Anecdotes. | LCSH: National Football League—Anecdotes. | LCGFT: Anecdotes.
Classification: LCC GV956.2.S8 M34 2026 | DDC 796.332/648—dc23

Published in the United States by
Firefly Books (U.S.) Inc.
P.O. Box 1338, Ellicott Station
Buffalo, New York
14205

Published in Canada by
Firefly Books Ltd.
50 Staples Avenue, Unit 1
Richmond Hill, Ontario
L4B 0A7

Cover design and page production: Stacey Cho
Interior design: Matt Filion

Printed in China | E

We gratefully acknowledge the financial support of the Government of Canada for our publishing program.

Previous Spread: Celebrations after the Seattle Seahawks defeat the New England Patriots at Super Bowl LX in Santa Clara, California.

Facing Page: San Francisco 49ers quarterback Joe Montana celebrates after scoring a touchdown at Super Bowl XIX on January 20, 1985.

PHOTO CREDITS

Associated Press
Brynn Anderson: 126
Associated Press: 17 (top), 20, 23 (bottom), 29 (bottom), 33, 41 (top), 49 (top), 145, 149, 152, 161
Doug Benc: 117 (top)
Vernon Biever: 19 (top), 19 (bottom), 31 (bottom), 37 (top), 38, 140, 153
Alex Brandon: 95
Gregory Bull: 109 (bottom)
Julio Cortez: 7
Tom DiPace: 72, 88, 89, 115, 144
David Drapkin: 92
Mark Duncan: 136
David Durochik: 166
Kara Durrette via AP: 150
Eric Gay: 97 (bottom)
Gerald Herbert: 106
Mark Humphrey: 99 (top), 148, 172
Andrew Innerarity: 71 (top), 71 (bottom)
Julie Jacobson: 154
Paul Jasienski: 107
Ryan Kang via AP: 119 (bottom), 125 (bottom), 129 (bottom)
Allen Kee: 158, 163
Perry Knotts via AP: 3–4, 11, 133
Charles Krupa: 134–35
Ashley Landis: 127
Ben Liebenberg; 12–13, 100, 113 (top), 122, 138
Jim Mahoney: 109 (top)
Lennox Mclendon: 61 (bottom)
Alex Menendez: 162
Al Messerschmidt: 5, 39, 45 (top), 45 (bottom), 46, 47, 49 (bottom), 50, 51, 53 (top), 53 (bottom), 54, 58, 164, 170
Peter Read Miller via AP: 119 (top)
Doug Mills: 63 (bottom)
NFL: 57 (top), 59, 61 (top), 64, 65, 67 (top), 68, 69, 141
Cooper Neill via AP: 176–177
Chris O'Meara: 99 (bottom)
Michael Owens via AP: 125 (top)
Gregory Payan: 105 (top), 105 (bottom), 142
David J. Phillip: 113 (bottom)
Pittsburgh Tribune-Review via AP: 147
Gene Pusckar: 9
Susan Ragan: 73
Kevin Reece: 91 (top)
Charlie Riedel: 103
Todd Rosenberg: 173
Kevin Sabitus via AP: 174
Amy Sancetta: 168
Phil Sandlin: 31 (top), 159
Reed Saxon: 55, 67 (bottom)
Patrick Semansky: 114
Marc Serota: 156
Matt Slocum: 146
Paul Spinelli: 63 (top), 94, 175
Vic Stein via AP: 14
Ray Stubblebine: 37 (bottom)
Mark J. Terrill: 93, 101
Elaine Thompson: 91 (bottom), 97 (top)
Tony Tomsic: 15, 17 (bottom), 21, 23 (top), 24, 25, 26, 29 (top), 32, 35 (top), 35 (bottom), 41 (bottom), 43, 57 (bottom), 160
George Walker IV: 129 (top), 171
Cliff Welch: 27, 42
Kathy Willens: 110, 111
Matt York: 120

Icon Sportswire
Robin Alam: 102
Rich Graessle: 117 (bottom)
Bob Kupbens: 130, 131, 132
Doug Murray: 121
James D. Smith/Icon SMI: 183
Cliff Welch: 123

Front cover: AP Photo/Doug Benc
Back cover: Nick Tre. Smith/Icon Sportswire

56
87

CONTENTS

INTRODUCTION | 10
SUPER BOWL SUMMARY | 178
INDEX | 180

★ ★ ★

THE GAMES

I | 14
II | 16
III | 18
IV | 20
V | 22
VI | 24
VII | 26
VIII | 28
IX | 30
X | 32
XI | 34
XII | 36
XIII | 38
XIV | 40
XV | 42
XVI | 44
XVII | 46
XVIII | 48
XIX | 50
XX | 52
XXI | 54
XXII | 56
XXIII | 58
XXIV | 60
XXV | 62
XXVI | 64
XXVII | 66
XXVIII | 68
XXIX | 70
XXX | 72
XXXI | 74
XXXII | 76
XXXIII | 78
XXXIV | 80
XXXV | 82
XXXVI | 84
XXXVII | 86
XXXVIII | 88
XXXIX | 90
XL | 92
XLI | 94
XLII | 96
XLIII | 98
XLIV | 100
XLV | 102
XLVI | 104
XLVII | 106
XLVIII | 108
XLIX | 110
50 | 112
LI | 114
LII | 116
LIII | 118
LIV | 120
LV | 122
LVI | 124
LVII | 126
LVIII | 128
LIX | 130
LX | 132

A football sits on the line of scrimmage during Super Bowl LX.

CONTENTS

★ ★ ★

BEST AND WORST OF THE SUPER BOWL

GREATEST SUPER BOWL QUARTERBACKS | 136

GREATEST SUPER BOWL RECEIVERS | 138

GREATEST SUPER BOWL RUNNING BACKS | 140

GREATEST SUPER BOWL DEFENSES | 142

GREATEST SUPER BOWL TEAMS | 144

BEST SUPER BOWL CATCHES | 146

BEST SUPER BOWL RUNNING PLAYS | 148

BEST SUPER BOWL INTERCEPTIONS | 150

BEST SUPER BOWL COACHES | 152

BEST PERFORMANCE BY A PLAYER ON A LOSING TEAM | 154

BEST PLAYERS TO NEVER WIN A SUPER BOWL | 156

WORST SUPER BOWL QUARTERBACKS | 158

BIGGEST SUPER BOWL BLUNDERS | 160

MOST MEMORABLE SUPER BOWL DRIVES | 162

MOST MEMORABLE SUPER BOWL FIELD GOALS | 164

MOST MEMORABLE SUPER BOWL COMMERCIALS | 166

MOST MEMORABLE SUPER BOWL HALFTIME SHOWS | 168

MOST FREQUENT SUPER BOWL CITIES | 170

SUPER BOWL ONE-HIT WONDERS | 172

TEAMS SHUT OUT OF THE SUPER BOWL | 174

David Tyree makes his helmet catch to keep the New York Giants' fourth-quarter drive alive in their eventual Super Bowl XLII victory.

INTRODUCTION

★ ★ ★

Of all the hundreds of millions of words written about the Super Bowl, these few from legendary sportswriter Dave Kindred best capture the essence of the Big Game: "If there had been a Super Bowl back then, Nero wouldn't have burned Rome. He'd have been too busy schmoozing with corporate chieftains who arrived by sedan chairs and reclined under purple robes as grapes were dropped into their mouths."

That's the Super Bowl, alright; an event so grandiose it is adorned with Roman numerals. Having just celebrated Super Bowl LX, the NFL championship game, now 60, is entering its Golden Years. It has been an amazing journey to this point in its evolution. From the first NFL versus AFL clash in a half-full Los Angeles Memorial Coliseum to the modern-era showcase that fills 70,000-seat stadiums, with the action being broadcast and streamed to millions around the world, everything in and about the Super Bowl has grown in stature.

Case in point: The Green Bay Packers arrived in L.A. a week before Super Bowl I and were allowed to stay well off the beaten path at the Santa Barbara Inn. They practiced at the University of California, Santa Barbara virtually free from the sporting media. Compare that to what transpires today. The competing teams are sequestered in their hotel and adhere to the league's ongoing custom of closed practices.

The NFL has done away with what used to be hailed as Media Day, a Tuesday afternoon mingle with the players where no question was too absurd. At one such event, New England Patriots' quarterback Tom Brady was asked by a female reporter wearing a white wedding gown and standing in the media mist if he wanted to get married. He just laughed and said, "No, I'm a one-woman man."

In 2016, at Super Bowl 50, the NFL scrapped Media Day and replaced it with "Monday Opening Night." Essentially, Opening Night extends the Super Bowl's pre-game festivities to a full week. As if that was necessary.

Born of NFL commissioner Pete Rozelle and rooted by coach Vince Lombardi, the Super Bowl found its place on the sporting map when, in 1969, New York Jets' quarterback Joe Namath guaranteed — and delivered — a win over the heavily favored Baltimore Colts. Namath became an instant star, setting the stage for such Super Bowl stars as Pittsburgh's Lynn Swann, San Francisco's Jerry Rice, New England's Brady and a slew of others.

That's not to say every Super Bowl has been superb. For the longest time, the games were overwhelmingly, predictably one-sided. The Dallas Cowboys crushed the Miami Dolphins by 21 points in Super Bowl VI; the Dolphins beat Minnesota by 17 in Super Bowl VIII; the Los Angeles Raiders destroyed the Washington Redskins by 29 in Super Bowl XVIII. This was followed by the Chicago Bears 36-point mauling of the Patriots (Super Bowl XX) and the San Francisco 49ers 45-point decimation of the Denver Broncos (Super Bowl XXIV). Those games were done as soon as the opening kick-off was in the air.

No doubt, there have still been some blowouts along the way, but the majority of Super Bowls over the last few decades have been mostly dramatic. Consider the St. Louis Rams' last-play victory over the Tennessee Titans (Super Bowl XXXIV); New England's three-point wins against the Rams (XXXVI), the Carolina Panthers (XXXVIII) and the Philadelphia Eagles (XXXIX) along with two losses to the New York Giants by a combined seven points (XLII, XLVI). And let's not forget the first overtime game in Super Bowl history (LI), with the Patriots erasing a 25-point deficit for a 34–28 win over the Atlanta Falcons in the game of our lives.

Good or dull, the undeniable truth about the Super Bowl is that it really doesn't matter which two teams are in it or where the game is played. There is so much more to it now. There are the corporate schmooze-fests and non-stop partying, pre-game concerts plus a halftime show with A-list artists strutting their stuff. Add to that mix are the TV commercials that run at a cost of more than $7 million for a 30-second spot.

At 60, it's safe to say the Super Bowl has proven its worth and resilience. It has survived the strike-shortened season of 1982, the devastation and fall-out from 9/11, Hurricane Katrina and the COVID-19 pandemic. All that and it keeps on getting better.

Just imagine what the next 60 years have in store.

New England Patriots quarterback Tom Brady throws a pass during Super Bowl LI versus the Atlanta Falcons. The Patriots defeated the Falcons 34–28 in overtime in the game of a lifetime.

Seattle Seahawks running back Kenneth Walker III runs the ball during Super Bowl LX against the New England Patriots.

THE GAMES

SUPER BOWL | ONE

I

JANUARY 15, 1967

GREEN BAY **PACKERS 35** | **10** KANSAS CITY **CHIEFS**

PATH TO THE SUPER BOWL

NFL: CHAMPIONSHIP – GREEN BAY 34 VS. DALLAS 27

AFL: CHAMPIONSHIP – KANSAS CITY 31 VS. BUFFALO 7

WHERE	ATTENDANCE	TV AUDIENCE	HALFTIME
MEMORIAL COLISEUM, LOS ANGELES, CALIFORNIA	61,946	51 MILLION	UNIVERSITIES OF ARIZONA AND MICHIGAN BANDS

Green Bay fullback Jim Taylor rushes the ball as Kansas City linebacker E.J. Holub tries to stop him.

Most everything about the first World Championship Game between the AFL and NFL — the game set to decide which league was indeed the mightiest — was not quite so super. (That great name would come later, too.) The pregame entertainment was provided by the University of Arizona and Grambling University (Michigan) marching bands accompanied by star trumpeter Al Hirt. The U.S. national anthem was played by the Arizona and Michigan marching bands. The halftime show featured — wait for it — the Arizona and Michigan marching bands.

Then there was the crowd. While the game drew 61,946 fans, it was the number of empty seats at the Los Angeles Memorial Coliseum (more than 30,000) that cheapened the look of this historic clash. Unfortunately, the game didn't provide many thrills, either.

Green Bay was supposed to win and uphold the NFL's honor as the senior league. The Packers had the best players, the best quarterback in Bart Starr and the best coach, Vince Lombardi, whose name would one day adorn the Super Bowl trophy.

With all that in their favor, the Packers hit the field and slept through the first half. It was safety Willie Wood who awakened his teammates with a 50-yard interception return that set up the first of three second-half touchdowns. In his book *Instant Replay*, Packers offensive lineman Jerry Kramer wrote about what that did to their rivals.

"The Kansas City kid playing opposite me leaned on me, uttered a loud groan and applied as much pressure on me as a good feather duster," wrote Kramer. "I knew the game was over."

With all the drama sucked out of it, the first World Championship Game wasn't much for making memories, unless you're into marching bands. What the Packers did was save the NFL from the embarrassment of losing to the upstart AFL. They also drew the winner's share of $15,000 per man. That was almost half of what some players earned for the regular season — inspiration aplenty to make a return appearance to the second World Championship Game.

MVP

BART STARR | QB

In 1956, Bart Starr was the Packers' 17th-round draft pick (200th overall from the University of Alabama), which meant he was going to watch veteran quarterbacks Tobin Rote and Babe Parilli until he earned a chance. Three years later, Starr became the starter, and after losing the 1960 NFL championship to the Philadelphia Eagles, he helped lead the Packers to seven league titles in a nine-year span.

In the first World Championship Game against Kansas City, Starr shrugged off a sluggish first half to be at his best. He called the right plays at the right times and got the Green Bay running game established to set up a passing attack aimed at receiver Max McGee. For completing 16 of 23 throws for 250 yards and two touchdowns, Starr was named the game's MVP, an award he happily shared with his teammates and their head coach, Vince Lombardi.

LISTEN UP

SUPER BOWL I IS THE ONLY SUPER BOWL IN HISTORY TO HAVE BEEN BROADCAST ON TWO DIFFERENT TV NETWORKS SIMULTANEOUSLY.

TAKING IT TO THE MAX

At 35 with nagging injuries, Max McGee was no longer a Green Bay starter. So he figured he could go out the night before the World Championship Game and have some fun. That meant drinking — a lot of drinking. During the pregame warmup, a thoroughly hungover McGee told Boyd Dowler not to get hurt, which is exactly what happened. Dowler injured a shoulder in the first quarter and was done for the day. McGee had figured there was no chance he'd be playing, so he hadn't even bothered to bring his helmet out of the dressing room. Grabbing a teammate's, he ran onto the field and into history. Off a juggled, one-handed catch, McGee raced 37 yards to score the first touchdown in Super Bowl history. He finished the afternoon with seven catches for 138 yards and two touchdowns. As the years have gone by, McGee's heroics and his 100-proof hijinks have proved more memorable than the game itself, although the marching bands got a lot of play.

★ ★ ★

SUPER BOWL | TWO

II

JANUARY 14, 1968

GREEN BAY **PACKERS 33** | **14** OAKLAND **RAIDERS**

PATH TO THE SUPER BOWL

NFL: DIVISION – GREEN BAY 28 VS. LOS ANGELES 7
CHAMPIONSHIP – GREEN BAY 21 VS. DALLAS 17

AFL: CHAMPIONSHIP – OAKLAND 40 VS. HOUSTON 7

WHERE	ATTENDANCE	TV AUDIENCE	HALFTIME
ORANGE BOWL, MIAMI, FLORIDA	75,546	39.1 MILLION	GRAMBLING UNIVERSITY BAND

Much like its predecessor, the 1968 World Championship Game between the NFL and AFL champions wasn't driving people wild with anticipation. The Green Bay Packers had just won the NFL crown by eliminating the Dallas Cowboys in the fabled Ice Bowl, a game that was played in Arctic-like conditions; the temperature with the windchill factored in was minus-48 Fahrenheit. In the AFC title game, the Oakland Raiders vandalized the Houston Oilers by a score of 40–7 to earn their measure of respect. On offense, the Raiders had quarterback Daryle Lamonica, nicknamed the Mad Bomber for his love of throwing the deep pass. The receivers were good, the running game more than adequate, and yet it was the Raiders' defensive unit that was touted as the strength of the team. At defensive end, there was 6-foot-8, 275-pound Ben Davidson, who wore a handlebar moustache and loved to beat on quarterbacks; at linebacker was the sure-tackling Dan Conners; and in the secondary there was Willie Brown, a future Hall of Famer.

But even with all that going for them, the Raiders were listed as 13½-point underdogs by Las Vegas bookies. And so it happened just as it had in the first World Championship Game: Oakland hung in as long as it could, just as the Kansas City Chiefs did, until the Packers put their foot on the gas and sped away in the second half.

Receiver Max McGee, the hero of the first World Championship, made a 35-yard catch to set up a touchdown run by Donny Anderson. The Packers added the backbreaker when cornerback Herb Adderley returned an interception 60 yards to make the score 31–7. The Raiders added a late touchdown, not that it mattered. The Packers were once again on top of the football world. To that point, they had won nine consecutive playoff games, earning their status as one of the greatest football teams ever assembled.

THE BIG GOOD-BYE

There was only one high-profile storyline coming into and out of the 1968 World Championship: the future of head coach Vince Lombardi. The players noticed a change in him as he prepared them for the game against Oakland. At one point in a team meeting, Lombardi tried to address the players but couldn't talk without choking up. That confirmed to the Packers that they were about to play their last game for him. Some of the veteran players chose to dedicate the second half to their coach. The Packers won and then carried Lombardi off the field on their shoulders. Eventually, Lombardi moved upstairs to the general manager's office and named Packers' assistant coach Phil Bengtson as the new head coach. A year later, Lombardi left Green Bay to coach the Washington Redskins. He guided them to their first winning record in 14 years. He died of cancer on September 3, 1970, at the age of 57. The NFL announced it was naming the Super Bowl trophy in his memory.

LISTEN UP

SUPER BOWL II WAS THE FIRST GAME IN FOOTBALL HISTORY TO DRAW $3 MILLION AT THE GATE.

Coach Vince Lombardi is carried off the field by his players following Green Bay's win in Super Bowl II.

MVP

BART STARR | QB

Again, as it was at the first World Championship, Green Bay quarterback Bart Starr was voted the game's MVP. Statistically, Starr completed 13 of 24 passes for 202 yards and a touchdown. His play calling and ball handling kept Oakland off balance. But in the fourth quarter, Starr hurt his right hand in a sack by the mustachioed Ben Davidson. That sent backup Zeke Bratkowski into the fray to finish things off for the Packers. Starr's showing against Oakland matched how he played during the 1967 season. Bothered by injuries, he completed 54.76 percent of his throws for 1,823 yards, reasonable numbers for any passer. The oddity was he also threw more interceptions (17) than touchdowns (9). The 17 interceptions were the most Starr ever threw in a single season. But in the playoffs, and in the Super Bowl, he could always be counted on to make the plays that mattered.

SUPER BOWL | THREE

III

JANUARY 12, 1969

NEW YORK **JETS** **16** / **7** BALTIMORE **COLTS**

PATH TO THE SUPER BOWL

AFL: NEW YORK 27 VS. OAKLAND 23

NFL: DIVISION – BALTIMORE 24 VS. MINNESOTA 14
CHAMPIONSHIP – BALTIMORE 34 VS. CLEVELAND 0

WHERE	ATTENDANCE	TV AUDIENCE	HALFTIME
ORANGE BOWL, MIAMI, FLORIDA	75,389	41.7 MILLION	FLORIDA A&M UNIVERSITY BAND

All it took to make the Super Bowl truly super was the biggest, most improbable upset in NFL history.

There weren't many football experts with the gumption to say the upstart New York Jets would topple an NFL goliath such as the Baltimore Colts. It wasn't supposed to be in the cards. The Colts had MVP quarterback Earl Morrall, with the old gunslinger, Johnny Unitas, in reserve. They got to the Super Bowl by crushing the Cleveland Browns, 34–0. The Jets had squeaked past the Oakland Raiders, 27–23, in the AFL title game.

In the Super Bowl, hotshot quarterback Joe Namath's play calling got the Jets moving either by short passes or handoffs to running back Matt Snell, who scored the game's first touchdown on a 4-yard run. Up by seven points, it marked the first time in Super Bowl history that an AFL team had taken a lead over an NFL rival. The rest of the game was a blend of Baltimore miscues and the Jets grinding it out with their running game. Snell, who was drafted by the New York Giants but signed with the Jets, was given the ball 30 times and rushed for a then record 121 yards. He also had four catches for 41 yards.

While the Jets kept moving the ball downfield and added three field goals from Jim Turner, the Colts were at a loss to do anything on offense. Morrall threw three interceptions and missed a wide-open Jimmy Orr in the Jets' end zone. That mistake, according to Colts players, was the stake in the heart. It seemed that even when they called the right play and had a man open, it wasn't good enough. Unitas, who was physically unable to start at quarterback because of an elbow injury, came on in relief and guided Baltimore to its only touchdown, a run by Jerry Hill. When the game ended, the Super Bowl had come of age as a sporting event — while the Jets secured their legacy as the ones who accomplished the impossible.

CHUMPS NO MORE

The Jets entered the Super Bowl with a chip the size of a cinder block on their shoulders. The NFL establishment considered the AFL a junior partner, one not nearly good enough to be mentioned in the same breath as the senior league, as the first two World Championships had shown. Former NFL quarterback Norm Van Brocklin was asked for his opinion of Namath before the Super Bowl and answered, "I'll tell you about Joe Namath on Sunday night — after he plays his first pro game." Despite the bad blood, the AFL and NFL had already planned a merger for the 1970 NFL season. It was the Jets' stunning beat-down of the Colts, however, that truly gave the AFL its credibility.

LISTEN UP

JOE NAMATH MADE HIS FAMOUS GUARANTEE THAT THE JETS WOULD DEFEAT THE COLTS. THEY DID, IN FACT, AND BECAME THE FIRST AFL TEAM TO BEAT AN NFL TEAM IN THE SUPER BOWL.

New York Jets running back Matt Snell rushes the ball in the fourth quarter of Super Bowl III.

MVP

JOE NAMATH | QB

The story of Joe Namath's guaranteeing a win for the Jets has taken on supersized proportions over the years. He wasn't scrummed by reporters furiously taking notes while he said his Jets were going to win. Namath made the guarantee on the Thursday before the game. He was at the Miami Touchdown Club receiving a player-of-the-year award when a fan heckled, "Hey, Namath, we're going to kick your ass." To which Namath replied, "I've got news for you. We're going to win the game. I guarantee it." The Namath guarantee wasn't reported until Saturday. It became a much bigger deal after the game. Even though his statistics were modest — he completed 17 of 28 passes for 206 yards, no touchdowns, no interceptions — Namath was named the MVP. The lasting image of this Super Bowl was Namath leaving the field after the game with his right forefinger raised in the air to indicate the Jets were, in fact, number one.

SUPER BOWL | FOUR

IV

JANUARY 11, 1970

KANSAS CITY **CHIEFS** **23** | **7** MINNESOTA **VIKINGS**

PATH TO THE SUPER BOWL

AFL: DIVISION – KANSAS CITY 13 VS. NEW YORK 6
CHAMPIONSHIP – KANSAS CITY 17 VS. OAKLAND 7

NFL: DIVISION – MINNESOTA 23 VS. LOS ANGELES 20
CHAMPIONSHIP – MINNESOTA 27 VS. CLEVELAND 7

WHERE	ATTENDANCE	TV AUDIENCE	HALFTIME
TULANE STADIUM, NEW ORLEANS, LOUISIANA	80,562	44.3 MILLION	CAROL CHANNING

Kansas City quarterback Len Dawson prepares to hand off to running back Mike Garrett during Super Bowl IV.

Given that Super Bowl IV was the last championship game before the merger of the AFL and the NFL, it seems fitting that the Kansas City Chiefs, the first AFL team to play in the Super Bowl, got one last shot at legitimacy before the two loops officially became one.

Kansas City's first appearance had ended in abject humiliation. For that very reason, betting houses analyzed Kansas City versus the Minnesota Vikings and established the Chiefs as 13-point underdogs. The Vikings had pillaged their NFL brethren all season, posting a 12-2 regular-season record before plundering the Cleveland Browns for the NFL title. Led by the defensive line of Jim Marshall, Carl Eller, Alan Page and Gary Larsen — the Purple People Eaters — Minnesota played the game like muggers in Central Park. Even their quarterback Joe Kapp went out of his way to run into tacklers before they ran into him.

The Chiefs were far more strategic. They showed different alignments on defense and built their offensive attack on confusion and skill. Kansas City came at the Minnesota defense with what they called "stacks" — formations where running backs or receivers lined up behind one another to confuse defenders. The Chiefs also used the shotgun formation, ran end-arounds on quick counts, and relied on their speed to flummox Minnesota. It was like watching a team from the future playing against one from the 1950s.

The first big break in the game occurred in the second quarter. Leading 9–0 on three field goals, Kansas City recovered a Minnesota fumble on the Vikings' 9-yard line. Chiefs coach Hank Stram sent in a play from the sidelines — the 65 Toss Power Trap. Kansas City quarterback Len Dawson was surprised. He has been quoted as saying the play wasn't in the team's game plan nor had it been practiced in weeks. Dawson called it in the huddle and handed the ball to Mike Garrett, who ran untouched into the end zone. That made the score 16–0. And when the Vikings got their wits about them and scored a touchdown, Dawson threw a hitch pass to receiver Otis Taylor, who broke a tackle and scampered 46 yards for the clinching touchdown. For the Chiefs, it was splendid retribution for losing in their first World Championship appearance in 1967.

LISTEN UP

THIS WAS THE LAST SUPER BOWL BEFORE THE AFL MERGED WITH THE NFL. BECAUSE THE CHIEFS WON, EACH LEAGUE WON TWO SUPER BOWL TROPHIES BEFORE JOINING TOGETHER.

MVP

LEN DAWSON | QB

Quarterback Len Dawson was headed to a Tuesday-afternoon quarterbacks' meeting when head coach Hank Stram pulled him aside and said NBC news was going to report a federal investigation into sports gambling and that Dawson was going to testify. Apparently, a man named Donald Dawson — no relation to Len — was caught with $400,000 and the quarterback's phone number. NFL commissioner Pete Rozelle said the "investigation by unattributable comment to news media representatives is totally irresponsible." Len Dawson read a statement to the media saying he had nothing to do with this sports gambling business. After, he sliced the Vikings' defense to pieces, completing 12 of 17 passes for 142 yards, to win the Super Bowl.

THE MENTOR

Hank Stram was made for the Super Bowl. Everything about him shouted "big time," so much so that he referred to himself in third person as "the mentor." Knowing how big a persona the Chiefs' coach was, the NFL Films crew asked him to wear a microphone during Super Bowl IV. He got $500 for doing it; NFL Films got a treasure trove of Stramisms, words that didn't make much sense, such as *rats*, *smoosh*, *pump head*, *sausage stuffers* and *puss bellies*, a term he reserved for the game officials. But his trademark line was "Keep matriculating the ball down the field, boys." For many listeners, it was the first time they'd heard the word *matriculating* used in a football game; for some it was the first time they'd heard it, period. After Kansas City scored on the 65 Toss Power Trap, a gleeful Stram shouted, "The mentor!" That he was.

★ ★ ★

SUPER BOWL | FIVE

V

JANUARY 17, 1971

BALTIMORE COLTS 16 / 13 DALLAS COWBOYS

PATH TO THE SUPER BOWL

AFC: DIVISION – BALTIMORE 17 VS. CINCINNATI 0
CONFERENCE CHAMPIONSHIP – BALTIMORE 27 VS. OAKLAND 17

NFC: DIVISION – DALLAS 5 VS. DETROIT 0
CONFERENCE CHAMPIONSHIP – DALLAS 17 VS. SAN FRANCISCO 10

WHERE	ATTENDANCE	TV AUDIENCE	HALFTIME
ORANGE BOWL, MIAMI, FLORIDA	79,204	48 MILLION	FLORIDA A&M UNIVERSITY BAND

Having endured public scorn for losing Super Bowl III to the New York Jets, the Baltimore Colts promised a better result. What they delivered in their bout with the Dallas Cowboys was a championship game of miscues and misfires that took until the final five seconds to be decided. For the record, Baltimore and Dallas committed 11 turnovers. The winners, the Colts, made seven. Dallas was called for 10 penalties for 133 yards.

The Cowboys scored first, turning a pair of stalled drives into two field goals. The Colts responded with the old tip-drill touchdown. Quarterback Johnny Unitas threw to Eddie Hinton, who had the ball tip off his hands right to Dallas defensive back Mel Renfro, who somehow also had the ball glance off his hands — this time landing in the big mitts of Baltimore tight end John Mackey, who went 75 yards uncontested for a touchdown. How do you compete with such a dog's breakfast of a touchdown? You go out and miss the extra point, which the Colts did.

After Dallas scored on a touchdown toss from quarterback Craig Morton to Duane Thomas to give the Cowboys a 13–6 lead, there was a sense that Baltimore was about to be dumbstruck again. Unitas was injured and Baltimore replaced him with Earl Morrall (the pair had reversed roles in Super Bowl III). The Morrall in this story was a little luckier, however. He worked at getting the ball into scoring position so the hijinks could continue. And they did.

Baltimore's Hinton was running for a touchdown when he fumbled at the Dallas 10-yard line. The Cowboys and Colts went after the loose ball only to see it bounce through the end zone. No points; touchback for Dallas. Ball at the 20. The Colts then intercepted a Morton pass that was converted into a 2-yard scoring run by Norm Bulaich to tie the game. After another interception off Morton, the Colts got as close as they could for Jim O'Brien, whose 32-yard field goal gave Baltimore its first lead with five seconds left. Turned out there was just enough time remaining for Morton to throw another interception. Dallas defensive lineman Bob Lilly was so angry he threw his helmet downfield. It fell incomplete.

IF AT FIRST YOU DON'T SUCCEED

The Colts' win underscored a trend that was beginning. Teams losing in their first Super Bowl were more inclined to bounce back and win the next time they were in the big game. The Kansas City Chiefs lost in the first Super Bowl, then won in Super Bowl IV. Baltimore lost Super Bowl III but won it in V. Other teams, such as the Dallas Cowboys, Miami Dolphins and Oakland Raiders, would follow the script in the years ahead. It was proof of what the Super Bowl was becoming — a big-time show with an increasing number of fans wanting to be part of it. That juiced the expectations and made the game even more scrutinised than before, more important to win. That pressure got to some teams; others saw it as their shot at redemption. For the Colts in Super Bowl V, that was all they wanted and were only too happy to proclaim.

LISTEN UP

CHUCK HOWLEY WAS THE FIRST NON-QUARTERBACK AND FIRST PLAYER FROM THE LOSING TEAM TO BE NAMED SUPER BOWL MVP.

Baltimore Colts running back Norm Bulaich runs up the field during Super Bowl V.

MVP

CHUCK HOWLEY | LB

Dallas linebacker Chuck Howley became the first defensive player to win a Super Bowl MVP and also the first player from a losing team to be honored. His numbers against Baltimore included two interceptions and a fumble recovery, but he wasn't thrilled with the outcome. That's when the stories circulated that Howley was so upset by the loss he refused to accept MVP honors. In an interview with *Vice Sports*, Howley said that wasn't the case at all. He found out he had won when his teammates congratulated him for it. He was taking a shower at the time. "I don't refuse an award like that. Not at all," he said. "It was just something that was hard to accept, winning [the MVP award] and losing the ball game. I would much rather we won the game."

SUPER BOWL | SIX

VI

JANUARY 16, 1972

DALLAS **COWBOYS 24** | **3** MIAMI **DOLPHINS**

PATH TO THE SUPER BOWL

NFC: DIVISION – DALLAS 20 VS. MINNESOTA 12
CONFERENCE CHAMPIONSHIP – DALLAS 14 VS. SAN FRANCISCO 3

AFC: DIVISION – MIAMI 27 VS. KANSAS CITY 24
CONFERENCE CHAMPIONSHIP – MIAMI 21 VS. BALTIMORE 0

WHERE
TULANE STADIUM, NEW ORLEANS, LOUISIANA

ATTENDANCE
81,023

TV AUDIENCE
56.6 MILLION

HALFTIME
ELLA FITZGERALD, CAROL CHANNING, AL HIRT AND THE U.S. MARINE CORPS DRILL TEAM

Duane Thomas of Dallas eyes Miami linebacker Doug Swift during Super Bowl VI. Thomas collected 95 rushing yards and one touchdown in the win.

The Dallas Cowboys were back. Not since Super Bowl I and II had a team made it to back-to-back championships. The Cowboys dispatched bitter rival Minnesota in the divisional round and then relinquished only a field goal to the San Francisco 49ers in the conference championship. Coach Tom Landry had finally handed the reins to quarterback Roger Staubach, while Duane Thomas continued to provide an excellent ground game. Staubach, too, had shown he could be a timely runner, which made the offense that much more difficult to contain.

All of that complemented the Cowboys' defense — Doomsday, they called it. Bob Lilly was so good at defensive tackle he constantly drew two blockers. Chuck Howley and Lee Roy Jordan were outstanding at linebacker, while the defensive backfield was armed with talent — Mel Renfro, Cliff Harris, Cornell Green and Herb Adderley, who had won the first two Super Bowls with the Green Bay Packers.

In the AFC, the Miami Dolphins narrowly edged out Kansas City and then dethroned the reigning Super Bowl champs by a demoralizing score of 21–0 to advance to the title game. In the Super Bowl, however, Dallas' Doomsday Defense simply overwhelmed Miami.

In a game devoid of drama, the Cowboys took to the field and then took Miami's offense apart one play at a time. The Dolphins managed just 10 first downs and 185 net yards of offense. Quarterback Bob Griese threw an interception and also set a Super Bowl record for most yards lost on one play (29). He was under so much continuous pressure that he couldn't get the ball to his ace receiver, Paul Warfield. Running backs Jim Kiick and Larry Csonka, Miami's one-two punch, couldn't open any holes against Dallas. Csonka's 12-yard run in the first quarter was the best Miami could do all game. Dallas got touchdowns from running back Duane Thomas and receivers Lance Alworth and Mike Ditka. To Cowboys defender Green, the game came down to this: "The Dolphins were just happy to be in the game and the Cowboys wanted to win the game."

MVP

ROGER STAUBACH | QB

Staubach got the MVP honors, in part by completing 12 of 19 passes for 119 yards and two touchdowns. But it was his poise and gamesmanship that impressed fans and media. Staubach was only a 10th-round draft choice by Dallas in 1964. What scared away other NFL teams was his military commitment. He served as a Supply Corps officer in the war in Vietnam and graduated from the U.S. Naval Academy. Staubach was 27 when he was finally able to attend the Cowboys' training camp in 1969. Two years later, when starter Craig Morton lost his mojo, head coach Tom Landry switched quarterbacks. Staubach neatly assumed control of the offense and won 10 consecutive games, including Super Bowl VI. It was the start of something special for the Cowboys.

LISTEN UP

THE COWBOYS DID NOT ALLOW THE DOLPHINS TO SCORE A TOUCHDOWN, A FIRST IN SUPER BOWL HISTORY.

PRESIDENTIAL TREATMENT

No one warned Miami head coach Don Shula that "the president is on line 1." Instead, Shula picked up his phone and heard Richard Nixon's familiar voice. It wasn't a complete surprise, however, as Nixon had also called Washington Redskins head coach George Allen before they faced the San Francisco 49ers in the divisional playoffs. Nixon suggested Allen use a reverse play involving receiver Roy Jefferson. So Jefferson ran the reverse just as the president recommended. He was dropped for a 13-yard loss. The Redskins then missed on a field goal try and wound up losing 24–20.

In Super Bowl VI, Shula had his offense try a Nixon-endorsed pass to receiver Paul Warfield (already a well-run play in practice and in games). In the Super Bowl, the pass was broken up and the Dolphins were beaten by 21 points. Nixon, by then, was already sinking in the Watergate quagmire that would lead to his resignation.

★ ★ ★

SUPER BOWL | SEVEN

VII

JANUARY 14, 1973

MIAMI DOLPHINS 14	7 WASHINGTON REDSKINS

PATH TO THE SUPER BOWL

AFC: DIVISION – MIAMI 20 VS. CLEVELAND 14
CONFERENCE CHAMPIONSHIP – MIAMI 21 VS. PITTSBURGH 17

NFC: DIVISION – WASHINGTON 16 VS. GREEN BAY 3
CONFERENCE CHAMPIONSHIP – WASHINGTON 26 VS. DALLAS 3

WHERE
MEMORIAL COLISEUM,
LOS ANGELES, CALIFORNIA

ATTENDANCE
90,182

TV AUDIENCE
53.3 MILLION

HALFTIME
UNIVERSITY OF MICHIGAN BAND
AND WOODY HERMAN BAND

Miami's Bob Griese completed 8 of 11 passes for 88 yards and one touchdown as the Miami Dolphins won their first Super Bowl.

The image of Miami kicker Garo Yepremian — by way of Larnaca, Cyprus — desperately trying to throw a football only to have it intercepted and returned for a touchdown in the Super Bowl will live forever. And since the Miami Dolphins won the game, in spite of Yepremian's wounded duck, it's okay to look back in time and chuckle.

Of course, at that particular moment not everyone on the Miami Dolphins thought what they had witnessed was knee-slap funny. With one gaffe, the rival Washington Redskins had cut the Dolphins' lead in half, 14–7. It happened in the fourth quarter and gave Washington hope it could win the game. But that 14–7 score ended up being the final tally of a Super Bowl won by Miami's unsung heroes on its No-Name Defense. To this day, that defense is remembered for its starring role in the lowest-scoring Super Bowl on record.

Although the Dolphins were taken to school in Super Bowl VI, losing by 23 points to the Dallas Cowboys, their return performance was far more business-like. Miami came to win the game, not to frolic in Super Bowl week's growing reputation as a good place to have fun. It didn't take them long to get going either, as late in the first quarter, Dolphins quarterback Bob Griese put together a drive that took them to the Washington 28-yard line. On third down Griese connected with receiver Howard Twilley for the game's first score.

After Miami linebacker Nick Buoniconti intercepted a Washington pass in the second quarter, the offense moved downfield, with running back Jim Kiick scoring from the 1-yard line. In the final three minutes of the game, Yepremian lined up for his fateful 42-yard field goal attempt. The kick was blocked, and the 5-foot-8 Yepremian picked up the bouncing ball and tried to hoist it downfield. It was a pass that resembled more of a shot-put attempt than a Hail Mary, and Washington's Mike Bass intercepted and ran 49 yards for a touchdown. When the game ended and the media asked Yepremian what had happened on the botched field goal attempt, he put his response clear through the uprights: "This is the first time the goat of the game is in the winner's locker room."

MVP

JAKE SCOTT | S

Jake Scott made two interceptions in Super Bowl VII. His most critical came in the fourth quarter in the Miami end zone and was returned 55 yards. That gave his team a turnover and field position. It also made Scott an easy choice as the game's top player. For five years in a row, Scott was voted to the NFL Pro Bowl, and five times he was named to the league's first or second All-Pro team. Never a flashy player, Scott was a keynote contributor in Miami's No-Name Defense. That label was hung on them by Miami assistant coach Bill Arnsparger, the architect of a defense that included tackle Manny Fernandez, Pro Football Hall of Fame linebacker Nick Buoniconti and defensive backs Dick Anderson and Scott, who also showed his versatility by returning punts.

LISTEN UP

DESPITE THEIR PERFECT RECORD, MIAMI ENTERED THE SUPER BOWL AS JUST ONE-POINT FAVORITES OVER WASHINGTON.

PERFECTLY PERFECT

It took 40 years to happen, but the undefeated Dolphins of 1972 finally got their White House visit. It should have come in 1973 after Miami won the Super Bowl, but at that point in U.S. history president Richard Nixon was busy defending himself against the Watergate phone-tapping scandal. In 2013, U.S. president Barack Obama figured four decades was long enough to wait and invited the Dolphins to the White House. It was a reward for a remarkable feat, one that withstood the New England Patriots' streak in 2007. The Patriots won all 16 of their regular-season games and won two more in the playoffs, only to lose 17–14 to the New York Giants in Super Bowl XLII. Many of the '72 Dolphins toasted the New England loss since it maintained their lofty status as the only unbeaten team in NFL history — the absolute best.

★ ★ ★

SUPER BOWL | EIGHT

VIII

JANUARY 13, 1974

MIAMI **DOLPHINS** **24** | **7** MINNESOTA **VIKINGS**

PATH TO THE SUPER BOWL

AFC: DIVISION – MIAMI 34 VS. CINCINNATI 16
CONFERENCE CHAMPIONSHIP – MIAMI 27 VS. OAKLAND 10

NFC: DIVISION – MINNESOTA 27 VS. WASHINGTON 20
CONFERENCE CHAMPIONSHIP – MINNESOTA 27 VS. DALLAS 10

WHERE	ATTENDANCE	TV AUDIENCE	HALFTIME
RICE STADIUM, HOUSTON, TEXAS	71,882	51.7 MILLION	UNIVERSITY OF TEXAS BAND

Based solely on the regular season, the Miami Dolphins–Minnesota Vikings showdown looked relatively equal. Each club had a veteran quarterback who could run when needed. Bob Griese, of course, had helmed the ship in Miami's past two Super Bowl appearances. Minnesota's Fran Tarkenton had long been an NFL regular. Until recently, however, Tarkenton was often the lone bright spot on poor teams. Not so on his second go-round in Minnesota. Here the Vikings had rookie fullback Chuck Foreman — who rushed for 801 yards and caught 37 passes for 362 yards and six touchdowns — as well as Pro Bowl wide receiver John Gilliam. Miami had a running trio of Jim Kiick, Larry Csonka and the mercurial Mercury Morris, who had 954 yards and 10 touchdowns during the season. The Vikings' defense was good; Miami's was better. The two teams finished with the same record, 12-2.

But it was obvious from the start of Super Bowl VIII just how much better Miami was compared with Minnesota. On their first offensive drive, the Dolphins used nine plays — most along the ground — to reach Minnesota's 5-yard line. Power fullback Larry Csonka rammed the ball into the end zone to make it 7–0. On their second offensive drive, the Dolphins used nine plays — most along the ground — to reach Minnesota's 1-yard line. Running back Jim Kiick took the ball into the end zone to make it 14–0. Game statistics show that in the first quarter, Miami had gained 118 yards on 20 plays. Minnesota? Six plays, 25 yards and one first down.

The rest of the game continued along those same lines. In the second quarter, Garo Yepremian capped another long possession by Miami by kicking a 28-yard field goal to make it 17–0. Minnesota showed a spark of life with a drive that took the team to the Dolphins' 7-yard line. The Vikings ran the ball twice and gained zero yards. On fourth down, Minnesota ran the ball again and fumbled. Csonka later scored another touchdown, giving Miami 24 unanswered points. Minnesota finally reached the end zone on a 4-yard run by Tarkenton, but the damage was done. The Vikings had lost two Super Bowls by a combined score of 47–14.

SNOOZE ALERT

At this point in its history, the Super Bowl was stuck in a rut. The prelude to the game was good; the party antics were adding to the week's entertainment value. People came because it was the place to be. But the game itself? It never quite lived up to its advanced billing. Aside from Super Bowl III, and the wonkiness of Super Bowl V, the big game was the big ordinary. (In six of the seven Super Bowls from VI to XII, the average margin of victory was 16 points.) Things were becoming so routine that even the players were feeling it. Miami's Larry Csonka, a three-time Super Bowl veteran, was blunt about his emotions heading into Super Bowl VIII. "This isn't like it was the first two years. I wouldn't say that we're bored, but it's just not the same exciting adventure it was in the other years. I came here to talk about the Super Bowl, but I have so little conversation about it . . ."

LISTEN UP

THIS WAS THE FIRST TIME A TEAM PARTICIPATED IN THE SUPER BOWL THREE CONSECUTIVE TIMES AND THE SECOND TIME A TEAM WON TWICE IN A ROW.

Miami Dolphins running back Mercury Morris rushes up the field during Super Bowl VIII.

MVP

LARRY CSONKA | FB

Csonka was the first back to receive the Super Bowl MVP award. To earn it, he carried the ball 33 times for a record 145 yards. He scored the game's first touchdown and Miami's last touchdown of the day. Early in his NFL career, Csonka suffered through nagging injuries. When Don Shula took over as head coach, Csonka was reprogrammed not to run so upright. From then on he used his size (6-foot-3, 235 pounds) to slam into tacklers with as much force as they applied to him. Csonka worked especially well with Jim Kiick, who was more of an outside-the-offensive-tackle runner to Csonka's inside power punches. Together, they were hyped as bandits Butch Cassidy and the Sundance Kid. To prove just how effective they were against Minnesota, consider that quarterback Bob Griese attempted only seven passes, completing six for 73 yards.

★ ★ ★

SUPER BOWL | NINE

IX

JANUARY 12, 1975

PITTSBURGH **STEELERS** 16 | 6 MINNESOTA **VIKINGS**

PATH TO THE SUPER BOWL

AFC: DIVISION – PITTSBURGH 32 VS. BUFFALO 14
CONFERENCE CHAMPIONSHIP – PITTSBURGH 24 VS. OAKLAND 13

NFC: DIVISION – MINNESOTA 30 VS. ST. LOUIS 14
CONFERENCE CHAMPIONSHIP – MINNESOTA 14 VS. LOS ANGELES 10

WHERE
TULANE STADIUM,
NEW ORLEANS, LOUISIANA

ATTENDANCE
80,997
TV AUDIENCE
56 MILLION

HALFTIME
MERCER ELLINGTON AND
GRAMBLING UNIVERSITY BANDS

In the Super Bowl for the first time, the Pittsburgh Steelers were about to show just how intimidating their Steel Curtain defense could be. Their opponent, the hard-bitten Minnesota Vikings, were looking for their first win in three Super Bowl tries. Unfortunately for the Vikings and hard-luck quarterback Fran Tarkenton, they'd still be looking once Super Bowl IX was over.

In a game dominated by defense, Pittsburgh played to its strength. Its top lineman was Mean Joe Greene, who played in the NFL Pro Bowl 10 times and won numerous awards. The top linebacker was Jack Lambert, famed for his toothless aggression and rugged play. In the secondary, Pittsburgh had Mel Blount, who loved to dish up the big hits with his size and speed. The Steelers could be overwhelming on offense, too. From quarterback Terry Bradshaw to running back Franco Harris to receiver Lynn Swann, the Steelers had all the pieces to beat you any way they wanted. Pittsburgh was ready to rule the NFL.

In Super Bowl IX, Pittsburgh smothered Minnesota's offense. In a championship played under cold, damp conditions, the Vikings fumbled the football and watched it roll into their end zone. Quarterback Fran Tarkenton recovered the loose ball and was tackled by Dwight White for the first safety in Super Bowl history. When the first half ended, the score remained 2–0 for Pittsburgh.

The third quarter began with Minnesota losing control of the football, again, and Pittsburgh recovering. The Steelers responded with a 9-yard touchdown run from Franco Harris. The Vikings had a glimmer of hope in the fourth quarter when they blocked a punt from well inside Pittsburgh territory. Terry Brown recovered the ball in the Steelers' end zone for a touchdown. As would figure, Minnesota missed the extra point and trailed 9–6. On the Steelers' ensuing possession, they ate up the yards and most of the remaining time with an 11-play, 66-yard drive capped by Bradshaw's 4-yard touchdown toss to Larry Brown. That made the score 16–6, and a Tarkenton interception kept it that way.

A TASTE OF THINGS TO COME

With one Super Bowl trophy to put on their mantel, the Steelers decided they needed another as a bookend. Then it was "Why not win a third Super Bowl?" When all the blocking and tackling were done, the Steelers of the mid-to-late 1970s won four Super Bowls. They were football's first dynasty since the Green Bay Packers, who had won five championships in seven years between 1961 and 1967 (pre–Super Bowl NFL titles inclusive). The Steelers' image mimicked that of Pittsburgh the city, the scrap-iron town where the public wanted the players to work every bit as hard as they did. And that is what the Steelers did. From their Steel Curtain defense to their rugged running game, all of it was designed to enhance the team's reputation as a formidable foe, tough as steel.

LISTEN UP

THE PITTSBURGH STEELERS SET A RECORD FOR THE MOST ATTEMPTS TO RUSH IN A SINGLE SUPER BOWL GAME AT 57.

Minnesota's Fran Tarkenton receives a snap during Super Bowl IX. Hurried often by Pittsburgh's defense, Tarkenton threw three interceptions in the game.

MVP

FRANCO HARRIS | RB

Franco Harris was already a name before reaching Super Bowl IX. Three years earlier in a playoff matchup with the Oakland Raiders, Harris did the unimaginable. It was desperation time for the Steelers, trailing 7–6 on the scoreboard with 20 seconds left in the game. Quarterback Bradshaw threw a pass to John Fuqua. The ball went off Fuqua's hands and was deflected by Oakland's Jack Tatum. Before the ball hit the turf as an incompletion, Harris grabbed it seemingly off his shoe tops and ran to the end zone for the winning touchdown. Given the improbability of what had just won the game, the play was dubbed the Immaculate Reception and is considered one of the most improbable finishing plays in pro football. In Super Bowl IX, Harris turned 34 carries into 158 yards and a touchdown — which wasn't immaculate but still important — to win the MVP and help his team to its first Super Bowl win.

★ ★ ★

SUPER BOWL | TEN

X

JANUARY 18, 1976

PITTSBURGH **STEELERS 21** | **17** DALLAS **COWBOYS**

PATH TO THE SUPER BOWL

AFC: DIVISION – PITTSBURGH 28 VS. BALTIMORE 10
CONFERENCE CHAMPIONSHIP – PITTSBURGH 16 VS. OAKLAND 10

NFC: DIVISION – DALLAS 17 VS. MINNESOTA 14
CONFERENCE CHAMPIONSHIP – DALLAS 37 VS. LOS ANGELES 7

WHERE	ATTENDANCE	TV AUDIENCE	HALFTIME
ORANGE BOWL, MIAMI, FLORIDA	80,187	57.7 MILLION	UP WITH PEOPLE

Franco Harris bursts through the Dallas front line to collect some of his game-high 82-yards rushing in Super Bowl X.

When the Pittsburgh Steelers won Super Bowl IX, they did it with a commanding running game and a defense to match. One year later in Super Bowl X, Pittsburgh showcased another weapon in its quest for a second NFL championship — receiver Lynn Swann, whose skill and grace stood out from the Steelers' smash-mouth approach to running and defending. Swann, as his name befit, was akin to a ballet dancer among pro wrestlers. He ran clean pass routes and outmanoeuvred defensive backs, and if he got his hands on a football, it was sure to be a catch.

The interesting thing was Swann had almost no impact in the previous Super Bowl. His grand contribution was three receptions for 24 yards and one carry for a loss of 7 yards. Against the Dallas Cowboys on the Super Bowl's 10th birthday, however, Swann's performance was undeniably brilliant and included one of the greatest catches ever made in the history of the big game. On a deep throw from quarterback Terry Bradshaw, who was hemmed in at Pittsburgh's goal line, Swann outjumped Dallas defensive back Mark Washington, tipped the ball in the air and then caught it while falling toward the turf. Then, in the last few minutes of the fourth quarter, Swann beat Washington again, this time for a 64-yard touchdown grab.

Dallas scored first in Super Bowl X and didn't relinquish the lead until halfway through the fourth quarter. After Swann's 64-yard TD put Pittsburgh on top 21–10, the Cowboys answered back with a desperate drive that ended with a 34-yard touchdown throw to Percy Howard. It was Howard's second TD of the match, and it sliced Pittsburgh's lead to four points. Cowboys quarterback Roger Staubach had one last shot at winning, as Dallas got the ball back with 1:22 left on the clock. He marched Dallas from their own 39-yard line, but the Steelers' Glen Edwards intercepted his final pass of the afternoon.

With the win, the Steelers joined the Miami Dolphins and Green Bay Packers as back-to-back Super Bowl champions. It was an exclusive club, but Pittsburgh wasn't done yet.

MVP

LYNN SWANN | WR

Swann finished the game with four catches for a record 161 yards and a touchdown. That made him the first receiver to win the award. That he was even in the game was something to wonder about. In the AFC championship against the Oakland Raiders, Swann suffered a concussion. He was hospitalized for two days and could not take full practice in the week before the Super Bowl. In a bid to rattle his confidence, Dallas defensive back Cliff Harris said, "I'm not going to hurt anyone intentionally. But getting hit again while he's running a pass route must be in the back of Swann's mind." Swann's response was exactly what you'd expect: "He can't scare me or the team . . . Sure, I thought about the possibility of being reinjured. But it's like being thrown by a horse. You have to get up and ride again immediately or you may be scared the rest of your life."

LISTEN UP

STEELERS DEFENSIVE END L.C. GREENWOOD SET THE RECORD FOR THE MOST SACKS IN A SUPER BOWL GAME WITH FOUR.

THIS WAY TO THE HALL

As rivalries go, the Steelers–Cowboys games were highly anticipated. They were always a clash of will and styles — Pittsburgh with its pounding defense; Dallas with its multiple-set offense. Think of it as old school meets state of the art. And there is another way to measure how good these organizations were: a combined 18 players, coaches and management members have been inducted into the Pro Football Hall of Fame in Canton, Ohio. For the Steelers, owner Art Rooney, team administrator Dan Rooney, coach Chuck Noll and nine players from Mel Blount to Mike Webster have been enshrined. The Dallas list celebrates team administrator Tex Schramm, coach Tom Landry and four players, including Staubach at quarterback. The Steelers and Cowboys loathed one another on the field, but the fact remains they brought out the best in each other. Their games were highly intense and never dull.

★ ★ ★

SUPER BOWL | ELEVEN

XI

JANUARY 9, 1977

OAKLAND **RAIDERS** **32** / **14** MINNESOTA **VIKINGS**

PATH TO THE SUPER BOWL

AFC: DIVISION – OAKLAND 24 VS. NEW ENGLAND 21
CONFERENCE CHAMPIONSHIP – OAKLAND 24 VS. PITTSBURGH 7

NFC: DIVISION – MINNESOTA 35 VS. WASHINGTON 20
CONFERENCE CHAMPIONSHIP – MINNESOTA 24 VS. LOS ANGELES 13

WHERE	ATTENDANCE	TV AUDIENCE	HALFTIME
ROSE BOWL, PASADENA, CALIFORNIA	103,438	62.1 MILLION	LOS ANGELES UNIFIED ALL-CITY BAND

The Oakland Raiders finally returned to the dance after three consecutive losses in the AFC championship game. It was their second trip to the Super Bowl, their first in nine years since the drubbing handed to them by the Green Bay Packers in 1968. This trip was sweeter given that Oakland vanquished the reigning champs from Pittsburgh to get to Super Bowl XI. Once there, they crushed the Minnesota Vikings, 32–14, to win Oakland's first NFL championship.

Over the years, the Raiders had honed their identity as the bad boys of the NFL. Their colors were silver and black. Their boss was Al Davis, king of the renegades. Their fans would show up on game day wearing skeleton masks or shoulder pads with spikes on them. It was as if the Raiders were part motorcycle gang, part football team. Their attack had Ken "the Snake" Stabler at quarterback, Fred Biletnikoff at receiver and one of the best blocking lines in the league. Defensively, the Raiders bent the rules of engagement until they snapped. Defensive backs George Atkinson and Jack Tatum were headhunters, which made them extremely dangerous to play against.

Minnesota was making its fourth appearance in the Super Bowl, and much of its cast was still seeking its first championship. Fran Tarkenton at 37 was still a very capable quarterback, and Chuck Foreman was the team's top rusher. Overall, the Vikings had the players who could get the job done but couldn't make things work when they had to. Tarkenton threw two interceptions, while Foreman managed just 44 yards. His longest run was 7 yards. Oakland's Stabler completed 12 of 19 throws for 180 yards and a touchdown, while Clarence Davis ran for 137 yards. The Raiders set a Super Bowl record with 429 yards of offense. Minnesota had 323. Oakland got touchdowns from running back Pete Banaszak, who scored twice, and tight end Dave Casper. But it was defensive back Willie Brown who put the nail in Minnesota's coffin, as he intercepted a pass and returned it 75 yards for the Raiders' final touchdown of the day, truly putting the game out of reach.

SUPER BAD

The Vikings earned their place in infamy by losing four Super Bowls. That occurred over eight years with a combined score of 95–34. The 32–14 loss to Oakland came with the biggest margin of defeat (18 points), meaning the Vikings were getting worse the more often they played in the Super Bowl. The Vikings never held a lead in a Super Bowl; they never even scored in the first half of a Super Bowl. In their four appearances they turned over the ball 15 times; and they couldn't establish a running game of any kind, never accruing more than 72 yards on the ground and totaling 227 yards over four games. There are more numbers and trends that exhibit how poorly Minnesota did in those games, but the ones listed are some of the most poignant. As of 2016, the Vikings have yet to make a fifth visit to the Super Bowl.

LISTEN UP

THIS WAS MINNESOTA'S FOURTH LOSS. THEY HAVE NOT APPEARED IN THE SUPER BOWL SINCE.

Oakland's Clarence Davis explodes upfield for a few of his 137 rushing yards during Super Bowl XI.

MVP

FRED BILETNIKOFF | WR

In a game where Clarence Davis had 137 yards rushing, and quarterback Ken Stabler was coolly efficient, it was wide receiver Fred Biletnikoff who was named MVP. He won the award without gaining 100 yards, a Super Bowl first. He didn't score a touchdown, either. What he did accomplish — four catches for 79 yards — seemed small potatoes for a player of his stature. But three times in the game, Biletnikoff made the critical catch to keep drives alive, drives that would lead to a field goal or a touchdown. During the regular season and playoffs, Biletnikoff would wipe a glop of glue known as Stickum on his sock. When he needed a little dab, he would take it off his sock and apply it to his hands. The NFL eventually came up with a rule banning Stickum. It didn't bother Biletnikoff one bit.

★ ★ ★

SUPER BOWL | TWELVE

XII

JANUARY 15, 1978

DALLAS COWBOYS 27 | 10 DENVER BRONCOS

PATH TO THE SUPER BOWL

NFC: DIVISION – DALLAS 37 VS. CHICAGO 7
CONFERENCE CHAMPIONSHIP – DALLAS 23 VS. MINNESOTA 6

AFC: DIVISION – DENVER 34 VS. PITTSBURGH 21
CONFERENCE CHAMPIONSHIP – DENVER 20 VS. OAKLAND 17

WHERE	ATTENDANCE	TV AUDIENCE	HALFTIME
SUPERDOME, NEW ORLEANS, LOUISIANA	76,400	78.9 MILLION	TYLER APACHE BELLES, PETE FOUNTAIN AND AL HIRT

The biggest story in the countdown to Super Bowl XII was Roger Staubach versus Craig Morton.

Staubach and Morton used to be teammates in Dallas trying to outdo each other to become the Cowboys' number one pivot. In 1971 the duo would take turns as starter, and at one point, the pair took turns in-game under center: Coach Tom Landry had Staubach run in from the sidelines and run a play, and then he sent Morton out for the next play. It was one of the goofiest things football fans had ever seen. Finally, Staubach won the job outright, commanding the team in both their previous Super Bowl appearances — a win in Super Bowl VI and a loss in Super Bowl X. Morton was traded to the New York Giants in 1974, where he played two and a half years on terrible teams before being dealt to the Denver Broncos. There he found new life in his first season, guiding the Broncos to their first Super Bowl appearance.

With no disrespect to Morton, it was Denver's defense, not the offense, that rode roughshod over the Pittsburgh Steelers and Oakland Raiders on their way to the big game. Denver football fans called it the Orange Crush and predicted that Staubach would get squeezed, and he did, getting sacked five times for a loss of 35 yards.

But it was Morton who got the worst of it, as Dallas' thundering Doomsday Defense smothered him. Hurried and rushed all game, Morton threw four interceptions in the first half! It didn't help that the Broncos fumbled the ball four times, and further, that they couldn't seem to recover key Dallas fumbles, of which there were many.

A 3-yard touchdown run by rookie Tony Dorsett and two field goals gave the Cowboys a 13–0 lead at halftime. Dallas wide receiver Butch Johnson caught a 45-yard scoring pass from Staubach in the third quarter that made the score 20–3. The interception-prone Morton was benched for Norris Weese, and running back Rob Lytle scored Denver's only touchdown on a 1-yard plunge. That score was matched by a Dallas halfback option that saw Robert Newhouse throw a scoring pass to receiver Golden Richards. In a wild game that had 10 turnovers, 10 fumbles and 4 interceptions, the final was 27–10.

MORE IS MORE

Super Bowl XII was the first to be played in a domed stadium. During the previous 11 years, the NFL had positioned the game in southern climates. Luckily for the league, the weather was accommodating much of the time, allowing fans to sit outdoors. Soon, more cities built covered stadiums, thus giving them a chance to bid on hosting the Super Bowl and its now week-long festivities. The other big change in the coverage and exposure of the game was the switch in kickoff times. Instead of starting in the afternoon, the game began Sunday evening in Eastern Time. It allowed the game to run during prime time, which made it easier for sponsors to show their commercials. That would become a major attraction for companies and viewers in the years to come.

LISTEN UP

THIS IS THE ONLY TIME TWO PLAYERS HAVE BEEN NAMED MVP, BOTH FROM THE DALLAS DEFENSE, DUE TO THEIR INCREDIBLE EIGHT FUMBLE RECOVERIES.

Tony Dorsett gets a block from Herbert Scott during the Dallas Cowboys' romp of the Denver Broncos in Super Bowl XII.

MVPS

HARVEY MARTIN | DE
RANDY WHITE | DT

When the votes were tallied, the MVP of Super Bowl XII was not only a defensive lineman, it was two defensive linemen, Harvey Martin and Randy White. The voters wanted to select the Cowboys' entire defensive lineup but were told by the league, "Don't do that." Martin and White were hot on Morton's tail all game, pressuring him into bad throws, forcing him into interceptions, sacking him as often as they could. Martin also had the best postgame quote when the subject matter turned to Denver's Orange Crush defense: "Orange Crush is soda water, baby. You drink it. It don't win football games." As for Dallas' Doomsday Defense, it won a lot of games for the Cowboys, and because of them Dallas was again the toast of the NFL.

★ ★ ★

SUPER BOWL | THIRTEEN

XIII

JANUARY 21, 1979

PITTSBURGH STEELERS 35 | 31 DALLAS COWBOYS

PATH TO THE SUPER BOWL

AFC: DIVISION – PITTSBURGH 33 VS. DENVER 10
CONFERENCE CHAMPIONSHIP – PITTSBURGH 34 VS. HOUSTON 5

NFC: DIVISION – DALLAS 27 VS. ATLANTA 20
CONFERENCE CHAMPIONSHIP – DALLAS 28 VS. LOS ANGELES 0

WHERE	ATTENDANCE	TV AUDIENCE	HALFTIME
ORANGE BOWL, MIAMI, FLORIDA	79,484	74.7 MILLION	KEN HAMILTON AND VARIOUS CARIBBEAN BANDS

Franco Harris gets the ball in Super Bowl XIII. His 22-yard fourth-quarter rush was part of Pittsburgh's 28–3 scoring run before Dallas mounted a near comeback.

Here, finally, was a Super Bowl that lived up to the hype and hysteria. The reigning champs going toe to toe with recent back-to-back Super Bowl winners. It was a rematch of Super Bowl X, arguably the most exciting Super Bowl since the format had been established, and both teams were healthy and coming off absolutely dominant wins in their respective conference championships.

But as seemed to be the trend with Dallas and Super Bowls, fumbles took center stage, with both teams earning points off miscues.

The first drop of the game happened on the Cowboys' first possession, and seven plays later, Pittsburgh quarterback Terry Bradshaw hooked up with receiver John Stallworth for a touchdown, and the game was on.

Dallas tied the game on a Tony Hill reception three plays after the Cowboys recovered a Bradshaw fumble off a sack. They then went ahead 14–7 when linebacker Mike Hegman wrestled the ball from Bradshaw's grip and ran it 37 yards for a touchdown. That play got the Steelers' attention. They responded almost immediately with a 75-yard catch and run by Stallworth. Before the first half ended, Bradshaw passed to running back Rocky Bleier for 7 yards and another touchdown. The score at that point was 21–14 for Pittsburgh.

After a largely uneventful third quarter came the furious fourth, and for Dallas, the second costly drop of the game. On the kickoff following a Franco Harris touchdown for Pittsburgh, the Cowboys' Randy White fumbled. Pittsburgh recovered and Bradshaw connected with Lynn Swann for a score on the next play, leaving Dallas down 35–17 with less than seven minutes to play.

Roger Staubach then took over. He marched the Cowboys from their own 11-yard line down to Pittsburgh's red zone to set up a 7-yard touchdown pass to Billy Joe DuPree. With a little more than two minutes remaining, Dallas kept the ball after a successful on-side kick, and Staubach again passed his way down to inside the Steeler's 10-yard line and hit Butch Johnson for a 4-yard touchdown that had the Cowboys trailing 35–31.

With 22 seconds left, Dallas failed to recover their second on-side kick. For the Steelers it was their third Super Bowl triumph in five years.

MVP

TERRY BRADSHAW | QB

In the days leading up to Super Bowl XIII, Cowboys linebacker Thomas "Hollywood" Henderson kept providing soundbites when asked what he thought of Bradshaw. The ever-quoted, never dull Henderson said he wasn't impressed with the Steelers' quarterback, which would have been fine if he had stopped there. But Henderson couldn't, so he let loose with this memorable assessment: "He's so dumb he couldn't spell 'cat' if you spotted him the 'c' and the 'a.'" After the game, which saw Bradshaw throw for 318 yards and four touchdowns, Henderson was reminded of his pregame comments. He insisted he never called Bradshaw a bad quarterback; it was just that the Steelers' MVP couldn't spell.

LISTEN UP

THE COWBOYS SET THE RECORD FOR MOST POINTS BY A LOSING TEAM. THE 49ERS WOULD TIE THEM IN SUPER BOWL XLVII WHEN THEY LOST TO THE RAVENS 34–31.

A MISSED OPPORTUNITY

It could have been a splendid send-off for one of the NFL's best players. Instead, it lives on as a legendary gaffe whenever people talk about the Super Bowl and its greatest mistakes. That wasn't how Jackie Smith wanted to go out. He had spent 15 seasons with the woeful St. Louis Cardinals, playing at tight end and catching most everything thrown his way. He signed with Dallas in 1978, hoping to retire with a Super Bowl trophy. At 38 years old, Smith played sparingly during the regular season but was on the Cowboys' roster for Super Bowl XIII. In the third quarter, on a third-down pass from Staubach, Smith slipped in the Pittsburgh end zone while trying to catch the ball only to flub it. Had he made the reception, Dallas would have tied the score, 21–21. Instead they kicked a field goal. It was Smith's last game in the NFL. He is a member of the Pro Football Hall of Fame.

★ ★ ★

SUPER BOWL | FOURTEEN

XIV

JANUARY 20, 1980

PITTSBURGH **STEELERS 31** | **19** LOS ANGELES **RAMS**

PATH TO THE SUPER BOWL

AFC: DIVISION – PITTSBURGH 34 VS. MIAMI 14
CONFERENCE CHAMPIONSHIP – PITTSBURGH 27 VS. HOUSTON 13

NFC: DIVISION – LOS ANGLES RAMS 21 VS. DALLAS 19
CONFERENCE CHAMPIONSHIP – LOS ANGELES RAMS 9 VS. TAMPA BAY 0

WHERE	ATTENDANCE	TV AUDIENCE	HALFTIME
ROSE BOWL, PASADENA, CALIFORNIA	103,985	76.2 MILLION	UP WITH PEOPLE

Playing in Pasadena was almost like having home-field advantage for the Los Angeles Rams, who played their games at the nearby Memorial Coliseum. Coming off a mediocre 9-7 record in the regular season, the surprising Rams had a lot of ground to cover against the three-time Super Bowl–winning Steelers. Their starting quarterback, Pat Haden, broke his finger midway through the season, giving way to understudy Vince Ferragamo. He threw twice as many interceptions (10) as he did touchdowns (5) during the regular season, yet he pushed his team through the playoffs to get to the Super Bowl. The Rams also had Wendell Tyler, a top-notch running back who rushed for 1,109 yards in the regular season, with another 308 receiving yards and 10 touchdowns. He led the NFL by averaging 5.1 yards per carry. Add a quick and stingy defense, and the sum of their parts helped carry the Rams past the Dallas Cowboys and the Tampa Bay Buccaneers all the way to the big dance.

Making their fourth visit to the Super Bowl in six years, the Steelers were old hands in dealing with the press and pressure. Quarterback Terry Bradshaw, the MVP of the previous Super Bowl, and his two receiving threats, John Stallworth and Lynn Swann, were ready to pick up where they had left off a year ago. It seemed as if it was going to be a walk in the park for the veteran Steelers against the first-timer Rams; considering the lead changed sides six times, it's safe to say Pittsburgh had their hands full.

Trailing 13–10 at halftime, the Steelers went into the dressing room and got their act together. In the third quarter, Bradshaw threw deep to Swann, who made the 47-yard scoring catch seem as easy as flipping channels with a TV remote. The only player to steal the spotlight from Swann was Stallworth. He broke free and pulled in a long ball from Bradshaw to complete a 73-yard touchdown play to make the score 24–19 for the Steelers in the fourth. Stallworth added a 45-yard grab later in the game to set up Franco Harris, and his 1-yard touchdown run rounded out the scoring at 31–19. Afterward, several Steelers, including Bradshaw and head coach Chuck Noll, made it a point to say this was the toughest matchup of all their Super Bowls.

HERE TODAY, LONG GONE TOMORROW

This was the only Super Bowl the L.A. Rams would play in. By the start of the 1995 NFL season, the Rams had checked out of Southern California and settled in St. Louis, Missouri, a move made possible by the St. Louis Cardinals' packing up and going to Phoenix. But now, more than 20 years later, the Rams are heading back to La La Land in an act by owner Stan Kroenke that many consider risky. The Rams had a great following in Missouri and a lot of history (they won Super Bowl XXXIV), whereas football fans in Los Angeles were forced to find a new club to root for in the wake of the Rams' departure, and many of those fans chose the neighboring Oakland Raiders or San Diego Chargers. But perhaps bringing the Rams back to California will reinvigorate the team, which has not made the postseason since 2004.

LISTEN UP

THIS IS THE HIGHEST ATTENDED SUPER BOWL IN HISTORY. BRADSHAW ALSO STILL HOLDS FIRST PLACE IN YARDS PER PASS FOR THIS GAME (14.71).

Pittsburgh Steelers' J.T. Thomas dangerously tackles Los Angeles Rams running back Wendell Tyler at the goal line during the first quarter of Super Bowl XIV.

MVP

TERRY BRADSHAW | QB

Bradshaw was voted the game's MVP for the second year in a row. He completed 14 of 21 passes for 309 yards and two touchdowns. But he also threw three interceptions, giving more ammunition to the skeptics of the day who were convinced that the Steelers' outstanding offensive line and their fleet of fast receivers made Bradshaw better, not the other way around. Bradshaw never missed a chance to say that he was blessed to work with the many skilled players around him. And when those receivers or running backs got open, Bradshaw got them the ball because that's what he did in the big games. He made things happen.

SUPER BOWL | FIFTEEN

XV

JANUARY 25, 1981

OAKLAND **RAIDERS** **27** | **10** PHILADELPHIA **EAGLES**

PATH TO THE SUPER BOWL

AFC: WILD CARD – OAKLAND 27 VS. HOUSTON 7
DIVISION – OAKLAND 14 VS. CLEVELAND 12
CONFERENCE CHAMPIONSHIP – OAKLAND 34 VS. SAN DIEGO 27

NFC: WILD CARD – DALLAS 34 VS. LOS ANGELES 13
DIVISION – PHILADELPHIA 31 VS. MINNESOTA 16
CONFERENCE CHAMPIONSHIP – PHILADELPHIA 20 VS. DALLAS 7

WHERE	ATTENDANCE	TV AUDIENCE	HALFTIME
LOUISIANA SUPERDOME, NEW ORLEANS, LOUISIANA	76,135	68.3 MILLION	SOUTHERN UNIVERSITY BAND AND HELEN O'CONNELL

Oakland Raiders guard Gene Upshaw raises the game ball after winning Super Bowl XV in dominant fashion over the Philadelphia Eagles.

There was something oddly satisfying about the Oakland Raiders being the first NFL wild-card team to win a Super Bowl. The Raiders were a gang-tackling, rule-bending collection of castoffs and renegades who took on the personality of their part owner Al Davis. It was Davis' belief that the league's rules were for other guys, not him or his team. He wanted his squad to "just win, baby," and it did—a great many times.

In the playoffs, the Raiders started off at home and beat the Houston Oilers by 20 points. The next two games were on the road, where Oakland defeated the Cleveland Browns by two points and then the San Diego Chargers by seven. That put the Raiders in the Super Bowl against the Philadelphia Eagles, who had knocked off the Minnesota Vikings and Dallas Cowboys to represent the NFC.

Philadelphia had some recent history on its side, giving gamblers more cause to believe the Eagles would win. During the 1980 regular season, Philadelphia beat Oakland 10–7 in a heated affair that saw Raiders quarterback Jim Plunkett sacked eight times.

That certainly wasn't the case in the Super Bowl. Eagles quarterback Ron Jaworski had his first pass intercepted by Raiders linebacker Rod Martin. That resulted in a 2-yard touchdown catch by Oakland receiver Cliff Branch. Still in the first quarter, Plunkett lobbed a pass to running back Kenny King, who raced to the Philadelphia end zone for an 80-yard scoring play. At halftime, the Raiders were up 14–3 and telling themselves it wasn't enough of a lead.

On their first possession in the second half, they drove into Philadelphia territory and scored again on a Plunkett-to-Branch pass, this one covering 29 yards.

The Eagles managed to score a touchdown in the fourth quarter, but it wasn't enough. Jaworski had a wretched game, throwing three interceptions, all of them to Martin, as the Raiders took their second Super Bowl championship in four years.

Just win, indeed.

MVP

JIM PLUNKETT | QB

Jim Plunkett was the star of the Raiders' castoffs. Before signing with Oakland in 1978 as a free agent, he had been released by the New England Patriots and the San Francisco 49ers. It wasn't until 1980, when starting quarterback Dan Pastorini suffered a broken leg, that Plunkett got his chance to play. He immediately took control and boosted the Raiders to nine wins in an 11-game span—good enough for a wild-card position and his first foray into the NFL playoffs. In the Super Bowl, the 33-year-old Plunkett completed 13 of 21 passes for 261 yards and three touchdowns, making him the easy MVP choice. And for all he did in the 1980 season, Plunkett was also chosen as the league's comeback player of the year.

LISTEN UP

THE RAIDERS BECAME THE FIRST WILD-CARD TEAM TO WIN THE SUPER BOWL, DEFEATING THE HOUSTON OILERS, CLEVELAND BROWNS, SAN DIEGO CHARGERS AND PHILADELPHIA EAGLES.

TROPHY PRESENTATION TO RAIDER NATION

Never before had the Super Bowl trophy presentation become must-see television. With an Oakland win, eyeballs were sure to stay glued to the screen. Why? Davis had a beef with NFL commissioner Pete Rozelle and was suing the NFL for blocking the Raiders' efforts to move out of Oakland and into Los Angeles. Tradition had it that Rozelle would hand the Super Bowl trophy to the team owner inside the winner's dressing room. Would Davis tell Rozelle to stick it? Could the two men be on their best behavior for all of a minute or two? It turned out they could, though Rozelle kept both hands on the trophy in case his offer to shake Davis' hand was rebuffed on live television. Davis held the trophy and told his players and coaches, "This is the finest hour in the history of the Oakland Raiders." Sure enough, two years later, they became the Los Angeles Raiders.

★ ★ ★

SUPER BOWL | SIXTEEN

XVI

JANUARY 24, 1982

SAN FRANCISCO **49ers 26** / **21** CINCINNATI **BENGALS**

PATH TO THE SUPER BOWL

NFC: DIVISION – SAN FRANCISCO 38 VS. NEW YORK GIANTS 24
CONFERENCE CHAMPIONSHIP – SAN FRANCISCO 28 VS. DALLAS 27

AFC: DIVISION – CINCINNATI 28 VS. BUFFALO 21
CONFERENCE CHAMPIONSHIP – CINCINNATI 27 VS. SAN DIEGO 7

WHERE	ATTENDANCE	TV AUDIENCE	HALFTIME
PONTIAC SILVERDOME, PONTIAC, MICHIGAN	81,270	85.2 MILLION	UP WITH PEOPLE

For a few reasons, Super Bowl XVI was bound to be an exciting one. The San Francisco 49ers and Cincinnati Bengals were both making their championship debuts and coming off franchise-best regular-season records (13-3 and 12-4, respectively). They also had two of the best quarterbacks in the league: Joe Montana for the 49ers and Ken Anderson for the Bengals.

San Francisco made the leap to being a championship contender by defeating the Dallas Cowboys with "the Catch"—a late game-winning grab by receiver Dwight Clark in the Dallas end zone that started the 49ers' upward swing toward greatness. Cincinnati's AFC title was won outdoors, where the Bengals used the freezing temperature to their advantage, defeating the fair-weather San Diego Chargers, 27–7.

The 49ers and Bengals were each ready for a prime-time breakout based on the performances of their stars during the 1981 season. Montana took first place in pass completion percentage, while Anderson took second. San Francisco's Dwight Clark made 85 receptions, and Cincinnati's Pete Johnson rushed for 12 touchdowns.

During the first half of the Super Bowl, however, the Bengals could do little more than watch as the 49ers commanded the play. Montana ran for one touchdown and threw for another to fullback Earl Cooper. Heading into the second half, the Bengals were down by 20 points and seriously needing an offensive push. That's when Anderson went to work with a short touchdown run of his own before twice connecting with tight end Dan Ross for touchdowns.

The Bengals' defense kept San Francisco from the end zone in the second half, but the 49ers scored two field goals to edge Cincinnati, 26–21. The win was especially sweet for 49ers head coach Bill Walsh, who had taken the team from 2-14 to 6-10 to Super Bowl champions in his first three seasons at the helm. The triumph was validation for his West Coast Offense—and the 49ers weren't done winning with it yet.

START OF A LEGEND

The win in Super Bowl XVI marked the beginning of a 49ers dynasty and the sanctification of their coach, Bill Walsh. Before he took the job in San Francisco, Walsh spent eight seasons as an offensive assistant with Cincinnati and mentored Bengals quarterback Ken Anderson. Walsh had Anderson going after defenses with short passes from multiple offensive sets. In San Francisco, with Montana using his sure passing and quick thinking, this tactic became known as the West Coast Offense, and the 49ers ran it to perfection, winning three Super Bowls. George Seifert, who assumed the head coaching job in 1989 after Walsh moved to an upper management position, went on to win two more Super Bowls with the dynastic club.

LISTEN UP

THE BENGALS GAINED 356 YARDS TO THE 49ERS' 275, MARKING THE FIRST TIME THE LOSING TEAM HAD COMPILED MORE YARDS THAN THE WINNING TEAM.

Cincinnati Bengals running back Archie Griffin is tackled by San Francisco 49ers linebacker Milt McColl in a 26–21 loss in Super Bowl XVI.

MVP

JOE MONTANA | QB

Joe Montana had a knack for winning games that were seemingly lost. In 1980, the 49ers were being thumped by the New Orleans Saints, who held a 35–7 lead at halftime. With a few adjustments, Montana returned to the field for the third quarter and went on the attack. The final score was 38–35 for San Francisco in overtime. His play to Dwight Clark against the Dallas Cowboys in the conference championship was further proof that Montana was a quarterback who could be counted on to deliver in the clutch. Against Cincinnati, he completed 14 of 22 passes for 157 yards and a touchdown, while also running the ball in for the game's first score. For Montana, playoff MVP awards were about to become as automatic as an extra point attempt.

SUPER BOWL | SEVENTEEN

XVII

JANUARY 30, 1983

WASHINGTON **REDSKINS 27**

17 MIAMI **DOLPHINS**

PATH TO THE SUPER BOWL

NFC: WILD CARD – WASHINGTON 31 VS. DETROIT 7
DIVISION – WASHINGTON 21 VS. MINNESOTA 7
CONFERENCE CHAMPIONSHIP – WASHINGTON 31 VS. DALLAS 17

AFC: WILD CARD – MIAMI 28 VS. NEW ENGLAND 13
DIVISION – MIAMI 34 VS. SAN DIEGO 13
CONFERENCE CHAMPIONSHIP – MIAMI 14 VS. NEW YORK JETS 0

WHERE	ATTENDANCE	TV AUDIENCE	HALFTIME
ROSE BOWL, PASADENA, CALIFORNIA	103,667	81.8 MILLION	LOS ANGELES SUPER DRILL TEAM

Washington quarterback Joe Theismann checks the formation during the Redskins' defeat of the Miami Dolphins in Super Bowl XVII.

In a strike-shortened nine-game season, the Washington Redskins stood out as the team to beat. Their regular-season record was 8-1; their quarterback, Joe Theismann, was the league's most accurate passer with a 63 percent completion average; and they had John Riggins, a 230-pound running back who was no easy tackle for rival defenses.

The Miami Dolphins weren't slouches either. They touted the league's best defense, a unit popularly referred to as the Killer Bs. But the Bs' strength was their speed, and Washington's offensive line, known by Redskins supporters as the Hogs, was all muscle.

With that strong offensive front and a sturdy defense, Washington entered Super Bowl XVII as the prohibitive favorite. And yet at halftime, the Miami Dolphins were ahead, 17–10. Two huge touchdown strikes, covering 174 yards between them (a 76-yard touchdown pass from quarterback David Woodley to receiver Jimmy Cefalo and a 98-yard kickoff return by Fulton Walker), were the difference in the game's first two quarters.

The Redskins convinced themselves they hadn't been playing the game their way and needed to get back to what worked best for them — simply put, it was Riggins right, left and up the middle. As Coach of the Year Joe Gibbs told his Washington players at halftime, "This was the way it was supposed to be. If we [are] going to be world champions, we [have] to earn it by coming back."

Heading into the fourth quarter down 17–13, Washington's comeback plan was in motion. With the Hogs exerting their strength, the run game began to wear Miami down. Riggins managed to break through the tired Miami defensive line and showed everyone just how fast he could run. On fourth down with inches to go, Riggins took the handoff, cut to his left and powered past a Miami defender to score on a 43-yard touchdown run on a play cemented in Redskins lore as "70-chip."

With about two minutes remaining in the game, Theismann connected with Charlie Brown on a 6-yard touchdown pass that finished the Dolphins' chances. It was the Redskins' first Super Bowl victory and avenged their 14–7 loss to Miami in Super Bowl VII.

MVP

JOHN RIGGINS | RB

Riggins could have been the MVP of the playoffs, not just the Super Bowl. In their three playoff wins before earning their shot at an NFL championship, the Redskins called on Riggins a lot. His rushing total against the Detroit Lions, Minnesota Vikings and Dallas Cowboys was a productive 444 yards. Then, against Miami in Super Bowl XVII, "Riggo" turned his game up to a higher level. He rushed for a then-record 166 yards on 38 carries and scored the touchdown that decided the outcome. In the postgame celebrations, an unabashed Riggins told the media, "At least for tonight, Ron [Reagan] is president, but I'm the king." His 43-yard scoring romp has become a storied moment in Washington's football history. It is also regarded as one of the best touchdowns ever scored in the Super Bowl.

LISTEN UP

MVP JOHN RIGGINS HOLDS FIRST PLACE IN RUSHING ATTEMPTS WITH 38 AND THIRD PLACE IN RUSHING YARDS WITH 166.

THE SUPER BOWL THAT ALMOST WASN'T

Whatever the result of Super Bowl XVII, the game was going to come with an asterisk. The 1982 season came dangerously close to being shut down entirely — no regular season, no playoffs, no Super Bowl. The NFL Players Association wanted 55 percent of the league's gross revenues, while the league wanted to wait out the players as long as it could. In trying to fill the programming gap created by the strike, TV networks took on drastic measures. NBC broadcast just four Canadian Football League games before pulling the plug on three-down football. After 57 days of being on strike, the NFLPA signed a five-year agreement with the NFL, giving the players severance packages upon retirement, salary increases and bonuses relative to years in the league, among other amendments. The league decided to play a nine-game regular season with a seeding style of playoffs. It wasn't the normal way things were done (hence the asterisk), but the Redskins were happy enough to take the Super Bowl.

★ ★ ★

SUPER BOWL | EIGHTEEN

XVIII

JANUARY 22, 1984

LOS ANGELES **RAIDERS** **38** | **9** WASHINGTON **REDSKINS**

PATH TO THE SUPER BOWL

AFC: DIVISION – LOS ANGELES RAIDERS 38 VS. PITTSBURGH 10
CONFERENCE CHAMPIONSHIP – LOS ANGELES RAIDERS 30 VS. SEATTLE 14

NFC: DIVISION – WASHINGTON 51 VS. LOS ANGELES RAMS 7
CONFERENCE CHAMPIONSHIP – WASHINGTON 24 VS. SAN FRANCISCO 21

WHERE
TAMPA STADIUM, TAMPA, FLORIDA

ATTENDANCE
72,920

TV AUDIENCE
85.2 MILLION

HALFTIME
UNIVERSITY OF FLORIDA AND FLORIDA STATE UNIVERSITY BANDS

It was the play that gutted the Washington Redskins — a play that never should have been called in the first place. The Redskins were first and 10 at their 12-yard line with 12 seconds until halftime. They trailed the Los Angeles Raiders, 14–3.

The first half had already had one unlikely miscue go the way of the Raiders when Derrick Jensen blocked a Washington first-quarter punt and recovered the ball in the end zone for the game's first touchdown.

With a start like that, the smart thing to do at the end of the half would have been for Washington quarterback Joe Theismann to take a knee, run out the clock and retool the game plan at halftime. But Redskins coach Joe Gibbs didn't go for that. He wanted a touchdown to pull within one score of the lead, so he called for one of Washington's sneakier plays, "the rocket screen." Theismann ran the play and rolled to his right only to stop and throw back to his left where running back Joe Washington was waiting.

Also waiting, however, was L.A. Raiders linebacker Jack Squirek. He stepped in front of Washington to intercept the pass and run it 5 yards into the end zone untouched, making the score 21–3. The Raiders were expecting Theismann to make that play because the Redskins had run it successfully against them in the regular season. L.A. linebacker coach Charlie Sumner anticipated the play call and made a substitution, taking middle linebacker Matt Millen out and putting Squirek on the outside. It worked like a charm.

Although there were still two quarters left to play, the game was all but over.

The best the Redskins could do was score a touchdown on a 1-yard run by John Riggins, who was rendered ineffective by L.A.'s defense. The MVP of the previous Super Bowl, Riggins was limited to 64 yards on 26 carries. But ultimately it was the miscall that turned into a miscue and a pick six for the Raiders that took the air out of Washington. L.A. added 17 more points, including Marcus Allen's stunning 74-yard touchdown gallop — a run that has become one of the most replayed moments in Super Bowl history.

LOST YEARS

After winning Super Bowl XVIII, the once-proud Raiders plunged into a sharp decline. Bo Jackson was a bright spot. An out-of-this-world talent, he mixed pro baseball and football and excelled at both. Sadly he blew out his hip in a 1991 playoff game and was done with the NFL, and he was never quite the same on the diamond, either. It took 19 years from the Raiders' XVIII championship to make it back to the Super Bowl — and in that championship game in 2003 against Tampa Bay, the Buccaneers clobbered the Raiders, 48–21. Following that were years of constant change, bad player drafts and signings, and a carousel of coaches. Since 2003, no one has been able to bring the Raiders back to the postseason, never mind their glory days.

LISTEN UP

THE RAIDERS' 38 POINTS SCORED WAS A RECORD AT THE TIME FOR AN AFC TEAM, SINCE TIED IN 2023 BY THE KANSAS CITY CHIEFS AT SUPER BOWL LVII.

Los Angeles Raiders running back Marcus Allen outruns Washington Redskins linebacker Neal Olkewicz for a touchdown during Super Bowl XVIII.

MVP

MARCUS ALLEN | RB

Allen's Super Bowl performance shone a light on him like never before. He was a star player with the University of Southern California Trojans. In 1981, he became the first NCAA running back to top the 2,000-yard mark in one season. Drafted by the Raiders, he got right to work, showing he could carry the ball often and score touchdowns. His 74-yard scoring run in Super Bowl XVIII showed off his diverse skill set — his agility, speed and ability to read blocks and defenders. Against Washington, Allen finished with 191 yards, a then–Super Bowl record. "To make a run like that, in a game like that, on a play like that," said Allen, "was pure magic. It was beautiful."

SUPER BOWL | NINETEEN

XIX

JANUARY 20, 1985

SAN FRANCISCO **49ers** **38** | **16** MIAMI **DOLPHINS**

PATH TO THE SUPER BOWL

NFC: DIVISION – SAN FRANCISCO 21 VS. NEW YORK GIANTS 10
CONFERENCE CHAMPIONSHIP – SAN FRANCISCO 23 VS. CHICAGO 0

AFC: DIVISION – MIAMI 31 VS. SEATTLE 10
CONFERENCE CHAMPIONSHIP – MIAMI 45 VS. PITTSBURGH 28

WHERE	ATTENDANCE	TV AUDIENCE	HALFTIME
STANFORD STADIUM, STANFORD, CALIFORNIA	84,059	85.5 MILLION	U.S. AIR FORCE BAND "TOPS IN BLUE"

San Francisco 49ers running back Roger Craig rushes during Super Bowl XIX. Craig scored three touchdowns in the game.

When the San Francisco 49ers first appeared in the Super Bowl, it was a baptism by fire. They beat the Cincinnati Bengals by five points in Super Bowl XVI, and people saluted the emerging greatness of quarterback "Joe Cool" Montana.

In their second Super Bowl appearance, it was a championship-savvy San Francisco team, with talent at every position, taking on the Miami Dolphins and walloping them by 22 points. That was the story at the end of the game. The story heading in was about the two quarterbacks — Joe Montana and Dan Marino.

In just his second pro season, Miami's Marino went pass happy, throwing for 5,084 yards and 48 touchdowns. His primary targets were Mark Clayton and Mark "Super" Duper, who each had more than 70 catches and 1,300 yards for the season. Clayton scored 18 touchdowns, a then-NFL record. Montana, on the other hand, was an experienced Super Bowl quarterback and had just led his team to a 15-1 record. With these two men running the game, Super Bowl XIX was expected to be one of those games people would look back on with reverence.

After Miami had kicked a field goal to make it 3–0, Montana went to work. He threw to running back Carl Monroe for a 33-yard touchdown. Miami answered that with a Marino completion to Dan Johnson for a 2-yard touchdown. The game was shaping up to be the offensive showcase many people had anticipated. Then in the second quarter, San Francisco took charge.

Running back Roger Craig scored two touchdowns — one on a run and the other on a pass from Montana, who added a 6-yard scoring run of his own. Two Miami field goals made the score 28–16 at halftime, but the 49ers kept the pressure on. They scored 10 more points in the third quarter, but more importantly harried and hampered Marino, who was sacked four times in the second half after having been sacked just 14 times in the previous 18 games. The pressure also resulted in two critical Marino interceptions. "We knew all week, among us in the secondary," 49ers safety Eric Wright said, "that we would be the key to beating those guys."

For the 49ers, this marked their second Super Bowl championship in four years.

MVP

JOE MONTANA | QB

When San Francisco began crushing opponents under its cleats time and time again, it created an unexpected problem: who was the right 49ers player to receive Super Bowl MVP honors? Often it was Montana because he always found a way to win on the grandest stage of all. When it wasn't him, it was receiver Jerry Rice or running back Roger Craig or Ronnie Lott in the defensive backfield. For Super Bowl XIX, Montana's numbers were 24 completions in 35 pass attempts for 331 yards, three scoring passes, no interceptions and a run of 8 yards for a touchdown. It was definitely enough to earn him the MVP award.

LISTEN UP

THE DOLPHINS MADE ONLY NINE RUSHING ATTEMPTS, THE FEWEST IN ANY SUPER BOWL.

FROM THE COMFORT OF HOME

The San Francisco 49ers were the second NFL team to play for a Super Bowl in what was considered their home market (the L.A. Rams were first, doing so at Super Bowl XIV in 1980). The 49ers played their regular-season games at Candlestick Park, and they had to travel only 30 miles to play in Super Bowl XIX, hosted at Stanford Stadium on the campus of Stanford University.

U.S. president Ronald Reagan got to play his part in the game from the comfort of home, too. When he made the official coin toss to start the game, Reagan wasn't on the field, nor was he in the stadium or even the state for that matter. He was in the White House, where he would later be sworn in for a second term. The Dolphins called heads, Reagan flipped tails and the crowd cheered loudly for the 49ers. It was a sign of what was to come for both teams. (For the record: the only other president to do a Super Bowl coin toss is George H.W. Bush at Super Bowl XXXVI; he was on the field.)

★ ★ ★

SUPER BOWL | TWENTY

XX

JANUARY 26, 1986

CHICAGO **BEARS** **46** / **10** NEW ENGLAND **PATRIOTS**

PATH TO THE SUPER BOWL

NFC: DIVISION – CHICAGO 21 VS. NEW YORK GIANTS 0
CONFERENCE CHAMPIONSHIP – CHICAGO 24 VS. LOS ANGELES RAMS 0

AFC: WILD CARD – NEW ENGLAND 26 VS. NEW YORK JETS 14
DIVISION – NEW ENGLAND 27 VS. LOS ANGELES RAIDERS 20
CONFERENCE CHAMPIONSHIP – NEW ENGLAND 31 VS. MIAMI 14

WHERE	ATTENDANCE	TV AUDIENCE	HALFTIME
LOUISIANA SUPERDOME, NEW ORLEANS, LOUISIANA	73,818	92.6 MILLION	UP WITH PEOPLE

This wasn't a football game; it was a mauling inside a massacre wrapped up in bandages. For 60 minutes, the hapless New England Patriots couldn't escape the jaws of their mighty opponent, the Chicago Bears. No matter what the Patriots tried, they were battered and crushed and left with the worst beating in the Super Bowl's 20 years.

The 1985 Bears were an assemblage of strong personalities. The team had so much swagger they recorded "The Super Bowl Shuffle" (which hit number 41 on the Billboard Hot 100) before they were even guaranteed a playoff spot.

Head coach Mike Ditka and defensive coordinator Buddy Ryan were possibly the strongest personalities of the bunch. Although their relationship was strained, they managed to bring together an incredible team, including Jim McMahon, Willie Gault and Walter Payton. Of course their defense was one of the best in NFL history: their playoff results were 21–0, 24–0 and 46–10.

Ryan's defense had eight men in what's called the box (the area occupied by the defensive line and linebackers). The Bears would line up with eight defenders, then rush five to eight of them at the other team's quarterback. And these were no ordinary guys doing the rushing. There were heavyweights Richard Dent, William "the Refrigerator" Perry and Dan "the Danimal" Hampton on the line. Add Otis Wilson and the crazy-eyed Mike Singletary at linebacker, with Leslie Frazier and Dave Duerson in the secondary, and you had a defense that was too much for Patriots quarterback Tony Eason, who was chased out of the game in favor of Steve Grogan, who fared no better.

As for Chicago's offense, four different players scored touchdowns, including two from quarterback McMahon. The last touchdown was scored by the Fridge. With Chicago holding the ball on the New England 1-yard line, the defender was called to take a spot in the Bears' offensive backfield. The Fridge took the handoff and plowed his way clear into the end zone. It gave Chicago an insurmountable 41-point lead after three quarters.

THE GOOD HUMOR MAN

Jim McMahon and the spotlight were made for each other. McMahon was all about having fun and not taking anything too seriously. So when NFL commissioner Pete Rozelle fined him for wearing an Adidas headband, McMahon decided to wear one that said "Rozelle" on it instead. He also wore one that said POW-MIA, meaning prisoners of war, missing in action. But this was nothing compared to when a helicopter came too close to where the Bears were practising and McMahon dropped his drawers to moon it. "I was just showing them where it hurt," he said. Head coach Mike Ditka said of his quarterback, "He's relatively sane."

LISTEN UP

THE NEW ENGLAND PATRIOTS RUSHED FOR THE FEWEST YARDS IN SUPER BOWL HISTORY WITH SEVEN. TOTAL.

Dan "Danimal" Hampton sacks New England quarterback Steve Grogan in Super Bowl XX, a game dominated by Chicago's defense.

MVP

RICHARD DENT | DE

Someone from the Bears defense just had to win the top player honor, and that went to Richard Dent. New England finished the day with only 123 total yards. The team averaged 0.6 yards per rushing attempt and were one for 10 on third-down conversions. The quarterbacks were sacked seven times and threw two interceptions. Dent, from his defensive end position, had some nice numbers, including two forced fumbles, a pass knockdown and 1.5 sacks. Dent was voted into the Pro Football Hall of Fame in 2011, where he joined three other players from that 1985 team — Hampton, Singletary and Payton.

★ ★ ★

SUPER BOWL | TWENTY-ONE

XXI

JANUARY 25, 1987

NEW YORK **GIANTS** **39** | **20** DENVER **BRONCOS**

PATH TO THE SUPER BOWL

NFC: DIVISION – NEW YORK GIANTS 49 VS. SAN FRANCISCO 3
CONFERENCE CHAMPIONSHIP – NEW YORK GIANTS 17 VS. WASHINGTON 0

AFC: DIVISION – DENVER 22 VS. NEW ENGLAND 17
CONFERENCE CHAMPIONSHIP – DENVER 23 VS. CLEVELAND 20

WHERE
ROSE BOWL,
PASADENA, CALIFORNIA

ATTENDANCE
101,063

TV AUDIENCE
87.2 MILLION

HALFTIME
SOUTHERN CALIFORNIA–AREA HIGH SCHOOL
DRILL TEAMS AND DANCERS

New York Giants defensive backs Herb Welch and Kenny Hill wrap up Broncos wide receiver Vance Johnson during Super Bowl XXI.

The player who grabbed most of the spotlight in the days leading up to Super Bowl XXI was John Elway, the Denver Broncos' gifted young quarterback. During the regular season, his fourth as a pro, Elway guided Denver to an 11-5 record built on his arm (he passed for 3,485 yards and 19 touchdowns) and his legs (he ran for 257 yards — third best on the team that season). Then there was Elway's ability to produce fourth-quarter comebacks under intense pressure. He displayed all those skills in the AFC Championship win over the Cleveland Browns. With just over five minutes left to play in the game, and Denver starting from its 2-yard line, Elway produced what football people have hailed "the Drive." He made 15 plays over 98 yards to throw a touchdown pass to tie the score at 20–20. In overtime, he moved his offense into position to kick the game-winning field goal.

The New York Giants made it to the Super Bowl with a defense that promised to give Elway a run for his money. They called themselves the Big Blue Wrecking Crew, and leading the charge were Giants linebackers Harry Carson, Carl Banks and Lawrence Taylor, the latter considered one of the greatest defensive players in NFL history. He led the 1986 season with 20.5 sacks and returned an interception for a touchdown in the Giants' divisional playoff win over the 49ers. In New York's two playoff wins to get to the Super Bowl, their defense allowed just three points.

In the Super Bowl, however, the Broncos took a 10–9 lead at the end of the first half. Then they fell apart. Giants quarterback Phil Simms threw a pair of touchdowns, while his team's running game ate up yards as well as huge chunks of time off the clock.

Elway was irritated by the Giants defense, especially since Taylor and Banks had 14 combined tackles, while Leonard Marshall had two sacks and a forced fumble. New York scored 30 points in the second half — including a touchdown made possible because of a sneak play on a fourth down. As the Giants set up to punt, backup quarterback Jeff Rutledge snuck into the formation unnoticed, moved under center, called his own number and plunged ahead for two yards and a fresh set of downs. Simms finished the job and the Giants won their first NFL championship since 1956.

MVP

PHIL SIMMS | QB

Phil Simms was regarded as a good quarterback by the end of the 1986 regular season — good but not great because of the 22 interceptions he threw (one more than the number of touchdown passes he made). In the Super Bowl, however, Simms put together four quarters of flawless football. He completed 22 of 25 passes for 268 yards, three touchdowns and no interceptions. The most memorable catch was a pass that deflected off the hands of teammate Mark Bavaro and into the grasp of Phil McConkey, who jumped into the spotlight with several key plays that stumped Denver.

LISTEN UP

MVP QUARTERBACK PHIL SIMMS HOLDS THE COMPLETION RECORD FOR ANY SUPER BOWL WITH 88 PERCENT.

SUPER SOAKED

If you hate that sloppy end-of-game tradition where players dump the Gatorade bucket on the winning head coach, blame the Giants. They started this ritual throughout the course of the 1986 regular season, dumping ice and such all over their sideline boss, Bill Parcells. So as the last seconds of Super Bowl XXI ticked off the clock, two players snuck up behind Parcells and showered him with Gatorade. Parcells wasn't too happy about the dunking because there was just over a minute to go in the game. But that was probably the dunking Parcells treasures most of all, given it was his first Super Bowl victory. Now every championship-winning coach gets to have icy Gatorade poured down his back.

SUPER BOWL | TWENTY-TWO

XXII

JANUARY 31, 1988

WASHINGTON REDSKINS 42 / 10 DENVER BRONCOS

PATH TO THE SUPER BOWL

NFC: DIVISION – WASHINGTON 21 VS. CHICAGO 17
CONFERENCE CHAMPIONSHIP – WASHINGTON 17 VS. MINNESOTA 10

AFC: DIVISION – DENVER 34 VS. HOUSTON 10
CONFERENCE CHAMPIONSHIP – DENVER 38 VS. CLEVELAND 33

WHERE
JACK MURPHY STADIUM, SAN DIEGO, CALIFORNIA

ATTENDANCE
73,302

TV AUDIENCE
80.1 MILLION

HALFTIME
CHUBBY CHECKER AND THE ROCKETTES WITH 88 GRAND PIANOS

One of the most famous quarters in NFL history took place during Super Bowl XXII. The Washington Redskins were playing the Denver Broncos, who were back in their second consecutive title game. The Broncos and their quarterback John Elway vowed it would be different this year. They weren't going to get drop-kicked to the sidelines — no, they were going to prove they deserved a Super Bowl victory.

Within the first six minutes of the game, Denver kept its word — they were up 10–0 after a 56-yard touchdown pass from Elway to Ricky Nattiel and a 60-yard drive that ended with a field goal by Rich Karlis. Little did they know that those 10 points were all they would get.

Heading into the second quarter, the Washington Redskins woke up and went to work. By the time the first half ended, this Super Bowl was as good as over.

Washington scored five touchdowns on five consecutive possessions in just five minutes and 47 seconds, all in the second quarter. Quarterback Doug Williams had the game of his life — he threw two touchdown passes to Ricky Sanders, one for 80 yards and the other for 50. Williams got his other scoring passes on completions to Gary Clark and Clint Didier. Add in running back Timmy Smith's 58-yard rush for a touchdown and you've got the record for most points in the first half of any Super Bowl.

That wasn't the only feat achieved that day. Williams set two records, one for his 340 passing yards and the other for his four touchdown passes. Sanders' 193 receiving yards was also a new record (all three have since been beaten). However, Smith's record of 204 rushing yards still stands, as does the Redskins' team stat of six touchdowns on 602 yards of total offense.

On the other side of the scoreboard, Denver's offense started to crack after its first two possessions. Elway threw three interceptions and was sacked five times, and his team managed to rush just 97 yards. It was as complete a beat-down by Washington as any team has managed in a championship game.

THE HOG-SKINS

The players who made up the Redskins championship team had swagger and went out of their way to show they had a good time when winning games. The Fun Bunch led the way. This collection of receivers would celebrate a touchdown catch with a group leap. The NFL has never liked showboating and ruled the fun jump an excessive celebration, thus forcing it into early retirement. With Washington's offensive line, who had nicknamed themselves the Hogs, it was the fans that got to have the fun. In honor of their unfailing work, which often saw the starting five getting their noses dirty, their followers would wear plastic pig noses and snort loudly.

LISTEN UP

WASHINGTON'S ROOKIE RUNNING BACK TIMMY SMITH IS THE ONLY PLAYER TO RUSH MORE THAN 200 YARDS IN A SUPER BOWL GAME.

Players pile on the only fumble to occur in Super Bowl XXII — committed and recovered by Washington — in a game where everything went the way of the Redskins.

MVP

DOUG WILLIAMS | QB

Doug Williams underwent a root canal the day before Super Bowl XXII. The next afternoon, he gave one to Denver — without any freezing to soothe the pain. Williams was amazing against the Broncos, completing 18 out of 29 throws to cap a mega-show that earned him status as the first African-American quarterback to win an NFL title. That was all the talk before the game — how Williams would fare under so much scrutiny. After the game, the talk was all about his impressive play. He is also remembered for his answer to the question "How long have you been a Black quarter-back?" Williams casually replied: "I've been a quarterback since high school. I've been Black all my life."

★ ★ ★

SUPER BOWL | TWENTY-THREE

XXIII

JANUARY 22, 1989

SAN FRANCISCO **49ers** **20** | **16** CINCINNATI **BENGALS**

PATH TO THE SUPER BOWL

NFC: DIVISION – SAN FRANCISCO 34 VS. MINNESOTA 9
CONFERENCE CHAMPIONSHIP – SAN FRANCISCO 28 VS. CHICAGO 3

AFC: DIVISION – CINCINNATI 21 VS. SEATTLE 13
CONFERENCE CHAMPIONSHIP – CINCINNATI 21 VS. BUFFALO 10

WHERE	ATTENDANCE	TV AUDIENCE	HALFTIME
JOE ROBBIE STADIUM, MIAMI, FLORIDA	75,129	81.6 MILLION	SOUTH FLORIDA–AREA DANCERS AND PERFORMERS

Joe Montana steps back to pass in Super Bowl XXIII, a game famous for the 49ers' 92-yard drive to go ahead in the dying seconds of the contest.

San Francisco 49ers quarterback "Joe Cool" Montana was at it again. Seven years earlier in Super Bowl XVI he broke the hearts of the Cincinnati Bengals with a narrow 26–21 victory. The script for Super Bowl XXIII was different, but for Bengals fans, it was eerily similar.

Montana, now 32 years old, had been sharing regular-season duties with San Francisco quarterback of the future, Steve Young. But come the playoffs, coach Bill Walsh didn't hesitate when it came time to pick his field general. Montana had established himself as a calm and collected pocket passer who operated in the zone afforded him by his all-star blockers. He also had versatile running backs and a receiving corps set with game-breaking ability. It was all available to Montana, and he used every bit of it to get past a resilient Cincinnati team.

With the score tied 3–3 at halftime, the Bengals were the first to reach the end zone. Stanford Jennings took a kickoff and returned it 93 yards for a touchdown. Now behind 13–6 with one quarter left, the 49ers responded right on cue, moving the ball to Cincinnati's 14-yard line, where Montana went to Jerry Rice for the tying touchdown. Cincinnati then kicked a field goal with less than four minutes left in the game.

Down by three points, no one would have thought it foolish for San Francisco to get in field goal position, tie the game and take a chance in overtime. Instead, Montana painted his masterpiece — one that started with an unlikely bit of comedic relief. Standing at the 49ers' 8-yard line, Montana, who was typically a man of few words in the huddle, diverted from his typical no-nonsense play calling to instead point out Canadian comedian John Candy, who was in attendance. The unexpected announcement broke any tension the 49ers brought into the huddle, and they coolly went to work.

Montana threw a combination of short passes to his running back Roger Craig or tight end John Frank before hitting Rice or John Taylor for large gains. After 10 plays and over 80 yards, the 49ers were at the Cincinnati 10-yard line. Montana passed to Taylor for the winning touchdown with 34 seconds left in the game.

San Francisco head coach Bill Walsh said of his quarterback's record-setting 357-yard game and winning drive: "That was Joe Montana at his best."

MVP

JERRY RICE | WR

Jerry Rice had all the numbers to be the game's pivotal player. He caught 11 passes for a Super Bowl record 215 yards. Not counting the yards of his prize receiver, Montana managed just 142 yards passing. What San Francisco needed was what Rice provided. He did more than catch the ball; he gained crucial yards after making the catch. No matter how they tried to cover him, Cincinnati's defenders couldn't slow Rice or keep him away from the ball. On the winning drive, Rice got better with every catch, gaining 7 yards then 17 then 27. After the game, Rice told reporters he thought his quarterback deserved to be MVP — he would be in the following Super Bowl.

LISTEN UP

SAN FRANCISCO'S WIDE RECEIVER AND MVP JERRY RICE IS THE ONLY PLAYER TO RECEIVE MORE THAN 200 YARDS IN THE SUPER BOWL.

END OF THE LINE

On the eve of Super Bowl XXIII, the Bengals held a team meeting at their hotel. Running back Stanley Wilson told his teammates he had forgotten his playbook and went back to his room to get it. He never made it to the meeting. Instead, he was found passed out in his bathroom. Cincinnati head coach Sam Wyche broke down in tears when he told the rest of the team that Stanley had had a relapse with cocaine. "When I told the team Stanley wasn't going to play," Wyche recalled 10 years later, "I can remember them throwing their playbooks to the ground and putting their heads in their hands. I believe if we had Stanley in that ball game . . . It wouldn't have been close." Wilson, who had already scored two touchdowns in the playoffs, failed his drug test following the incident. It was his third failed test, and he was suspended from the NFL for life.

★ ★ ★

SUPER BOWL | TWENTY-FOUR

XXIV

JANUARY 28, 1990

SAN FRANCISCO **49ers** **55** / **10** DENVER **BRONCOS**

PATH TO THE SUPER BOWL

NFC: DIVISION – SAN FRANCISCO 41 VS. MINNESOTA 13
CONFERENCE CHAMPIONSHIP – SAN FRANCISCO 30 VS. LOS ANGELES RAMS 3

AFC: DIVISION – DENVER 24 VS. PITTSBURGH 23
CONFERENCE CHAMPIONSHIP – DENVER 37 VS. CLEVELAND 21

WHERE	ATTENDANCE	TV AUDIENCE	HALFTIME
LOUISIANA SUPERDOME, NEW ORLEANS, LOUISIANA	72,919	73.9 MILLION	PETE FOUNTAIN, DOUG KERSHAW AND IRMA THOMAS

Looking back, this game was over with three seconds to go in the first quarter. When tight end Brent Jones hauled in a 7-yard pass from quarterback Joe Montana, it put the San Francisco 49ers 10 points up on the here-they-flop-again Denver Broncos. After that, the 49ers would go on to score 14 points every 15 minutes to lay down the most one-sided beating in Super Bowl history. "I knew we were great, but I didn't think we were going to be this great," said defensive back Ronnie Lott, a four-time Super Bowl champion. "No question, this is the most talented 49er team I've been on."

San Francisco was ready to roll when the playoffs for the 1989 season began, having finished the year at 14-2. Switching from good in the regular season to great in the postseason, the 49ers walloped the Minnesota Vikings by 28 points before beating the Los Angeles Rams by 27 for the NFC title. In the AFC playoffs, quarterback John Elway and his Broncos had a far more difficult run. They beat the Pittsburgh Steelers by just 1 point thanks to a 71-yard drive in the fourth quarter. Against the Cleveland Browns in the AFC championship, Elway reminded the world of his talent by once again moving his offense downfield to produce a timely touchdown that carried Denver to the Super Bowl.

Broncos coach Dan Reeves, understanding just what his team was up against in the matchup against the three-time Super Bowl champion 49ers, tried to give his troops some confidence before the game. He suggested a Broncos win "could be the second-greatest upset in sports history. We could do what the American hockey team did against the Russians."

Well, they didn't. Elway completed only 10 of 26 passes for a mere 108 yards. He was sacked six times, compared to just once for Montana. All of the receiving yards for Denver combined didn't equal Jerry Rice's 148. San Francisco never fumbled the ball and had possession almost double the time that Denver did. Numbers don't lie — this was a landslide victory.

NO MORE SUPER JOE

Montana injured his elbow in the playoffs after the 1990 season, and the injury gave backup Steve Young a chance to prove himself to his coaching staff and teammates. For Montana, Young's performance, combined with his desire for a big-money deal on the new contract he was due, meant that his time in San Francisco was coming to an end. And in 1993, the 49ers dealt their superstar quarterback to the Kansas City Chiefs. Moving Montana was an emotional issue, both in the dressing room and in the Bay area. The fans felt obligated to choose sides, and many campaigned to keep Montana on the club. In the end, Montana got the challenge he needed with the Chiefs, lifting them into the playoffs for two consecutive seasons before retiring in 1995 — the same year Steve Young led the 49ers to their fifth title.

LISTEN UP

THE 45-POINT MARGIN OF VICTORY IS THE LARGEST IN A SUPER BOWL GAME.

Denver's John Elway is sacked by San Francisco's Danny Stubbs in the 49ers' record-setting Super Bowl win.

MVP

JOE MONTANA | QB

Montana put on a passing display that made it look as if the 49ers were playing against a nine-man defense. He threw for five touchdowns, three of them to his faithful sidekick Jerry Rice. At game's end, the media surrounded Montana and asked if winning the Super Bowl was getting to be a little too routine. He replied: "Each Super Bowl becomes more precious. The more, the merrier. They are all sweet, and this was the sweetest yet. It was so much fun; we couldn't wait to get back onto the field." And even though this would be Montana's last Super Bowl appearance, he remains one of the NFL's winningest playoff quarterbacks.

SUPER BOWL | TWENTY-FIVE

XXV

JANUARY 27, 1991

NEW YORK **GIANTS** **20** / **19** BUFFALO **BILLS**

PATH TO THE SUPER BOWL

NFC: DIVISION – NEW YORK GIANTS 31 VS. CHICAGO 3
CONFERENCE CHAMPIONSHIP – NEW YORK GIANTS 15 VS. SAN FRANCISCO 13

AFC: DIVISION – BUFFALO 44 VS. MIAMI 34
CONFERENCE CHAMPIONSHIP – BUFFALO 51 VS. LOS ANGELES RAIDERS

WHERE	ATTENDANCE	TV AUDIENCE	HALFTIME
TAMPA STADIUM, TAMPA, FLORIDA	73,813	79.5 MILLION	NEW KIDS ON THE BLOCK

"Wide right." Those two words have gone down as the most famous reference point for the Super Bowl's 25th anniversary game. That was the call from commentator Al Michaels as Scott Norwood's game-winning field goal attempt started sailing wide of the right goalpost.

The Buffalo Bills had their best season in franchise history, going 13-3 to win their division. To cap it all off, they were going to their first-ever Super Bowl. The New York Giants also had a 13-3 season, which was as well as the club had performed since they last won the Super Bowl four years earlier.

Even though the Giants had more experience, the Bills took them on and led the game for large chunks of time. Buffalo opted for a no-huddle offense directed by quarterback Jim Kelly and executed brilliantly by running back Thurman Thomas. Both teams kicked field goals in the first quarter and both got touchdowns in the second. Thanks to a safety, Buffalo was ahead 12–10 going into halftime. The Giants came back for the third ready to take the lead by both exhausting the Bills' defense with lots of short passes (including several to running back Ottis Anderson, who scored a touchdown) and punishing Buffalo's ball carriers with a heavy ground attack.

With the score 20–19 for New York and a little over two minutes left in the game, Kelly did his part, moving the ball as close as he could to the Giants' end zone. Then it happened. With eight seconds left in the game, Norwood attempted a 47-yard field goal to give Buffalo the championship. The snap was good; the hold was good . . . wide right.

There are people to this day who refuse to give Norwood a break, even though he was only one for five in field goal attempts on grass of 40 or more yards. Despite having made hundreds of successful kicks during his career with Buffalo, it was the one he missed that has stamped his football legacy. Scott Norwood — wide right.

STAR-SPANGLED FOOTBALL

This was the big game played against a bigger backdrop. The United States was heavily involved in the Gulf War, causing NFL officials to entertain the possibility of an attack during one of America's most iconic events. The security for Super Bowl XXV was tightened up, and every fan had to go through a metal detector. In the end, there was no attack on the Super Bowl, but kicker Scott Norwood did have to eventually flee Buffalo due to "the Miss." He kicked for one more season before moving to Virginia to sell insurance. It seemed the only time he would be back in the limelight was when the media called at Super Bowl time to ask him to relive his field goal attempt. Since then, Norwood has moved back to Buffalo and received the Distinguished Service Award in 2011 from Bills owner Ralph Wilson.

LISTEN UP

THE GIANTS SET A SUPER BOWL RECORD BY HAVING POSSESSION OF THE BALL FOR 40 MINUTES AND 33 SECONDS.

Buffalo Bills running back Thurman Thomas carries the ball through the New York Giants defensive line during Super Bowl XXV.

MVP

OTTIS ANDERSON | RB

Buffalo's Thurman Thomas was in high gear, rushing 15 times for 135 yards, plus a touchdown, and also catching five passes for 55 yards. Jim Kelly completed 18 of 30 passes for 212 yards. But neither Thomas nor Kelly received enough votes to be the game's most valuable player. Not wanting a repeat of Super Bowl V, when Dallas Cowboys linebacker Chuck Howley was given the award in a losing effort, voters selected Giants running back Ottis Anderson as Super Bowl MVP. His numbers were a respectable 21 carries for 102 yards and a touchdown. But selecting his teammate Jeff Hostetler would have made more sense, as he completed 20 of 32 passes for 222 yards and a touchdown. However, the voters liked how Anderson lugged the ball and ate up possession time, keeping the Bills' offense stuck on the sidelines.

★ ★ ★

SUPER BOWL | TWENTY-SIX

XXVI

JANUARY 26, 1992

WASHINGTON **REDSKINS 37** | **24** BUFFALO **BILLS**

PATH TO THE SUPER BOWL

NFC: DIVISION – WASHINGTON 24 VS. ATLANTA 7
CONFERENCE CHAMPIONSHIP – WASHINGTON 41 VS. DETROIT 10

AFC: DIVISION – BUFFALO 37 VS. KANSAS CITY 14
CONFERENCE CHAMPIONSHIP – BUFFALO 10 VS. DENVER 7

WHERE
METRODOME,
MINNEAPOLIS, MINNESOTA

ATTENDANCE
63,130

TV AUDIENCE
79.6 MILLION

HALFTIME
GLORIA ESTEFAN WITH BRIAN BOITANO
AND DOROTHY HAMILL

Washington's Earnest Byner gains some of his 49 rushing yards in Super Bowl XXVI. Byner was also good for a receiving touchdown in the Redskins' win.

A year after the "wide right" fiasco, the Buffalo Bills were back to play for an NFL championship in Super Bowl XXVI. The Bills had quarterback Jim Kelly and his no-huddle offense — the one that had put opposing defenses on their heels as Buffalo racked up an AFC-best 13-3 record. Their opposition, the Washington Redskins, was the only team with a better regular-season record (14-2) — they also had the most points in the league during those 16 games (485) and the second fewest points against (224). So if Bills fans thought it couldn't get worse than losing on a missed field goal, they were at least about to be presented with an alternative.

Things didn't start well for the Bills, as league MVP Thurman Thomas was held off the field for the first two plays because he couldn't find his helmet. As writer Sal Maiorana put it, "It was under the bench, which is probably where Thomas wishes it would have stayed." Washington's defense dominated early against the Bills, forcing Kelly to throw without much accuracy and to avoid the ground game, which pretty much took Thomas out of the mix. Still, both teams were held scoreless in the first quarter.

The Redskins exploded for 17 points in the second quarter, and it just got worse for Buffalo from there. In the second half the Washington defense continued to hurry Kelly. Over the course of the game, the Bills quarterback hoisted a record-setting 58 pass attempts (only 28 were complete), resulting in four interceptions (tying a Super Bowl record). He was also sacked four times.

Buffalo did play valiantly, with second-half scores from Thomas, Don Beebe and Pete Metzelaars. Scott Norwood even made a successful field goal, but it was all too late as Washington added 20 points of their own, the Buffalo defense unable to provide the critical stops the Bills needed in order to make a comeback a reality. The 37–24 Washington triumph gave the Redskins their third Super Bowl victory in 10 years and handed the Bills their second straight loss.

Redskins center Jeff Bostic said after the game: "If the rest of Washington ran as efficiently as this football team, there wouldn't be any deficit."

MVP

MARK RYPIEN | QB

The week before Super Bowl XXVI, *USA Today* reported that Washington quarterback Mark Rypien "scores low in charisma, is only average looking and has a lousy haircut." That may have all been true, but he also had a great arm, his share of toughness and an impeccable sense of timing. During training camp before the 1991 season, Rypien signed a one-year $1.25 million deal after contract disputes with Redskins management. This gamble paid off after the Super Bowl when Rypien signed a three-year $9 million contract with Washington, tying him for the third highest salary in the game. Rypien's success with Washington turned out to be fleeting, however. The next season he threw just 13 touchdowns, compared to 17 interceptions, and had the NFL's lowest passer rating. By early in the 1993 season he was no longer the team's starting quarterback.

LISTEN UP

THIS WAS THE FIRST SUPER BOWL DURING WHICH A TOUCHDOWN WAS OVERTURNED THANKS TO INSTANT REPLAY.

BULLETIN BOARD MATERIAL

Super Bowl teams shouldn't need extra motivation to win. But Buffalo defensive line coach Chuck Dickerson may have given some to the Washington Redskins because of an attempt at humor. The Redskins were led up front by a monstrous group of offensive linemen known as "the Hogs." During Super Bowl week, Dickerson gave an interview in which he said that Washington tackle Joe Jacoby was a "Neanderthal" who "slobbers a lot"; tackle Jim Lachey was a "ballerina in a 310-pound body"; and center Jeff Bostic was "ugly like the rest of them" and "ate grease." Redskins coach Joe Gibbs showed his team the videotape of Dickerson's analysis the night before the game, and the players testified that it fired them up. Bills head coach Marv Levy fired Dickerson four days after the Super Bowl.

★ ★ ★

SUPER BOWL | TWENTY-SEVEN

XXVII

JANUARY 31, 1993

DALLAS **COWBOYS 52** / **17** BUFFALO **BILLS**

PATH TO THE SUPER BOWL

NFC: DIVISION – DALLAS 34 VS. PHILADELPHIA 10
CONFERENCE CHAMPIONSHIP – DALLAS 30 VS. SAN FRANCISCO 20

AFC: WILD CARD – BUFFALO 41 VS. HOUSTON 38
DIVISION – BUFFALO 24 VS. PITTSBURGH 3
CONFERENCE CHAMPIONSHIP – BUFFALO 29 VS. MIAMI 10

WHERE	ATTENDANCE	TV AUDIENCE	HALFTIME
ROSE BOWL, PASADENA, CALIFORNIA	98,374	91 MILLION	MICHAEL JACKSON AND 3,500 LOCAL CHILDREN

Nothing stirs emotion in the NFL quite like the presence of the Dallas Cowboys — "America's Team" to some; an evil empire to others. And of course no band of Cowboys ever carried themselves with the swagger of these guys, from Troy Aikman, the quarterback with the movie star looks, to running back Emmitt Smith, defined by his toughness and determination, this was a Cowboys team that earned its greatness. The major parts were in place, starting with their 1-15 season in 1989 (Jimmy Johnson's first as head coach). Through the lessons learned on a three-year climb from the bottom to the very top, they developed into a brash, fast and talented club. It was at the expense of the Buffalo Bills that this boisterous bunch proved to the football world that they were the real deal.

A quick look at both teams' regular-season performances would show they were relatively on par in terms of total yards, touchdowns and passing attempts. And the Bills were actually leading their third consecutive Super Bowl appearance by a score of 7–0 before everything fell apart in the last five minutes of the first quarter.

In that time Buffalo quarterback Jim Kelly threw an interception and fumbled the ball, both plays allowing Dallas to convert touchdowns. Kelly then left the game in the second quarter because of injury, so backup Frank Reich came in. Dallas scored two more touchdowns, and the Bills' last scoring play came at the very end of the third quarter. The Cowboys scored three more touchdowns in the fourth — the most by any team in the final stanza. Dallas forced nine Buffalo turnovers, which they converted into 35 points, scoring in bunches so quickly that the Bills could barely process what was happening.

The first Bills Super Bowl loss was a heartbreaker; the second was dispiriting; and this one would be remembered as simply hopeless. "The unbelievable thing is that each year it keeps getting worse," said Buffalo's Steve Tasker. "And I have no idea why."

LEON LETT

He is featured in one of the most memorable plays in Super Bowl history, and it didn't have any bearing on the outcome of the game. With Dallas leading Buffalo 52–17 late in the fourth quarter, the Cowboys sacked Bills quarterback Frank Reich, who fumbled the ball and watched it bounce straight into the arms of Dallas defensive lineman Leon Lett at the Cowboys' 31-yard line. Lett took off down the field, rumbling toward the end zone with no one left to stop him. With roughly 5 yards to go, convinced he was home free, Lett extended his ball-holding hand triumphantly. He didn't see Bills receiver Don Beebe screaming in from behind and arriving just in time to knock the ball out of Lett's hand, forcing it through the end zone for a touchback. Had Lett scored, the Cowboys would have set a record for points by one team in a Super Bowl game.

LISTEN UP

THE BILLS HAD NINE TURNOVERS AGAINST DALLAS, A SUPER BOWL RECORD.

Don Beebe was Buffalo's only shining star in Super Bowl XXVII. Here he stops Leon Lett from making the score an abysmal 58–17 in favor of Dallas.

MVP

TROY AIKMAN | QB

It is every college football player's dream to become the first overall pick of the NFL Draft and to take his team on a climb to a Super Bowl victory. That is exactly what Dallas Cowboys quarterback Troy Aikman did after being selected with the first pick in 1989 out of UCLA. It wasn't all roses, though. Aikman transformed himself from a rookie with a 0-11 record and a one-to-two ratio of touchdowns to interceptions into a starting quarter-back with one of the best completion percentages in the NFL. In the playoffs for the 1992 season he firmly cemented his place as one of the game's best passers when he threw 89 consecutive passes without an interception to set a still-standing record. During the Super Bowl, Aikman completed 22 of 30 passes for 273 yards and four touchdowns.

★ ★ ★

SUPER BOWL | TWENTY-EIGHT

XXVIII

JANUARY 30, 1994

DALLAS **COWBOYS 30** | **13** BUFFALO **BILLS**

PATH TO THE SUPER BOWL

NFC: DIVISION – DALLAS 27 VS. GREEN BAY 17
CONFERENCE CHAMPIONSHIP – DALLAS 38 VS. SAN FRANCISCO 21

AFC: DIVISION – BUFFALO 29 VS. LOS ANGELES RAIDERS 23
CONFERENCE CHAMPIONSHIP – BUFFALO 30 VS. KANSAS CITY 13

WHERE
GEORGIA DOME,
ATLANTA, GEORGIA

ATTENDANCE
72,817

TV AUDIENCE
90 MILLION

HALFTIME
CLINT BLACK, TANYA TUCKER, TRAVIS TRITT,
AND WYNONNA AND NAOMI JUDD

Troy Aikman looks to hand off the ball to Emmitt Smith during Super Bowl XXVIII, a game in which Smith ran for 132 yards and two touchdowns.

If a team makes it to the Super Bowl for four consecutive years and never comes out victorious, could you call them chokers? If another team wins its second consecutive NFL championship (and fourth overall), could you call them a dynasty?

These were questions that could have been asked after Super Bowl XXVIII. After being humiliated in losses to the New York Giants, Washington Redskins and Dallas Cowboys, the Buffalo Bills seemed ready to claim football's ultimate prize in their second attempt against America's Team.

The Bills had beaten the Cowboys in their regular-season matchup that year. They both went on to post 12-4 records before the playoffs, and both teams made their march to the championship look easy. So football fans were treated to a Super Bowl rematch, an event so rare it had never happened before and hasn't happened since.

For the first time since they had faced the Giants, Buffalo went into the second half of the game with a lead, 13–6. Unfortunately, miscues at the most inopportune times cost the Bills their last good chance at a championship.

The game turned in favor of Dallas less than a minute into the third quarter. Bills running back Thurman Thomas fumbled the ball, allowing Cowboys safety James Washington to take it 46 yards for a touchdown to tie the game 13–13. After the Bills punted to finish their next drive, Cowboys running back Emmitt Smith rushed for 46 yards over six plays and then scored a touchdown to give Dallas the lead.

With visions of their last three Super Bowl losses popping up, Buffalo managed to hold Dallas off for a while, until a fourth-quarter interception by James Washington slashed any Buffalo hopes of a comeback.

Whether they're chokers or not, Buffalo has never been the same team since those four losses. Dallas won one more championship two years later for a total of five, putting them in the company of the Pittsburgh Steelers and San Francisco 49ers.

MVP

EMMITT SMITH | RB

The 1993 season began with a focus on Dallas Cowboys running back Emmitt Smith, and it ended that way as well. Smith missed the first two games of the season because of a contract dispute with Cowboys owner Jerry Jones, despite his having made three consecutive Pro Bowls and winning two rushing titles. The Cowboys lost those first two games without their stud running back, making Jones willing to move in Smith's direction at the negotiating table. Four days after that second loss, Smith became the highest-paid running back in the NFL. He rewarded his boss by claiming his third rushing title (even though he played in only 14 games). In the Super Bowl, Smith carried the ball 30 times for 132 yards and two touchdowns, with 92 of his yards coming during the second half.

LISTEN UP

THIS SUPER BOWL GAVE THE BILLS THE RECORD FOR MOST CONSECUTIVE GAMES PLAYED AND MOST CONSECUTIVE GAMES LOST.

JAMES WASHINGTON

It's rare for a defensive player to be the MVP of a Super Bowl. But Dallas safety James Washington had the kind of game that could have easily earned him the honor. During the first half, with the game tied 3–3, Buffalo's Thurman Thomas took a shovel pass and fumbled the ball when Washington hit him near midfield. That turnover led to a Dallas field goal and a 6–3 lead. In the second half, Washington seized the moment again on another Thomas fumble, scooping up the ball and racing 46 yards for a touchdown. "It seemed like I was running forever," said Washington. His interception of Jim Kelly early in the fourth quarter snuffed out any chance the Bills had to reverse the momentum of the game. The Cowboys scored 17 points off of turnovers that involved Washington, who also led the team with 11 tackles.

★ ★ ★

SUPER BOWL | TWENTY-NINE

XXIX

JANUARY 29, 1995

SAN FRANCISCO **49ers 49** | **26** SAN DIEGO **CHARGERS**

PATH TO THE SUPER BOWL

NFC: DIVISION – SAN FRANCISCO 44 VS. CHICAGO 15
CONFERENCE CHAMPIONSHIP – SAN FRANCISCO 38 VS. DALLAS 28

AFC: DIVISION – SAN DIEGO 22 VS. MIAMI 21
CONFERENCE CHAMPIONSHIP – SAN DIEGO 17 VS. PITTSBURGH 13

WHERE
JOE ROBBIE STADIUM, MIAMI, FLORIDA

ATTENDANCE
74,107

TV AUDIENCE
83.3 MILLION

HALFTIME
TONY BENNETT, PATTI LABELLE, ARTURO SANDOVAL AND THE MIAMI SOUND MACHINE

From the outset, everything about the 29th Super Bowl was a mismatch. The San Francisco 49ers had won four Super Bowls; they had quarterback Steve Young, the NFL's regular-season MVP and leader in both passing touchdowns and passing efficiency; and they had the best record of 13-3 leading up to the Super Bowl. They crushed the Chicago Bears by 29 points in one playoff game and beat the two-time defending Super Bowl champion Dallas Cowboys in another.

The San Diego Chargers, on the other hand, had won the AFC West with a pedestrian 11-5 record and squeaked through to the Super Bowl with wins over Miami and Pittsburgh that were so close the combined point differential for the Chargers was less than a touchdown.

When the two California-based teams met during the regular season in December, the 49ers emerged with a 38–15 win. The Super Bowl point spread, favoring San Francisco by 19.5, was the largest in the game's history.

It came as no surprise then that the 49ers scored the fastest touchdown in any Super Bowl, doing so just a minute and 24 seconds into the game. The score was Young to Jerry Rice for 44 yards on only the 49ers' third offensive play. Their next touchdown came just over three minutes later, when Young connected with running back Ricky Watters for 51 yards. The Chargers didn't give up so easily, though; their first touchdown followed after making 15 plays to exhaust the 49ers' defense.

If it seemed as if a back-and-forth battle would ensue between the two teams, the second quarter proved otherwise. San Francisco scored two more touchdowns, while San Diego managed only a field goal to make the score 28–10 going into halftime. The 49ers dominated the first half and never looked back, controlling the rest of the game in every measureable way.

A bright spot for San Diego was when Andre Coleman returned a kickoff for a 98-yard touchdown, setting a record for longest return (which has since been beaten twice). After a successful two-point conversion, the Chargers were still down 42–18, but Coleman's game stood out in one of the most lopsided Super Bowls of all time.

JERRY RICE

Before the San Francisco 49ers defeated the San Diego Chargers to win their fifth Super Bowl title, Jerry Rice was well on his way to being recognized as the greatest receiver in NFL history. By the time Super Bowl XXIX was over, there was little room for debate. With 10 catches, 149 yards and three touchdowns, Rice made it look easy against the Chargers. His career Super Bowl totals of 33 receptions, 589 receiving yards and eight touchdowns are the most by any receiver in Super Bowl history. "Jerry Rice with one arm is better than any receiver in the league with two arms," Young said.

LISTEN UP

SAN FRANCISCO QUARTERBACK STEVE YOUNG PASSED FOR A RECORD SIX TOUCHDOWNS; HE SURPASSED FORMER TEAMMATE JOE MONTANA, WHO PREVIOUSLY HELD THE RECORD WITH FIVE TOUCHDOWN PASSES.

Superstar receiver Jerry Rice collects a few of his Super Bowl all-time-record receiving yards in Super Bowl XXIX.

MVP

STEVE YOUNG | QB

Steve Young's career took a long and circuitous route to Super Bowl glory. The college star from Brigham Young University signed his first pro contract for 10 years and $40 million, not with an NFL team but with the United States Football League's Los Angeles Express in 1984 — an organization that folded two years later. Young landed with the Tampa Bay Buccaneers in 1986, but his NFL career got off to a rocky start as he went 3-16 in his first 19 starts and threw nearly twice as many interceptions as touchdowns. The San Francisco 49ers brought Young in to study under Joe Montana in 1987. By the time Young made his first Super Bowl appearance as a starter, he was riding a streak of four consecutive regular seasons as the NFL's passing efficiency leader. In the Super Bowl Young completed 24 of 36 passes for 325 yards and six touchdowns.

SUPER BOWL | THIRTY

XXX

JANUARY 28, 1996

DALLAS **COWBOYS** **27** | **17** PITTSBURGH **STEELERS**

PATH TO THE SUPER BOWL

NFC: DIVISION – DALLAS 30 VS. PHILADELPHIA 11
CONFERENCE CHAMPIONSHIP – DALLAS 38 VS. GREEN BAY 17

AFC: DIVISION – PITTSBURGH 40 VS. BUFFALO 21
CONFERENCE CHAMPIONSHIP – PITTSBURGH 20 VS. INDIANAPOLIS 16

WHERE	ATTENDANCE	TV AUDIENCE	HALFTIME
SUN DEVIL STADIUM, TEMPE, ARIZONA	76,347	94.1 MILLION	DIANA ROSS

Dallas' Daryl Johnston cuts through the Pittsburgh line for a short gain in Super Bowl XXX, a contest in which Pittsburgh eliminated much of the vaunted Dallas run game.

Whether you were a fan of football or soap operas, you could find your pleasure with the Dallas Cowboys. America's Team was living up to its name, finding the national spotlight on a weekly basis. They lured All-Pro cornerback and two-sport star "Neon" Deion Sanders away from San Francisco in a highly publicized courtship that ended with Sanders becoming the second-highest-paid Cowboy. Not to be forgotten, Emmitt Smith rushed for 25 touchdowns (a record he held for almost 10 years). Combine that talent with quarterback Troy Aikman (fresh off a $50 million deal) and wide receiver Michael Irvin, as well as new firecracker coach Barry Switzer, and it was all larger than life in Big D.

In fact, to some, the Cowboys seemed a little too comfortable with their recent Super Bowl success and front-runner status heading into the big game. Pittsburgh Steelers' new head coach Bill Cowher sought to make the Cowboys' casual attitude about facing his team a rallying point for the Steelers: "Make them respect you" was a message he sent loud a clear.

The Steelers hadn't been to a Super Bowl since 1979, when they won their fourth championship. Under Cowher, Pittsburgh was making a comeback, having gone from 7-9 to 11-5 in his first season. This 30th Super Bowl was a grind-it-out affair between two NFL dynasties.

Dallas started off strong, taking a 13–0 lead with about six minutes to go in the first half. Pittsburgh quarterback Neil O'Donnell found Yancey Thigpen for a touchdown with just 17 seconds to go before halftime, putting Pittsburgh within one touchdown of the lead.

Pittsburgh, despite Cowher's efforts, was always playing catch-up in this game. Dallas raced ahead to a 20–7 lead in the third quarter, and after a Pittsburgh touchdown run by Bam Morris in the fourth to make the difference three points (20–17), O'Donnell threw an interception into the arms of Cowboys cornerback Larry Brown. Brown had already intercepted O'Donnell in the third quarter, and his second pick of the day set up the Cowboys for an Emmitt Smith touchdown to go ahead 27–17. The miscues by O'Donnell spoiled a fine effort by the Pittsburgh defense, which held Aikman to just 209 yards passing and Smith to just 49 yards on the ground.

MVP

LARRY BROWN | CB

Dallas Cowboys cornerback Larry Brown will go down as one of the least likely Super Bowl MVPs of all time. The 320th overall pick in the 1991 NFL Draft, Brown was the kind of player teams could find anywhere. And yet while Brown was never considered one of the greatest Cowboys of his era, he had a way of making a big impact in important games. None more so than his two interceptions of Pittsburgh's Neil O'Donnell in Super Bowl XXX, which made the difference in the Cowboys' third Super Bowl title in four years. "I was reading the quarterback all the way, and I felt he thought the receiver was going to go out," said Brown of his second interception. "I think there was some miscommunication." Brown immediately turned his newfound fame into dollars by signing a lucrative contract with the Oakland Raiders, with whom he lasted just two seasons.

LISTEN UP

THIS WAS THE FIRST TIME THE STEELERS PLAYED IN THE SUPER BOWL AND LOST. THE COWBOYS' VICTORY TIED THEM WITH SAN FRANCISCO FOR THE MOST WINS WITH FIVE.

THE NFL'S GREATEST RIVALRY?

One of the NFL's greatest rivalries was forged when the Pittsburgh Steelers and Dallas Cowboys both rose to prominence during the 1970s and were fierce combatants in those still-early Super Bowl days. The NFL's television reach was growing larger year by year, and the Steelers and Cowboys became synonymous with greatness, developing fan bases all over North America. From 1971 to 1980, the Dallas Cowboys represented the NFC in five Super Bowls and the Pittsburgh Steelers represented the AFC in four. The teams matched up for two of those, with the Steelers winning both. So it was hard to ignore Super Bowl XXX when they clashed again. This time, however, the Cowboys finally got the upper hand on their old nemesis. And even though the names and faces had changed, legions of Cowboys fans thought of Super Bowl XXX as payback.

SUPER BOWL | THIRTY-ONE

XXXI

JANUARY 26, 1997

GREEN BAY **PACKERS 35** | **21** NEW ENGLAND **PATRIOTS**

PATH TO THE SUPER BOWL

NFC: DIVISION – GREEN BAY 35 VS. SAN FRANCISCO 14
CONFERENCE CHAMPIONSHIP – GREEN BAY 30 VS. CAROLINA 13

AFC: DIVISION – NEW ENGLAND 28 VS. PITTSBURGH 3
CONFERENCE CHAMPIONSHIP – NEW ENGLAND 20 VS. JACKSONVILLE 6

WHERE
LOUISIANA SUPERDOME, NEW ORLEANS, LOUISIANA

ATTENDANCE
72,301

TV AUDIENCE
87.9 MILLION

HALFTIME
THE BLUES BROTHERS (DAN AYKROYD, JOHN GOODMAN AND JAMES BELUSHI) WITH JAMES BROWN AND ZZ TOP

Brett Favre scores on a 2-yard rush in the second quarter of Super Bowl XXXI, giving Green Bay a 27–14 lead.

The Super Bowl is usually too big to be taken over by one personality, but New England coach Bill Parcells did a pretty good job sucking up a lot of attention during the run-up to Super Bowl XXXI. Reports said there was a rift between Parcells and Patriots owner Robert Kraft, so deep that Parcells was determined to join the division-rival New York Jets immediately after the season.

If the Parcells drama was the sideshow of Super Bowl XXXI, then the main event featured two of the game's great quarterbacks in their primes: Green Bay's Brett Favre and New England's Drew Bledsoe. Favre led the 1996 season with 39 touchdowns, while Bledsoe had the most completed passes with 373. They also tied with a low 2.4 percent interception rating.

But it was the Packers who were favored to win by a point spread of 14, and it was the Packers who struck early, with a touchdown on their opening drive and then an interception converted into a field goal. The Patriots replied with a pair of touchdowns to take a 14–10 lead at the end of the opening quarter. Seventeen unanswered points, including a Super Bowl record 81-yard pass from Favre to Antonio Freeman, made it 27–14 for Green Bay at the half.

The Patriots came into the second half determined to gain some control. They managed to hold the Packers off and even pull to within one score late in the third quarter. However, that was erased on the ensuing kickoff when Desmond Howard returned a kick 99 yards for a touchdown.

"That kick return kind of turned it their way," Parcells said following the game. "Until that point, I thought we still had an opportunity to win."

The game wasn't over, so there's a chance that New England could have stormed back, but Bledsoe, who'd already been picked off twice to that point, threw two fourth-quarter interceptions, and the Green Bay defense never let New England have a sniff.

The storyline of two great quarterbacks in their prime was a good one but a short one. Both Favre and Bledsoe would pass the torch to two new up-and-coming leaders — Aaron Rodgers and Tom Brady, respectively. As for the Parcells narrative, he chose not to fly home with the Patriots from New Orleans and quickly accepted a role with the New York Jets.

MVP

DESMOND HOWARD | KR/PR

It was the first time a special teams player had been named Super Bowl MVP. But Desmond Howard had both the stats and a flare for the dramatic — his 99-yard kickoff return crushed the New England Patriots' hopes of mounting a second-half comeback. The Patriots had just scored to climb within a touchdown of the lead. Howard's timing was impeccable. "I knew that sooner or later I was going to scorch 'em," said Howard. Overall, Howard set a Super Bowl record with 244 return yards (154 on kickoffs, 90 on punts), and his touchdown became the signature moment of the first Packers Super Bowl win in 29 years. "That kickoff return by Desmond Howard was the big play [of the game] and I credit him for it," said Parcells. "That was a huge play."

LISTEN UP

BOTH TEAMS COMBINED FOR 24 POINTS IN THE FIRST QUARTER, SETTING A SUPER BOWL RECORD.

THE MINISTER OF DEFENSE

When Reggie White left the Philadelphia Eagles at the peak of his career in 1993 and decided to sign with the Green Bay Packers, it was the moment that changed the franchise. Green Bay hadn't been a home for star players since the 1960s; and success hadn't exactly been the Packers' trademark in the years since Vince Lombardi was on the sidelines. Reggie White changed all of that by choosing to play in the league's smallest market in frozen Wisconsin. White, known as one of the NFL's all-time greatest sack artists, set a Packers record for sacks during his six seasons in Green Bay with 68.5 (that has since been broken by Kabeer Gbaja-Biamila). White currently sits in second all-time in the NFL with 198.0 career sacks.

★ ★ ★

SUPER BOWL | THIRTY-TWO

XXXII

JANUARY 25, 1998

DENVER **BRONCOS 31** / **24** GREEN BAY **PACKERS**

PATH TO THE SUPER BOWL

AFC: WILD CARD – DENVER 42 VS. JACKSONVILLE 17
DIVISION – DENVER 14 VS. KANSAS CITY 10
CONFERENCE CHAMPIONSHIP – DENVER 24 VS. PITTSBURGH 21

NFC: DIVISION – GREEN BAY 21 VS. TAMPA BAY 7
CONFERENCE CHAMPIONSHIP – GREEN BAY 23 VS. SAN FRANCISCO 10

WHERE
QUALCOMM STADIUM, SAN DIEGO, CALIFORNIA

ATTENDANCE
68,912

TV AUDIENCE
90 MILLION

HALFTIME
BOYZ II MEN, SMOKEY ROBINSON, MARTHA REEVES, THE TEMPTATIONS AND QUEEN LATIFAH

Those making predictions about Super Bowl XXXII can be forgiven if they thought the championship was going to be a lopsided affair — especially if they believed in the tenet that history likes to repeat itself.

The matchup pitted the reigning Super Bowl champion Green Bay Packers, a franchise that had won every Super Bowl it had ever played, against the snakebitten Denver Broncos, four-time Super Bowl losers.

But if prognosticators probed a bit further, they'd see that this contest was more even than the playoff tables showed. In the regular season Green Bay had tied for the best record in the league (13-3) and were winners of the NFC Central. Denver, on the other hand was a wild-card entry. However, their 12-4 record was second best in the entire AFC, and the Broncos scored the most points in the NFL; only five points against separated the Denver and Green Bay defenses.

Underdogs or not, Bronco John Elway, the 37-year-old quarterback with more wins at that point than any other in NFL history, was the media's darling. The three-time Super Bowl loser now had a chance to go out on top.

That was the opportunity that awaited Elway in the fourth quarter as he led Denver's offense onto the field, tied 24–24 with 3:27 to play and the ball at Green Bay's 49-yard line. The next few plays weren't classic Elway; in fact, he made only one pass on that final drive, a 23-yard strike that brought Denver to the Packers' 8-yard line. The rest was left up to running back Terrell Davis, who eventually plunged in for the winning score. His three touchdowns in the game set a Super Bowl single-game record for most rushing touchdowns.

But Elway finally adding a Super Bowl win to his legacy is the enduring storyline of this game. "There have been a lot of things that go along with losing three Super Bowls and playing for 14 years and being labeled as a guy who has never been on a winning Super Bowl team," Elway said. That all changed on January 25, 1998.

THE HELICOPTER RIDE

Most Super Bowl games have a signature play, a moment that can define the rest of the game. The signature moment of Super Bowl XXXII wasn't a touchdown throw or big tackle, but an 8-yard quarterback scramble. It didn't exactly change the game, but it said everything about the determination of 37-year-old John Elway to win the game. With the score tied at 17–17 in the third quarter, the Broncos faced third and six at the Green Bay 12-yard line. Unable to find an open receiver, Elway took off down the middle of the field, diving and absorbing ferocious hits from Packers safeties LeRoy Butler and Mike Prior, as well as linebacker Brian Williams. Their opposing hits spun Elway in midair like a helicopter before crashing to the ground. "When I saw him do that and then get up pumping his fist, I said, 'It's on,'" said Broncos All-Pro tight end Shannon Sharpe. "That's when I was sure we were going to win."

LISTEN UP

MVP RB TERRELL DAVIS SET A RECORD WITH THREE RUSHING TOUCHDOWNS, WHICH WAS TIED IN SUPER BOWL LVII BY QB JALEN HURTS.

John Elway goes on a helicopter ride courtesy of Green Bay defenders LeRoy Butler, Mike Prior and Brian Williams. It was a defining play in Denver's first championship.

MVP

TERRELL DAVIS | RB

In today's era, Terrell Davis' second-half Super Bowl performance that included 90 yards and two touchdowns might never have taken place because of concussion protocol. Davis was kicked in the head during the first half, began suffering from a migraine and was questionable to continue playing. "In the second quarter, I really couldn't see straight," Davis said. "I had gotten dinged a little, and I knew a migraine was coming on. But I also knew there was a good chance it could go away." Go away it did; Davis came back for the third quarter and the rest is history. His time with the Broncos was short — he played in the NFL for only seven seasons because of injuries. But his legacy remains, as he is Denver's all-time rushing leader in yards and touchdowns.

★ ★ ★

SUPER BOWL | THIRTY-THREE

XXXIII

JANUARY 31, 1999

DENVER BRONCOS 34 / 19 ATLANTA FALCONS

PATH TO THE SUPER BOWL

AFC: DIVISION – DENVER 38 VS. MIAMI 3
CONFERENCE CHAMPIONSHIP – DENVER 23 VS. NEW YORK JETS 10

NFC: DIVISION – ATLANTA 20 VS. SAN FRANCISCO 18
CONFERENCE CHAMPIONSHIP – ATLANTA 30 VS. MINNESOTA 27

WHERE
PRO PLAYER STADIUM, MIAMI, FLORIDA

ATTENDANCE
74,803

TV AUDIENCE
83.7 MILLION

HALFTIME
STEVIE WONDER, GLORIA ESTEFAN, BIG BAD VOODOO DADDY AND TAP DANCER SAVION GLOVER

Denver's Ed McCaffrey gains a few of his 72 yards receiving during the Broncos' 34–19 victory in Super Bowl XXXIII.

It was again hard to escape the John Elway narrative during the week of Super Bowl XXXIII. The once downtrodden Denver Broncos were back for their second consecutive Super Bowl, and while there was no official word on this being Elway's last season in the NFL, it was all but assumed.

This time, though, the narrative had some drama — the Broncos would face their former coach, Dan Reeves, who was now leading the Atlanta Falcons. On top of that, Denver's new coach was Mike Shanahan, who had worked under Reeves in 1991 as the Broncos' offensive assistant but was fired after supposedly trying to undermine Reeves' relationship with Elway. If Shanahan needed any extra incentive to make it two Super Bowls in a row, he had all he needed in Reeves.

On the field, it turned out that John Elway really did save the best for last. He not only raised his second consecutive Vince Lombardi Trophy but also delivered his best of five Super Bowl performances. He completed 18 of 29 passes for 336 yards and rushed a touchdown on the final scoring play of his career. As the *Denver Post* put it, "Welcome to 7's Heaven."

For a game that eventually turned into a blowout, it was still relatively close during the third quarter when the Falcons drove deep into Broncos territory, trailing 17–6. But the second interception of the game tossed by Atlanta's Chris Chandler proved costly. Denver's Darrien Gordon returned the pick 58 yards, leading to a Denver touchdown and a 24–6 lead. Chandler's third intercepted pass was the nail in the coffin. Gordon also snared it and returned for 50 yards; his 108 interception-return yards gave the defensive back the Super Bowl record. It also set up Elway for a play he and coach Shanahan had scripted just for such a moment.

Another big play — a 39-yard completion to Terrell Davis — and a short gain put the Broncos on Atlanta's 3. Denver ran a quarterback draw and Elway marched into the end zone to seal the game and his career.

The Falcons had a decent total of 337 yards of offense, but the Broncos held them to just two touchdowns, both in the fourth quarter.

"They got the turnovers," said Atlanta linebacker Jessie Tuggle. "They put us in a position in this game where we were trying to play catch-up and trying our best not to make things worse. They made it where we couldn't play our normal game."

LISTEN UP

QUARTERBACK JOHN ELWAY EARNED THE MVP AWARD IN HIS FINAL NFL GAME.

MVP

JOHN ELWAY | QB

John Elway ended his NFL career in fairy tale fashion. As one of the greatest quarterbacks of his era, Elway had spent the first 14 years of his career listening to those who questioned whether he could win "the big game" — three Super Bowl defeats in an otherwise brilliant career can do that to a player. But after leading Denver to its second consecutive Super Bowl title, throwing for the third-most yards in a Super Bowl game and earning MVP honors, Elway had proven he could come through when it mattered most.

"I am just thrilled that we won. I'm thrilled to be a part of this team. This is what we play for, and to have this opportunity two years in a row is unbelievable."

SATURDAY NIGHT FEVER

Atlanta Falcons safety Eugene Robinson earned his place in NFL infamy on the day before Super Bowl XXXIII. Earlier on that Saturday, he received the Athletes in Action/Bart Starr Award, given annually to a player who best exemplifies outstanding character and leadership in the home, on the field and in the community. That night, he was arrested on charges of trying to solicit an undercover police officer who was posing as a prostitute. Robinson returned the award but still played in the game, giving up an 80-yard touchdown to Rod Smith during the first half. Several Falcons players, speaking anonymously to the media, suggested that the incident had taken their focus off beating the Broncos.

SUPER BOWL | THIRTY-FOUR

XXXIV

JANUARY 30, 2000

ST. LOUIS RAMS 23 | 16 TENNESSEE TITANS

PATH TO THE SUPER BOWL

NFC: DIVISION – ST. LOUIS 49 VS. MINNESOTA 37
CONFERENCE CHAMPIONSHIP – ST. LOUIS 11 VS. TAMPA BAY 6

AFC: WILD CARD – TENNESSEE 22 VS. BUFFALO 16
DIVISION – TENNESSEE 14 VS. WASHINGTON 13
CONFERENCE CHAMPIONSHIP – TENNESSEE 33 VS. JACKSONVILLE 14

WHERE
GEORGIA DOME, ATLANTA, GEORGIA

ATTENDANCE
72,625

TV AUDIENCE
88.5 MILLION

HALFTIME
PHIL COLLINS, CHRISTINA AGUILERA, ENRIQUE IGLESIAS, TONI BRAXTON AND AN 80-PERSON CHOIR

Tennessee's Kevin Dyson places the ball over the goal line and looks vainly to officials after having been brought down just short of securing a last-second score.

During the 1990s, Super Bowl games had earned the reputation of being blowouts handed down by the game's heavyweights. By the time Super Bowl XXXIV rolled around, fans were starving for a close game. Boy, did they get their wish.

The St. Louis Rams were making their first Super Bowl appearance since they'd lost Super Bowl XIV when the club was stationed out of Los Angeles. The Tennessee Titans, formerly of Houston, were playing in their first-ever Super Bowl and coming off a franchise-best 13-3 season.

St. Louis' offense came as advertised: great receptions by Marshall Faulk and Isaac Bruce fired from the excellent arm of Kurt Warner, who had a regular-season completion percentage of 65.1. The Rams' one problem, though, was getting through the red zone. They repeatedly drove the length of the field, reached the red zone and left with a field goal. This happened three times in the first half for a 9–0 lead; St Louis had 294 yards of offense, compared to 89 for the Titans.

St. Louis did manage a touchdown, but then the Titans answered with back-to-back touchdown drives of their own and tied the game on a field goal with just three minutes left to play. Less than a minute later, Warner hit Bruce for a 73-yard touchdown to make it 23–16 St. Louis.

Tennessee was led by quarterback Steve McNair and running back Eddie George, and both performed admirably in the loss. McNair, only the second Black quarterback to ever play in the Super Bowl, was excellent in completing 22 of 36 passes for 214 yards. The 64 yards he rushed set a rushing record for quarterbacks in the Super Bowl. George, stymied in the first two quarters, ran for 82 yards and two touchdowns in the second half.

Down 23–16 with 1:48 remaining, McNair had his work cut out for him. He and the Titans worked the ball to the Rams' 10-yard line with six seconds remaining. It all came down to one last play. McNair fired a slant to Kevin Dyson, who was tackled by linebacker Mike Jones. It looked as though Dyson was going to score, but Jones clamped down and stopped Dyson 1 yard shy of the tying touchdown.

"Somehow he got his whole body around, and got his left hand on my left knee," said Dyson of Jones. "I couldn't extend my leg and get that extra few inches we needed. I was down, and that was it. It was over."

LISTEN UP

RAMS LINEBACKER MIKE JONES MADE THE PLAY OF HIS LIFE WHEN HE TOOK DOWN TITANS WIDE RECEIVER KEVIN DYSON IN THE LAST SIX SECONDS, JUST 1 YARD SHY OF TENNESSEE'S TYING THE GAME.

MVP

KURT WARNER | QB

There have been several unlikely Super Bowl MVPs, but the story of Kurt Warner's journey from grocery store bag boy to Super Bowl–winning quarterback is the stuff of Hollywood screenplays. After going undrafted in the 1994 NFL Draft, Warner played in the Arena Football League for three years. The Rams signed him in 1998 and sent him to their European affiliate before naming him as their third-string quarterback. He was promoted to second string before the 1999 season, but starter Trent Green injured himself in the preseason, so Warner stepped up as the Rams' leader. He ended up leading the league with 41 touchdowns and a passer rating of 109.2. He led the Rams to their first Super Bowl in St. Louis and still holds the record for most passing yards in the game with 414.

DICK VERMEIL

When head coach Dick Vermeil arrived in St. Louis in 1997, the Rams were tied for the worst record in the NFL to that point in the 1990s. Vermeil had coached the Philadelphia Eagles from 1976 to 1982, before retiring at age 46 because of burnout — he was known as a workaholic who would routinely sleep at the office. Now he was back at age 60, leaving behind a television career and ready to have another go at trying to win the Vince Lombardi Trophy. "Fourteen years ago I left coaching because I had to. I'm not embarrassed to say it," Vermeil said at his media introduction. "Today I'm back because I have to be. I have a passion for this damn game . . . I didn't want to be 65 and regret not taking advantage of an opportunity." At 63, he finally had his Super Bowl ring.

★ ★ ★

SUPER BOWL | THIRTY-FIVE

XXXV

JANUARY 28, 2001

BALTIMORE **RAVENS** **34** | **7** NEW YORK **GIANTS**

PATH TO THE SUPER BOWL

AFC: WILD CARD – BALTIMORE 21 VS. DENVER 3
DIVISION – BALTIMORE 24 VS. TENNESSEE 10
CONFERENCE CHAMPIONSHIP – BALTIMORE 16 VS. OAKLAND 3

NFC: DIVISION – NEW YORK GIANTS 20 VS. PHILADELPHIA 10
CONFERENCE CHAMPIONSHIP – NEW YORK GIANTS 41 VS. MINNESOTA 0

WHERE
RAYMOND JAMES STADIUM, TAMPA, FLORIDA

ATTENDANCE
71,921

TV AUDIENCE
84.3 MILLION

HALFTIME
AEROSMITH, *NSYNC, BRITNEY SPEARS, MARY J. BLIGE AND NELLY

Since the 1980s, the NFL had been trending in the direction of more and more offense, with players like Joe Montana, Jerry Rice, Emmitt Smith and Walter Payton owning the record books with their offensive zeal. Quite a few Super Bowls during that time had point differentials of 20 or more. So by the turn of the millennium, it seemed unlikely that a team could win a Super Bowl as a defense-first club.

Then came the Baltimore Ravens, winners of Super Bowl XXXV. No other Super Bowl champion had been so singularly associated with the defensive side of the ball than the Ravens. Baltimore came in as a wild-card team, defeating the Denver Broncos, Tennessee Titans and Oakland Raiders before facing the New York Giants in the Super Bowl, where they dominated as well, allowing just 152 yards, forcing five turnovers and making four sacks, all without surrendering an offensive touchdown. Consider that the Ravens surrendered a total of 23 points in four postseason wins, or that over the 20 games played during the regular season and playoffs, only five times did their opponents manage to score more than 10 points against them.

During the Super Bowl, the Ravens' offense was good but not great. Quarterback Trent Dilfer completed just 12 of 25 pass attempts for 153 yards and a touchdown, with one Baltimore touchdown coming off an interception return and another off a kickoff. Dilfer's numbers shouldn't have been good enough to win an NFL title, but when New York's Kerry Collins completed only 15 of 39 pass attempts for 109 yards and four interceptions, they were more than adequate.

"I don't mean to disrespect anyone, but we're definitely the best defense of all time," said Ravens linebacker Ray Lewis. "The thing is, the Giants didn't know. You just don't know until you play us, but our defense is a buzz saw." And considering the Giants spent most of their time on their side of half, it seems like that's a lesson they'll never forget.

DILFER SHOWN NO RESPECT

Trent Dilfer was a 28-year-old quarterback in his contract year, with free agency on the horizon; he had just won the Super Bowl and was awarded the winners' trip to Disney World. That's a combination for most that has teams giddy with excitement, but not for Dilfer, it seems. Even the Ravens — for whom Dilfer went 7-1 in the regular season and 4-0 in the playoffs — opted not to keep the quarterback. Instead, they went out on the free-agent market and signed the Kansas City Chiefs' Elvis Grbac to a five-year, $30 million contract. Dilfer had to settle for the Seattle Seahawks and a backup roll, carrying the clipboard for second-year starter Matt Hasselbeck. He stayed there four years and started 12 games.

LISTEN UP

BACK-TO-BACK KICKOFFS WERE RETURNED FOR TOUCHDOWNS — THE ONLY TIME IN SUPER BOWL HISTORY.

Trent Dilfer hands the ball to Jamal Lewis during Super Bowl XXXV. Lewis ran for 102 yards and one touchdown in Baltimore's victory.

MVP

RAY LEWIS | LB

One year before he was named MVP of Super Bowl XXXV, Baltimore Ravens linebacker Ray Lewis and two associates were indicted on charges of murder and aggravated assault after two people were killed outside a party they attended in Atlanta. Lewis' attorney struck a deal for him to plead guilty to obstruction of justice and have the murder charge dropped in exchange for testimony against his two associates, who were later found not guilty. As part of that deal, Lewis received one year of probation, allowing him to return to the NFL.

During Super Bowl week in Tampa, Lewis came across as defiant instead of remorseful. His coach, Brian Billick, took aim at the media for what he felt was an unfair line of questioning about the incident one year earlier. "It's inappropriate, and you're not qualified," Billick said of the media. Lewis' legal issues are likely why Trent Dilfer was awarded the annual trip to Disney World, normally given to the Super Bowl MVP.

SUPER BOWL | THIRTY-SIX

XXXVI

FEBRUARY 3, 2002

NEW ENGLAND **PATRIOTS** **20** / **17** ST. LOUIS **RAMS**

PATH TO THE SUPER BOWL

AFC: DIVISION – NEW ENGLAND 16 VS. OAKLAND 13
CONFERENCE CHAMPIONSHIP – NEW ENGLAND 24 VS. PITTSBURGH 17

NFC: DIVISION – ST. LOUIS 45 VS. GREEN BAY 17
CONFERENCE CHAMPIONSHIP – ST. LOUIS 29 VS. PHILADELPHIA 24

WHERE	ATTENDANCE	TV AUDIENCE	HALFTIME
LOUISIANA SUPERDOME, NEW ORLEANS, LOUISIANA	72,922	86.3 MILLION	U2

New England Patriots kicker Adam Vinatieri kicks a game-winning 48-yard field goal for a last-play win over the St. Louis Rams in Super Bow XXXVI.

Back in the early days of the 2001 season, there wasn't a more unlikely Super Bowl champion than the New England Patriots or a less likely MVP than Tom Brady. Not much had been expected of the Patriots, as they were coming off a 5-11 record from the previous season. They were 0-2 when starting quarterback Drew Bledsoe suffered a sheared blood vessel in his chest, so backup quarterback Tom Brady, the 199th selection in the NFL Draft just 17 months earlier, had to step up. Any hope for a better season seemed lost.

Just to make the challenge that much greater, the first opponent the Brady-led Patriots would face was the offensive powerhouse of Peyton Manning and the Indianapolis Colts, who were 2-0. New England's upset win of 44–13 against the Colts proved to be a harbinger of things to come. Still, the notion of the Patriots winning a Super Bowl seemed preposterous, even when Brady finished with an 11-3 regular-season record.

Bledsoe (who had signed a record 10-year, $103-million contract the previous March) was medically cleared to return by Week 11, but head coach Bill Belichick stayed with Brady through the end of the regular season. But when Brady suffered a sprained ankle during the second quarter of the AFC Championship Game against the Pittsburgh Steelers, it was Bledsoe who came in to save the day.

On Tuesday night of Super Bowl week, however, Belichick announced it would be Brady who'd lead the Patriots against the vaunted St. Louis Rams, who were 14-point favorites. It proved to be a wise decision, as the Patriots were ahead of the Rams for the majority of the game. But St. Louis mounted a comeback and scored a touchdown to tie the score at 17–17 with one minute and 37 seconds remaining.

Instead of taking a knee to go into overtime, Brady and the Patriots moved the ball downfield to give kicker Adam Vinatieri a chance at a field goal. With seven seconds left, his kick sailed through the uprights from 48 yards out for one of the most stunning upsets in Super Bowl history.

MVP

TOM BRADY | QB

A quarterback who completes 16 of 27 passes for 145 yards isn't normally going to be a Super Bowl MVP. But on a New England team devoid of star players, someone had to win it. Brady essentially earned the award on the game's final drive. While television announcer and Hall of Fame coach John Madden was screaming for the Patriots to kneel down, kill the clock and play for overtime, Brady and head coach Bill Belichick decided to take an aggressive approach by going for the win. It was a brave move for a rookie quarterback, but it paid off when the Patriots won their first-ever Super Bowl. "That wasn't even on my mind," Brady said of going to overtime. "I was planning to go out there and win the game."

LISTEN UP

QUARTERBACK TOM BRADY, THE 199TH SELECTION OF THE PATRIOTS IN 2000, EARNED MVP STATUS AS HE LED HIS TEAM TO THEIR FIRST-EVER SUPER BOWL VICTORY.

POST-9/11 SUPER BOWL

Super Bowl XXXVI was supposed to be played on January 27, 2002. That was before terrorists attacked the United Sates on September 11, 2001, leading to the unprecedented postponement of a week of NFL games. Postponing a week had a domino effect on the rest of the calendar, and in order to play a full season, the Super Bowl needed to be pushed back a week. However, much of New Orleans, the host city, had been booked for the National Automobile Dealers Association Convention, which, after some negotiation, agreed to swap weekends with the Super Bowl to accommodate the NFL schedule.

The game proceeded without incident, under the watch of heightened security. Military vehicles were routine in the streets of New Orleans, and fighter jets made sweeps over the city the night before the game. It was the first Super Bowl game designated as a National Special Security Event. Up until Super Bowl XXXVI, that designation had been reserved for presidential inaugurations, political conventions and United Nations meetings.

★ ★ ★

SUPER BOWL | THIRTY-SEVEN

XXXVII

JANUARY 26, 2003

TAMPA BAY BUCCANEERS 48 | **21 OAKLAND RAIDERS**

PATH TO THE SUPER BOWL

NFC: DIVISION – TAMPA BAY 31 VS. SAN FRANCISCO 6
CONFERENCE CHAMPIONSHIP – TAMPA BAY 27 VS. PHILADELPHIA 10

AFC: DIVISION – OAKLAND 30 VS. NEW YORK JETS 10
CONFERENCE CHAMPIONSHIP – OAKLAND 41 VS. TENNESSEE 24

WHERE	ATTENDANCE	TV AUDIENCE	HALFTIME
QUALCOMM STADIUM, SAN DIEGO, CALIFORNIA	67,603	88.6 MILLION	SHANIA TWAIN, NO DOUBT AND STING

Another dramatic coaching debacle was the center of attention leading up to the Super Bowl. Fiery Tampa Bay Buccaneers head coach Jon Gruden had the Oakland Raiders in his sights. During four seasons as head coach of the Raiders, Gruden had compiled a regular-season record of 38-26 and taken the Black and Silver as far as the AFC Championship. But Raiders owner Al Davis didn't like Gruden's style, so when Tampa Bay came calling in February of 2002 (with a year still remaining on Gruden's contract), Oakland sold their coach for an unprecedented $8 million and four draft picks.

Coaching drama aside, Super Bowl XXXVII was essentially going to come down to Tampa Bay's top-ranked defense (they allowed only 196 points against) as compared to Oakland's league-best offense (they scored 450 points). And as so often happens in championship football, when two great forces collide, defense usually wins.

The Buccaneers, in fact, looked very much like a team that knew what was coming every time the Raiders had the ball. They sacked Raiders quarterback Rich Gannon five times and picked him off five times, returning three of those for touchdowns. There was a span in which the Buccaneers racked up 34 unanswered points, during which Oakland made just two first downs and never ran a play inside the Tampa 40-yard line.

Not used to being on the losing side of things was three-time Super Bowl champion Jerry Rice, who was in his first season with the Raiders. He may have been the oldest player on the team, but he led all receivers in yards during both the regular season and the championship game. This included a 48-yard pass from Gannon in the fourth quarter; however, Oakland's late offensive surge never challenged Tampa Bay's lead.

So did Gruden's Buccaneers have an idea what was coming based on the intelligence of their head coach? "I've never been involved in a game where everything we ran in practice played out so identically," said Tampa Bay safety John Lynch. At 39, Gruden became the youngest coach ever to win a Super Bowl.

BARRET ROBBINS

Oakland Raider Barret Robbins was the starting All-Pro center on an offensive line that most teams dream about. He flew completely under the radar during Super Bowl week until the day before, when he was reported missing after being absent during a walk-through and team meeting. Robbins eventually turned up and was so incoherent that Raiders coach Bill Callahan had no choice but to take him off the starting roster in favor of backup Adam Treu. It turned out that Robbins hadn't taken his depression medication that day and was suffering from later-diagnosed bipolar disorder. He played one more season for the Raiders but was released in the summer of 2004 after testing positive for a prohibited steroid.

LISTEN UP

OAKLAND RAIDERS QUARTERBACK RICH GANNON THREW FIVE INTERCEPTIONS FOR A SUPER BOWL RECORD.

Oakland cornerback Darrien Gordon is tackled during Super Bowl XXXVII by Tampa Bay safety John Howell and linebacker Nate Webster.

MVP

DEXTER JACKSON | FS

It was a day when Tampa Bay's best offense was its defense. So it was only fitting that the Most Valuable Player in Super Bowl XXXVII was Dexter Jackson, whose two first-half interceptions set the pace for Tampa's domination. "We had the No. 1 defense and nobody gave us any credit," Jackson said. "We [the defense] felt like we were one of the strong points of the team. We just didn't get any attention." Tampa Bay drafted Jackson out of Florida State University, where the once highly prized quarterback prospect had converted to safety. Good thing too, as Jackson was one of only 15 defensive players throughout the 2002 season to return for more than 100 yards after intercepting.

SUPER BOWL | THIRTY-EIGHT

XXXVIII

FEBRUARY 1, 2004

NEW ENGLAND **PATRIOTS** **32** **29** CAROLINA **PANTHERS**

PATH TO THE SUPER BOWL

AFC: DIVISION – NEW ENGLAND 17 VS. TENNESSEE 14
CONFERENCE CHAMPIONSHIP – NEW ENGLAND 24 VS. INDIANAPOLIS 14

NFC: WILD CARD – CAROLINA 29 VS. DALLAS 10
DIVISION – CAROLINA 29 VS. ST. LOUIS 23
CONFERENCE CHAMPIONSHIP – CAROLINA 14 VS. PHILADELPHIA 3

WHERE
RELIANT STADIUM, HOUSTON, TEXAS

ATTENDANCE
71,525

TV AUDIENCE
89.8 MILLION

HALFTIME
JANET JACKSON, JUSTIN TIMBERLAKE, P. DIDDY, KID ROCK AND NELLY

Deion Branch eyes defensive back Dante Wesley during Super Bowl XXXVIII. Branch collected 10 receptions for 143 yards and one touchdown.

Occasionally a team comes out of nowhere and makes it to the Super Bowl. That was certainly the case for the 2003 Carolina Panthers, a club that finished 11-5 for their first showing above .500 in six seasons and that was just two seasons removed from a disastrous 1-15 campaign.

Their opponents, the New England Patriots, had an incredible season and came into the Super Bowl with a 16-2 record, having won their last 14 games. They were definitely favored to win, but the Panthers made them work hard for their second Super Bowl victory in three years.

It was an odd seesaw affair that was at times an all-out offensive showcase and at others a series of impressive defensive stops. Case in point: it took 26 minutes and 57 seconds for the game's first points to be scored — a Tom Brady touchdown pass to Deion Branch — but then took 3 minutes and 5 seconds for the two teams to combine for 24 points. What looked like it could be 0–0 at the half turned into a 14–10 New England lead.

The third quarter progressed much like the first 26:57 of the first half, and the fourth quarter was like the final 3:05.

The offense broke out 11 seconds into the fourth on a pass from Brady to running back Antowain Smith. About two minutes later, the Panthers scored when DeShaun Foster rushed for a 33-yard touchdown. On their next turn with the ball, Carolina quarterback Jake Delhomme threw a record 85-yard pass to Muhsin Muhammad, giving his team their first lead of the day, 22–21, with 6:53 to play.

The Patriots then scored with just under three minutes remaining and added a two-point conversion before the Panthers responded with a game-tying score to make it 29–29 with 1:08 to play. John Kasay's kickoff for Carolina went out of bounds, allowing New England to scrimmage at its own 40-yard line. Five plays later Adam Vinatieri booted the game-winner for New England.

MVP

TOM BRADY | QB

Two Super Bowls, two Super Bowl MVP trophies — not bad for 26-year-old Tom Brady. Becoming the youngest quarterback ever to win two Super Bowls cemented Brady's status as a winning leader and raised the question of where he might rank among the game's all-time greats. His Super Bowl XXXVIII performance, which saw him complete 32 passes for 354 yards and three touchdowns, clearly demonstrated his evolution as a quarterback, especially when compared with his MVP-winning game two years earlier where he was only 16 of 27 for 145 yards. "Tom's going to be mentioned with the better quarterbacks playing now and in the past," Patriots coach Bill Belichick said. "You can't deny his production. He's a winner."

LISTEN UP

THIS GAME HAD DRAMA: IT WAS THE HIGHEST-SCORING FOURTH QUARTER EVER (37 POINTS), WAS WON ON A LAST-SECOND 41-YARD FIELD GOAL AND HAD A HALFTIME "WARDROBE MALFUNCTION" THAT SENT SHOCKWAVES THROUGH THE ENTIRE ENTERTAINMENT INDUSTRY.

DISTRACTIONS AND WARDROBE MALFUNCTIONS

Despite the entertaining football game, Super Bowl XXXVIII is remembered most for its halftime show. The controversial finale featured Justin Timberlake ripping off one of Janet Jackson's breast coverings, revealing her nipple, as he sang "bet I'll have you naked by the end of this song," from his hit "Rock Your Body."

However, there was a second non-football incident that took place at Super Bowl XXXVIII. This one, though, didn't make it to air. As the teams took the field for the start of the second half, someone dressed as a game official walked toward where the ball sat on its tee awaiting kickoff and began disrobing down to his jockstrap before breaking into a dance. When security gave chase, it was Patriots linebacker Matt Chatham who took down the intruder. "Was I surprised?" asked Chatham. "Hell no. I play for Bill Belichick. You don't think we watched film on that guy all week? I'd seen everything there is to see."

SUPER BOWL | THIRTY-NINE

XXXIX

FEBRUARY 6, 2005

NEW ENGLAND **PATRIOTS 24** | **21** PHILADELPHIA **EAGLES**

PATH TO THE SUPER BOWL

AFC: DIVISION – NEW ENGLAND 20 VS. INDIANAPOLIS 3
CONFERENCE CHAMPIONSHIP – NEW ENGLAND 41 VS. PITTSBURGH 27

NFC: DIVISION – PHILADELPHIA 27 VS. MINNESOTA 14
CONFERENCE CHAMPIONSHIP – PHILADELPHIA 27 VS. ATLANTA 10

WHERE	ATTENDANCE	TV AUDIENCE	HALFTIME
ALLTEL STADIUM, JACKSONVILLE, FLORIDA	78,125	86.1 MILLION	PAUL MCCARTNEY

The NFL's decision to hold a Super Bowl in Jacksonville seemed only slightly more ill-advised than its decision to put a franchise in the northern Florida city in the first place.

Jacksonville's lack of adequate hotel space had always been a concern, and for the Super Bowl, visitors were either staying out of town or bunking on cruise ships anchored offshore. Combine those headaches with the often cool and wet weather, and you can understand the sense that the NFL's showcase event wouldn't be returning anytime soon.

The real conversation about Super Bowl XXXIX, however, revolved around dynasty. With a win, the New England Patriots would match the Dallas Cowboys as the only other team to win three Super Bowls in four years, and quarterback Tom Brady's postseason record would hit a sterling 9-0.

The Philadelphia Eagles, whose only championship appearance had come in a loss to the Oakland Raiders in Super Bowl XV, were experiencing as much a sense of relief as celebration when, after three consecutive NFC Championship losses from 2002 to 2004, they finally won the conference championship to reach their first Super Bowl in 24 years.

The Patriots and Eagles were tied 7–7 at the half and 14–4 after three quarters before New England broke things open with a touchdown and field goal to take a 10-point lead with 8:40 left to play. Perhaps it was nerves on the part of quarterback Donovan McNabb or a rejuvenated New England defense, but on the next play, McNabb threw his second of three interceptions, giving the Patriots possession. With time winding down, the Eagles also seemed to be scrimmaging with a puzzling lack of urgency rather than using a no-huddle offense to utilize every second that was left. They did manage to score another touchdown to pull within three points, but it was too late.

The Patriots won their third Super Bowl and have continued to have great success. The Eagles, however, haven't gone 13-3 since that 2004 season and have made it back to the conference championship only once since then.

TERRELL OWENS

After three consecutive defeats in the NFC Championship Game, the Philadelphia Eagles made the big move to acquire receiver Terrell Owens from the San Francisco 49ers heading into the 2004 season. Owens, controversial because of his frank comments about other NFL players, was the kind of game-changing receiver the Eagles had been lacking.

His impact was immediate, as the Eagles raced out to a 13-1 start before Owens was injured on December 19th. Despite skepticism he could effectively return, Owens had nine catches for 122 yards in Super Bowl XXXIX. That, however, proved to be the high point of his tenure as an Eagle. Two months later he hired agent Drew Rosenhaus, who demanded the Eagles renegotiate the contract Owens had signed just one year earlier. Owens was eventually suspended for four games by the Eagles during the 2005 season for public comments — many directed at quarterback Donovan McNabb — and subsequently released.

LISTEN UP

THE PATRIOTS' VICTORY TIED THEM WITH THE DALLAS COWBOYS FOR THREE SUPER BOWL WINS IN FOUR YEARS.

Tom Brady calls out coverage during Super Bowl XXXIX. The win gave New England its third championship in four seasons.

MVP

DEION BRANCH | WR

There was a case for New England quarterback Tom Brady to win his third Super Bowl MVP trophy in four years, as he completed 23 of 33 passes for 236 yards and two touchdowns.

But a record-tying performance by Patriots receiver Deion Branch (11 catches for 133 yards, a mark held by Jerry Rice and Dan Ross) was enough to give the nod to Branch. "Deion made some big plays tonight," Brady said. "We figured out a way to get him the ball to begin the second half and he made the plays. I'm really happy for him."

The Super Bowl performance capped a fantastic postseason for Branch. He racked up 264 yards receiving, 41 yards rushing and two touchdowns in three postseason games. Considering he was injured for much of the regular season, and limited to just 35 receptions for 454 yards and four touchdowns, it was truly an MVP-worthy performance.

SUPER BOWL | FORTY

XL

FEBRUARY 5, 2006

PITTSBURGH STEELERS 21 | 10 SEATTLE SEAHAWKS

PATH TO THE SUPER BOWL

AFC: WILD CARD – PITTSBURGH 31 VS. CINCINNATI 17
DIVISION – PITTSBURGH 21 VS. INDIANAPOLIS 18
CONFERENCE CHAMPIONSHIP – PITTSBURGH 34 VS. DENVER 17

NFC: DIVISION – SEATTLE 20 VS. WASHINGTON 10
CONFERENCE CHAMPIONSHIP – SEATTLE 34 VS. CAROLINA 14

WHERE	ATTENDANCE	TV AUDIENCE	HALFTIME
FORD FIELD, DETROIT, MICHIGAN	68,206	90.7 MILLION	THE ROLLING STONES

Receiver Antwaan Randle El tosses a touchdown pass to Hines Ward on a reverse play. The novel play came with less than nine minutes remaining in Super Bowl XL.

After the Pittsburgh Steelers captured their fourth Super Bowl, they came up with a slogan for the following season: "One for the Thumb in '81," a reference to their quest to complete a set of five Super Bowl rings. It turned out to be a much longer wait — 26 years in fact — before the Steelers would get that fifth ring.

Head coach Bill Cowher, who had taken the Steelers to four AFC Championship Games and one prior Super Bowl, was determined to get a ring after 14 years with the team. And of course running back Jerome Bettis, the heart and soul of the Steelers for 10 seasons, had a chance to close out his Hall of Fame–worthy career with a championship in his hometown of Detroit.

The Steelers were actually long shots to get to the Super Bowl after having finished 11-5 on the year by virtue of winning their final four games to secure the no. 6 seed. No team had ever come from the bottom seed to win a Super Bowl. The Seattle Seahawks, meanwhile, had finished with the NFC's best record at 13-3 and had scored the most points in the NFL.

But overall, Seattle's first Super Bowl appearance was a series of miscues and missed opportunities, compounded by frustration with officiating. The Seahawks were flagged seven times for 70 yards compared to the Steelers' three for 20. They also had two missed field goals, and quarterback Matt Hasselbeck tossed a critical interception deep in Pittsburgh territory.

The Steelers' 7–3 first-half lead was extended on the second play of the second half when running back Willie Parker scampered for a 75-yard record-setting touchdown. Seattle added a touchdown of its own to bring the game within four points, but it was the closest they would come.

Ben Roethlisberger, at age 23, became the youngest quarterback to guide his team to a Super Bowl title. This despite his terrible line of 9 for 21 passing for 123 yards and two interceptions. Bettis contributed 14 carries for 43 yards in what, as expected, proved to be the final game of his storied career.

"It's been an incredible ride," he said. "I'm a champion. I think the Bus' last stop is here in Detroit."

MVP

HINES WARD | WR

His name was routinely left out among the greatest receivers of his era, and yet few receivers enjoyed as much success year in and year out as Pittsburgh's Hines Ward. His performance in Super Bowl XL was too good to ignore, though. He had five catches for 123 yards and a touchdown against Seattle, earning him the MVP nod. Ward's recognition might as well have been for his consistency and durability as the Steelers' most reliable offensive weapon for his six years with the team. "Words can't describe — from a third-rounder that came in and had to overcome so much — to get to this position," Ward said. "I'm very elated right now." Ward remains the franchise's receiving leader in yards (12,083), receptions (1,000) and touchdowns (85).

LISTEN UP

THE STEELERS WON THEIR FIRST SUPER BOWL IN 26 YEARS, FOR A FRANCHISE TOTAL OF FIVE; PITTSBURGH'S WILLIE PARKER BROKE THE RECORD FOR LONGEST RUSH (75 YARDS).

SUPER BOWL GADGET PLAY

Trick plays weren't very common in the history of the Super Bowl. But midway through the fourth quarter, leading 14–10 with the ball on the Seattle 43-yard line, Steelers head coach Bill Cowher called for a handoff on a reverse to receiver Antwaan Randle El, who happened to be a former quarterback at the University of Indiana. As Randle El came around, he launched the ball toward Hines Ward for a touchdown that helped seal the game's fate. "That's something we've been doing for a long time," Randle El said. "We hit that one earlier in the season for a touchdown and we had it set up for this game. When [Cowher] called it, my eyes lit up and I had to try not to give it away. What went through my mind was hope."

SUPER BOWL | FORTY-ONE

XLI

FEBRUARY 4, 2007

INDIANAPOLIS **COLTS** **29** | **17** CHICAGO **BEARS**

PATH TO THE SUPER BOWL

AFC: WILD CARD – INDIANAPOLIS 23 VS. KANSAS CITY 3
DIVISION – INDIANAPOLIS 15 VS. BALTIMORE 6
CONFERENCE CHAMPIONSHIP – INDIANAPOLIS 38 VS. NEW ENGLAND 34

NFC: DIVISION – CHICAGO 27 VS. SEATTLE 24
CONFERENCE CHAMPIONSHIP – CHICAGO 39 VS. NEW ORLEANS 14

WHERE	ATTENDANCE	TV AUDIENCE	HALFTIME
DOLPHIN STADIUM, MIAMI, FLORIDA	74,512	93.2 MILLION	PRINCE

The Indianapolis Colts' Kelvin Hayden runs back a fourth-quarter interception 56 yards for a touchdown to clinch Super Bowl XLI.

If NFL games were simply a battle of quarterbacks, then Super Bowl XLI would have been one of the biggest blowouts of all time. On one hand there was Indianapolis Colts quarterback Peyton Manning, the NFL's leader in passer rating for three consecutive regular seasons, a two-time regular-season MVP and the best player on the planet to never win a Super Bowl. On the other hand was the Chicago Bears' Rex Grossman, who ranked 24th in passer rating and 28th in completion percentage for starters in the regular season. He also had only three more touchdowns than interceptions (23-20).

Manning's Super Bowl performance was efficient, even in the heavy rain. He completed 25 of 28 passes for 247 yards and threw one touchdown and one interception — but it was definitely a team effort.

"Everyone thinks this is about Peyton's legacy," said Colts defensive end Dwight Freeney. "But listen — this is a 53-man team. Peyton doesn't do everything by himself, and at the end of the day defense wins championships. That still holds up."

Not only did the Indianapolis defense hold Chicago's offense to just two touchdowns and a field goal, their mental game stayed strong after the Bears returned a touchdown for 92 yards off of the opening kickoff. Most important, though, with the Colts up 22–17 heading into the final 15 minutes, the Indianapolis defense came through when it mattered most.

Just three minutes into the fourth quarter, Grossman's throw was intercepted by Kelvin Hayden, who returned it for a 56-yard touchdown. It seemed that even with the unstoppable Devin Hester returning kicks, a top-notch defense featuring Brian Urlacher and a strong running game, the Bears couldn't overcome the limitations of their quarterback.

"We wanted to put the ball in Grossman's hands," said Colts corner Nick Harper. "Now I can say what I'd really felt all week: We'd seen the film, and we knew there was no way in hell they were going to beat us in the passing game."

MVP

PEYTON MANNING | QB

Peyton Manning holding the Vince Lombardi Trophy was a powerful image, enough to silence the critics who'd insisted Manning was a player not cut out for the pressure of playoff football. It was a reputation that followed him right back to the University of Tennessee, where he was never able to lead his team to victory over rival Florida. Before beating the Bears in Super Bowl XLI, the Colts had been defeated by the eventual Super Bowl champions for the previous three seasons, twice against New England and once against Pittsburgh, even though they had had incredibly successful regular seasons. "We worked hard in years past also, and it's been hard not only to lose in the playoffs, but to watch these other teams hoist that trophy, knowing they were the ones who beat you," said Manning. "You realize how badly you want to be up there."

LISTEN UP

THIS WAS A SUPER BOWL OF FIRSTS, WITH A WIN FOR 31-YEAR-OLD PEYTON MANNING, AN OPENING KICKOFF TOUCHDOWN RETURN AND TONY DUNGY BECOMING THE FIRST AFRICAN-AMERICAN COACH TO WIN.

AN AFRICAN-AMERICAN FIRST

For the first 40 years of the Super Bowl, an African-American head coach had never led his team to the championship game. Of course there were no Black head coaches at all until the Los Angeles Raiders hired Art Shell in 1989, and still the vast majority of NFL head coaching jobs have remained the domain of white men. So when two Black head coaches met in Super Bowl XLI — Indianapolis' Tony Dungy and Chicago's Lovie Smith — it was truly an NFL milestone. It was also a reunion of two coaches who'd been together in Tampa Bay, where Dungy was the Buccaneers' head coach and Smith his defensive coordinator.

"I just told Lovie how proud I was of this whole moment," Dungy said after the game.

★ ★ ★

SUPER BOWL | FORTY-TWO

XLII

FEBRUARY 3, 2008

NEW YORK **GIANTS** **17** / **14** NEW ENGLAND **PATRIOTS**

PATH TO THE SUPER BOWL

NFC: WILD CARD – NEW YORK GIANTS 24 VS. TAMPA BAY 14
DIVISION – NEW YORK GIANTS 21 VS. DALLAS 17
CONFERENCE CHAMPIONSHIP – NEW YORK GIANTS 23 VS. GREEN BAY 20

AFC: DIVISION – NEW ENGLAND 31 VS. JACKSONVILLE 20
CONFERENCE CHAMPIONSHIP – NEW ENGLAND 21 VS. SAN DIEGO 12

WHERE
UNIVERSITY OF PHOENIX STADIUM, GLENDALE, ARIZONA

ATTENDANCE
71,101

TV AUDIENCE
97.5 MILLION

HALFTIME
TOM PETTY AND THE HEARTBREAKERS

The New England Patriots may have been all anyone could talk about before Super Bowl XLII, as they were coming off an undefeated regular season — the first during the era of the 16-game schedule — and had the highest single-season scoring performance of any offense in NFL history. But it was the unheralded New York Giants who became all anyone talked about after Super Bowl XLII.

The Giants were a wild-card team that had begun their season 0-2 and won three straight road playoff games before coming from behind to defeat the 12-point-favorite Patriots for their first NFL title in 17 years.

The game was a rematch of one played five weeks earlier when the Patriots beat the Giants 38–35 during the final weekend of the regular season. The result wouldn't affect the standings, but it could have tarnished New England's perfect season, so both teams played their starters from the beginning all the way to the dramatic finish.

What the Giants learned from that loss was that their best chance to take down the Patriots would be to upset Tom Brady's rhythm, which meant winning the battle in the trenches. Giants defensive coordinator Steve Spagnuolo opted to play three natural ends — Justin Tuck, Michael Strahan and Osi Umenyiora — among the four defensive linemen to try to take advantage of New York's athleticism along its front. They also mixed up their blitz packages to contradict looks they had given New England during their Week 17 meeting.

New England had been a strong running team all season but ran just 16 times for 45 yards against the Giants. The result was Brady being sacked five times on 48 pass attempts — his second-highest total of the season — as the Pats were held to their lowest point total of the year when it mattered most. There was also the New York Giants' 83-yard march that featured the most unbelievable catch in Super Bowl history — but more on that later.

GREATEST CATCH EVER?

New York Giants receiver David Tyree had made only 54 catches in his entire NFL career before Super Bowl XLII. He had three receptions in that game, and the final one couldn't have come at a more favorable time or in more dramatic fashion. Regarded as the most unlikely catch in NFL history, Tyree's grab came with the Giants facing third and five from their own 44-yard-line with 1:15 to play and trailing 14–10. Manning took the snap and escaped several grasping defensive linemen before heaving the ball downfield. Tyree got both hands on it, but New England safety Rodney Harrison knocked his left hand away, leaving Tyree to secure the ball with his right hand against his helmet. How he maintained possession as they both fell to the ground appeared to defy both the laws of physics and probability. Four plays later, Manning threw the winning touchdown to Plaxico Burress.

LISTEN UP

WITH THE GIANTS' VICTORY, QUARTERBACK ELI MANNING AND HIS BROTHER PEYTON BECAME THE FIRST SET OF BROTHERS TO WIN BACK-TO-BACK SUPER BOWLS AND MVP HONORS.

New York's David Tyree catches the ball with his fingertips and his head to complete a 32-yard reception as New England's Rodney Harrison tries to knock the ball loose.

MVP

ELI MANNING | QB

New York Giants quarterback Eli Manning had always been seen as a lighter version of his older brother Peyton: not as physically gifted, not as cerebral and certainly not as charismatic or engaging when it came to dealing with the public or media. But Eli Manning, who entered the league six years after Peyton, ended up matching his older sibling in both Super Bowl wins and MVP awards. Manning's numbers in Super Bowl XLII — 19 of 34 pass attempts for 255 yards, two touchdowns and an interception — weren't legendary, but his performance on the Giants' final 83-yard drive was. "I talked about it before with Peyton," said Eli. "You want to be down four [points], where you have to score a touchdown. Because if you're down three, maybe we settle for the field goal."

★ ★ ★

SUPER BOWL | FORTY-THREE

XLIII

FEBRUARY 1, 2009

PITTSBURGH STEELERS 27 | 23 ARIZONA CARDINALS

PATH TO THE SUPER BOWL

AFC: DIVISION – PITTSBURGH 35 VS. SAN DIEGO 24
CONFERENCE CHAMPIONSHIP – PITTSBURGH 23 VS. BALTIMORE 14

NFC: WILD CARD – ARIZONA 30 VS. ATLANTA 24
DIVISION – ARIZONA 33 VS. CAROLINA 13
CONFERENCE CHAMPIONSHIP – ARIZONA 32 VS. PHILADELPHIA 25

WHERE	ATTENDANCE	TV AUDIENCE	HALFTIME
RAYMOND JAMES STADIUM, TAMPA, FLORIDA	70,774	98.7 MILLION	BRUCE SPRINGSTEEN AND THE E STREET BAND

Through the first 42 years of the Super Bowl, no team had less of an association with the NFL's big show than the Arizona Cardinals, which as a franchise had made the postseason only four times, winning just one game in four decades. The fact that Arizona was facing the Pittsburgh Steelers, a franchise trying to become the first to win six Super Bowls, provided sharp contrast for the storylines heading into this game.

The 43rd Super Bowl is remembered mostly for an unlikely return touchdown and an unbelievable winning catch, but the game's fourth quarter was a stellar back-and-fourth offensive battle.

Pittsburgh linebacker James Harrison's interception return came with just seconds remaining in the first half. While the goal-line pick was significant enough on its own, the 240-pound Harrison rumbling 100 yards for the longest interception return in Super Bowl history swung the pendulum and gave the Steelers a 16–7 lead, and a huge emotional boost.

The game was far from over, however. Arizona's Larry Fitzgerald had the quarter of his lifetime in the fourth. With the score 20–7 and a little more than 11 minutes remaining, Arizona quarterback Kurt Warner repeatedly connected with Fitzgerald to score a touchdown at 7:41. Two drives later the Cardinals earned a safety on a Steelers penalty in the end zone to bring the score to 20–16. On the ensuing possession, Warner and Fitzgerald connected again, this time on a 64-yard touchdown strike. In just under nine minutes the Cardinals transformed the game, scoring 16 points, with Fitzgerald making five receptions for 95 yards and two touchdowns.

Then Pittsburgh's Santonio Holmes put his grip on the game's MVP award by dragging his toes in bounds in the back corner of the end zone as he stretched to haul in the game-winning score with 35 seconds left to play.

On the other end of that pass was Ben Roethlisberger. The 26-year-old Pittsburgh quarterback was the engine behind Pittsburgh's offense, completing 21 of 30 passes for 256 yards and a touchdown on the game-winning 78-yard drive.

KURT WARNER'S REDEMPTION

By the time he got to his first Super Bowl game during his first full season back in January of 2000 with the St. Louis Rams, Kurt Warner already had an NFL career unlike any other, emerging out of nowhere to become a champion and league MVP. But in the years between Warner's second and third Super Bowl appearances, a lot had happened. He'd been replaced twice — once in St. Louis where the Rams opted to go with Marc Bulger, and later in New York where the Giants benched him one-third of the way through Eli Manning's rookie season. When he arrived in Arizona in 2005, it appeared he might fade away in the desert on a team that had no real success during the Super Bowl era (they hadn't been over .500 since 1984). Instead, against the Steelers, Warner came just short of becoming the first quarterback to win Super Bowls with two different franchises.

LISTEN UP

PITTSBURGH'S HEAD COACH MIKE TOMLIN BECAME THE YOUNGEST COACH AT 36 YEARS AND 323 DAYS TO EVER WIN AN NFL TITLE. HIS RECORD WAS BROKEN BY SEAN MCVAY (36 YEARS 20 DAYS), WINNER OF SUPER BOWL LVI.

Pittsburgh Steelers linebacker James Harrison returns an interception for a 100-yard touchdown during the second quarter of Super Bowl XLIII.

MVP

SANTONIO HOLMES | WR

It would not have made much sense to give the MVP honors to anyone besides Pittsburgh Steelers receiver Santonio Holmes. He not only covered 131 yards with nine receptions but also caught the game-winning touchdown that cemented his team in NFL history with six Super Bowl victories. That final drive was full of well-executed plays by quarterback Ben Roethlisberger and Holmes, who ran over half his total yardage in those last few minutes of the game. When Roethlisberger's throw evaded three Arizona defenders, Holmes caught the ball with his toes barely dragging through the corner of the end zone for the touchdown. "I dared the team," Holmes said. "Just give me the ball, give me the chance to make plays and I will do it for you."

SUPER BOWL | FORTY-FOUR

XLIV

FEBRUARY 7, 2010

NEW ORLEANS **SAINTS 31** | **17** INDIANAPOLIS **COLTS**

PATH TO THE SUPER BOWL

NFC: DIVISION – NEW ORLEANS 45 VS. ARIZONA 14
CONFERENCE CHAMPIONSHIP – NEW ORLEANS 31 VS. MINNESOTA 28

AFC: DIVISION – INDIANAPOLIS 20 VS. BALTIMORE 3
CONFERENCE CHAMPIONSHIP – INDIANAPOLIS 30 VS. NEW YORK JETS 17

WHERE	ATTENDANCE	TV AUDIENCE	HALFTIME
MIAMI GARDENS, MIAMI, FLORIDA	74,059	106.5 MILLION	THE WHO

Lance Moore scores a controversial two-point conversion in the fourth quarter of Super Bowl XLIV to give the New Orleans Saints a 24–17 lead.

The story surrounding Super Bowl XLIV was one of redemption, which is one of the most powerful narratives in sports. The New Orleans Saints were four seasons removed from a 3-13 record, before which they were forced to evacuate their city along with tens of thousands of others in the wake of Hurricane Katrina. They played that 2005 season out of San Antonio, Texas, and many people wondered if the Saints would ever return home. But go home they did, and they went on to become the ultimate comeback story.

The Saints got to the Super Bowl after a franchise-best 13-3 season, riding the talent and guts of quarterback Drew Brees to knock off the Indianapolis Colts 31–17 and capture their first title. The Colts were no pushover. They had an incredible 14-2 season, and quarterback Peyton Manning had a 68.8 percent completion rating, second only to Drew Brees at 70.6 percent.

The Colts led the game 10–6 at the half, at which time Saints head coach Sean Payton made one of the gutsiest calls in Super Bowl history, gambling with an on-side kick that New Orleans recovered and then turned into a touchdown. "That was a huge turning point," said Indianapolis defensive back Melvin Bullitt. "They caught us off guard. It was gutsy. If we would have got it, the game might have been a blowout."

Instead, New Orleans was up 13–10 and the game's momentum had changed. Indianapolis got a touchdown and New Orleans got a field goal, giving the Colts a one-point lead heading into the fourth. Brees then engineered a nine-play 59-yard touchdown drive, completing passes to seven different receivers without any incompletions to make it 24–17 after a successful two-point conversion. Saints cornerback Tracy Porter turned out the lights when he intercepted Manning and returned a 74-yard touchdown.

The city that had played Super Bowl host more than any other (six) now had its own reason to celebrate. "Louisiana, by way of New Orleans, is back," said the Saints' owner, Tom Benson, as he clutched the Vince Lombardi Trophy. "And it shows the whole world."

MVP

DREW BREES | QB

After the 2005 NFL season, his fifth with the San Diego Chargers, Drew Brees was damaged goods and looking for a place to make a comeback. He had torn the labrum in his throwing shoulder, requiring a series of off-season procedures that put his future in doubt. The New Orleans Saints, in need of a comeback themselves, turned out to be the perfect fit for Brees. The quarterback moved his family to New Orleans and became a catalyst in the city's recovery effort through his several charitable endeavors. It also didn't hurt that he was becoming the best quarterback in franchise history. During Super Bowl XLIV, he completed 32 of 39 passes for 288 yards and two touchdowns. "Four years ago, whoever thought this would be happening?" Brees said. "Eighty-five percent of the city was under water . . . Most people not knowing if New Orleans could ever come back or if the organization or team would ever come back."

LISTEN UP

THE SAINTS BECAME THE THIRD TEAM TO WIN THEIR FIRST SUPER BOWL IN THEIR FIRST AND ONLY APPEARANCE. THE OTHER TWO ARE THE TAMPA BAY BUCCANEERS AND NEW YORK JETS.

BOUNTYGATE

When New Orleans captured its first Super Bowl, it felt like football's ultimate feel-good story. Then came Bountygate, the NFL's investigation into allegations of Saints coaches paying out bonuses for injuring opposing players, beginning during the 2009 season. Among the alleged targets was Minnesota Vikings quarterback Brett Favre, who the Saints played during the NFC Championship Game that New Orleans won to advance to the Super Bowl. In March of 2012 the NFL issued sanctions and suspensions against Saints head coach Sean Payton (one year), defensive coordinator Gregg Williams (indefinite, though it was overturned a year later), general manager Mickey Loomis (eight games) and assistant head coach Joe Vitt (six games). Several players were also suspended, but NFL commissioner Paul Tagliabue overturned those on appeal.

SUPER BOWL | FORTY-FIVE

XLV

FEBRUARY 6, 2011

GREEN BAY **PACKERS 31** | **25** PITTSBURGH **STEELERS**

PATH TO THE SUPER BOWL

NFC: WILD CARD – GREEN BAY 21 VS. PHILADELPHIA 16
DIVISION – GREEN BAY 48 VS. ATLANTA 21
CONFERENCE CHAMPIONSHIP – GREEN BAY 21 VS. CHICAGO 14

AFC: DIVISION – PITTSBURGH 31 VS. BALTIMORE 24
CONFERENCE CHAMPIONSHIP – PITTSBURGH 24 VS. NEW YORK JETS 19

WHERE	ATTENDANCE	TV AUDIENCE	HALFTIME
COWBOYS STADIUM, ARLINGTON, TEXAS	103,219	111 MILLION	BLACK EYED PEAS

Green Bay Packers wide receiver James Jones holds onto the football as Pittsburgh Steelers cornerback Ike Taylor attempts to tackle him during Super Bowl XLV.

Super Bowl XLV was a matchup rich in NFL tradition and history. The Pittsburgh Steelers, leaders in NFL titles with six, were playing the Green Bay Packers — winners of three Super Bowls including the very first one — at the home of the Dallas Cowboys, who just happened to be fierce rivals of both of them.

Super Bowl week, however, is most remembered for the severe winter weather that essentially shut down the city of Dallas. Fortunately, temperatures rose by the weekend when the Steelers and Packers met in one of the most anticipated Super Bowls in recent history.

The Steelers made it to the championship game after a 12-4 record, despite their starting quarterback Ben Roethlisberger missing the first four games because of a suspension; the Packers came in as an NFC wild-card team after finishing the season 10-6. Green Bay was still the favorite to win, though, because of quarterback Aaron Rodgers, who had emerged as a bona fide star after taking over from future Hall of Famer Brett Favre in 2008.

The Packers raced out to a 21–3 lead in the first 27 minutes of the game. This included two touchdown passes from Rodgers and a 37-yard interception that was returned for a touchdown by safety Nick Collins. The Steelers, however, came back with a pair of touchdowns, one just before halftime and another early in the third quarter.

Pittsburgh's momentum was halted when running back Rashard Mendenhall fumbled the ball, courtesy of linebacker Clay Matthews. The Packers took over at their 45-yard line, and five plays later, Rodgers hit Greg Jennings for an 8-yard touchdown that made it 28–17. Pittsburgh managed to claw within three points, but Green Bay sealed the deal with a field goal with just over two minutes remaining.

Roethlisberger wasn't able to repeat the final-drive heroics he had performed against Arizona three years earlier. Instead, Rodgers brought the Vince Lombardi Trophy back to Wisconsin for the first time in 14 years.

MVP

AARON RODGERS | QB

When Aaron Rodgers left high school, none of the major colleges wanted him, so he went to Butte College in northern California to prove he was good enough. His determination paid off. A year later, he was at the University of California, and two years after that he was drafted by the Green Bay Packers at 24th overall. The selection seemed as much a curse as a blessing, since Rodgers would have to wait to play behind the legendary Brett Favre and would presumably always be measured against him. But three years after Favre left Green Bay, Rodgers led the Packers to their fourth Super Bowl title, completing 24 of 39 passes for 304 yards and three touchdowns. "That's kind of been the journey of my career," said Rodgers. "Waiting for an opportunity and making the most of it . . . This was another opportunity that doesn't come around that often."

LISTEN UP

THE 45TH STAGING OF THE SUPER BOWL WAS THE FIRST SINCE SUPER BOWL II TO NOT HAVE CHEERLEADERS. THE REASON? GREEN BAY AND PITTSBURGH WERE TWO OF SIX TEAMS AT THE TIME THAT DIDN'T HAVE A CHEERLEADING SQUAD.

PRESIDENTIAL BULLETIN BOARD MATERIAL

In the days leading up to the NFC Championship Game between Chicago and Green Bay, President Barack Obama let it be known that he was pulling for the Bears: "If the Bears win, I'm going, no doubt." So when Chicago lost to the Packers, Charles Woodson, Green Bay cornerback and motivational leader of the group, told his team that "the President don't wanna watch us go to the Super Bowl. Guess what? We'll go see him." Woodson ended up getting injured just before halftime during the Super Bowl, but his quest to win a championship in his 13th season inspired his teammates in the second half. When the Packers visited the White House the following August, the president gave Woodson his due respect. "Charles, you're a man of your word," Obama said. "And I've learned something that every NFL quarterback knows: Don't mess with Charles Woodson."

★ ★ ★

SUPER BOWL | FORTY-SIX

XLVI

FEBRUARY 5, 2012

NEW YORK **GIANTS 21** / **17** NEW ENGLAND **PATRIOTS**

PATH TO THE SUPER BOWL

NFC: WILD CARD – NEW YORK GIANTS 24 VS. ATLANTA 2
DIVISION – NEW YORK GIANTS 37 VS. GREEN BAY 20
CONFERENCE CHAMPIONSHIP – NEW YORK GIANTS 20 VS. SAN FRANCISCO 17

AFC: DIVISION – NEW ENGLAND 45 VS. DENVER 10
CONFERENCE CHAMPIONSHIP – NEW ENGLAND 23 VS. BALTIMORE 20

WHERE	ATTENDANCE	TV AUDIENCE	HALFTIME
LUCAS OIL STADIUM, INDIANAPOLIS, INDIANA	68,658	111.3 MILLION	MADONNA

When the New England Patriots and New York Giants arrived in Indianapolis for Super Bowl XLVI, you could still feel the sting of what had occurred four years earlier, when the Patriots' date with perfection had been stripped away by the Giants' victory over them.

These were different Patriots, though, with only a handful of players remaining from the team that had accomplished the NFL's only 16-0 regular season. But the principal characters on both teams remained the same — Patriots quarterback Tom Brady and head coach Bill Belichick, and Giants quarterback Eli Manning and head coach Tom Coughlin.

Brady was ahead of Manning during the regular season in most measures, and New England had a better record too, having gone 13-3, while the Giants squeaked into the postseason with a dismal 9-7 record. However, odds-makers still saw this as a close game, installing New England as just 2.5-point favorites.

The Giants jumped out to a 9–0 lead on a safety and a touchdown before the Patriots scored 17 unanswered points, as New England quarterback Tom Brady set a Super Bowl record with 16 consecutive completions. But just as they had rallied during the regular season to gain a wild-card spot, New York saved its best for last.

The Giants started with two field goals to take them into the fourth quarter only two points down, 17–15. New York's defense also got to work, holding Brady to just 7 of 17 passes for 75 yards during his team's final three drives, the last of which took place under desperate circumstances. The Giants had just scored the go-ahead touchdown but left 57 seconds on the clock. The Patriots, though, couldn't capitalize and were again held to their lowest point total of the season in the biggest game of the year.

"When somebody has your number, there's just nothing you can do about it," said Giants defensive end Osi Umenyiora of his team's hold over the Patriots. "Apparently we've found the way to beat an unbeatable team."

BIG BROTHER

Although Eli's brother Peyton Manning did not play a single down for the Indianapolis Colts during the 2011 season because of injuries, his presence loomed large over Super Bowl week in Indianapolis. As the Colts finished the regular season with the NFL's worst record of 2-14, it became clear they would secure a top draft position and get the opportunity to select Stanford quarterback Andrew Luck. So while visitors to Super Bowl week were mostly interested in the Giants and Patriots, the citizenry of Indianapolis was fixated on the drama unfolding between Manning and Colts owner Jim Irsay, who was skeptical that his quarterback would play another game for his team. Of course little brother Eli had the spotlight when it mattered most, celebrating his second Super Bowl win and second Super Bowl MVP award, this time in the city his older brother had helped put on the NFL map.

LISTEN UP

THE GIANTS WERE THE FIRST TEAM IN NFL HISTORY TO GO TO THE SUPER BOWL WITH A NEGATIVE POINT DIFFERENTIAL (400–394) IN THE REGULAR SEASON.

New York's Ahmad Bradshaw scores one of the weirdest game-winning touchdowns in Super Bowl history. New England allowed Bradshaw to score quickly to keep as much time on the clock as possible for the last possession of the game.

MVP

ELI MANNING | QB

It's not as famous as the catch David Tyree made off the side of his helmet four years earlier, but Eli Manning's throw to receiver Mario Manningham late in the fourth quarter of Super Bowl XLVI belongs among the greatest plays in the game's history. Manning had again engineered a game-winning drive to defeat the New England Patriots. Trailing 17–15 with 3:46 to play, the Giants scrimmaged at their own 12-yard line. It was from there that Manning hit Manningham with a perfect 38-yard pass down the sideline that ultimately changed the result of the Super Bowl. When the Giants eventually scored on an Ahmad Bradshaw rush, there was no doubt who had been the game's most valuable player. "It's been a wild game. It's been a wild season," said Manning, who completed 30 of 40 passes for 296 yards and a touchdown. "We had a bunch of guys who never quit."

SUPER BOWL | FORTY-SEVEN

XLVII

FEBRUARY 3, 2013

BALTIMORE **RAVENS** **34** | **31** SAN FRANCISCO **49ers**

PATH TO THE SUPER BOWL

AFC: WILD CARD – BALTIMORE 24 VS. INDIANAPOLIS 9
DIVISION – BALTIMORE 38 VS. DENVER 35
CONFERENCE CHAMPIONSHIP – BALTIMORE 28 VS. NEW ENGLAND 13

NFC: DIVISION – SAN FRANCISCO 45 VS. GREEN BAY 31
CONFERENCE CHAMPIONSHIP – SAN FRANCISCO 28 VS. ATLANTA 24

WHERE
MERCEDES-BENZ SUPERDOME,
NEW ORLEANS, LOUISIANA

ATTENDANCE
71,024
TV AUDIENCE
108.4 MILLION

HALFTIME
BEYONCÉ AND
DESTINY'S CHILD

Darkness descends over Super Bowl XLVII during the 34-minute power outage that halted the then one-sided contest.

The 47th Super Bowl game is best remembered for a few different reasons. It was the first championship game where the head coaches were brothers. It was more than likely going to be the last game in the controversial career of defensive great Ray Lewis. But the biggest story that came out of Super Bowl XLVII was the 34 minutes when no football was actually played.

With the Ravens dominating the 49ers by a score of 28–6, San Francisco desperately needed something to turn the momentum of the game around. They got it early in the third quarter when half the lights in the Superdome went out.

The game was stopped immediately, and an eerie quiet fell over the crowd. When the lights came back on about half an hour later, the game resumed, though now the 49ers had the momentum. "Was it tough getting back out there?" Baltimore's Ray Rice asked rhetorically after the game. "It was pretty tough."

What started out as a blowout turned into an absolute nail-biter.

The 49ers had arrived in New Orleans on the strength of their dynamic young quarterback, Colin Kaepernick. For a team so used to postseason success, the 49ers had struggled for close to a decade. They were now ready to take on the Ravens, who arrived at the Super Bowl as the underdog.

Kaepernick struggled early in the game and the Ravens took advantage. They opened up a 22-point lead after receiver Jacoby Jones returned the second half's opening kickoff for a 108-yard score (a Super Bowl record), just moments before the lights went out. The power returning woke San Francisco up, and they began their comeback with a Michael Crabtree touchdown reception, a Frank Gore touchdown rush, a Kaepernick 15-yard touchdown run and a field goal. The 49ers outscored the Ravens 23–3 in about 12 minutes to bring themselves within two points.

But the run ended there. After both Gore and Kaepernick cut up the Ravens with their legs in the second half, they abandoned the run and option game when they had the chance to go ahead for good. With two minutes remaining and the ball at the Baltimore 5, the 49ers threw three passes to Crabtree, all incomplete.

Baltimore held on for the win and their second championship.

LISTEN UP

A 34-MINUTE POWER OUTAGE IN THE THIRD QUARTER MADE THIS THE LONGEST SUPER BOWL GAME AT FOUR HOURS AND 14 MINUTES.

MVP

JOE FLACCO | QB

Joe Flacco picked an excellent time to get hot. The Baltimore quarterback had a near-perfect playoff run by leading his team from a wild-card spot to road wins over the Denver Broncos and New England Patriots. To cap that off, he completed 22 of 33 passes for 287 yards and three (first-half) touchdowns in the Super Bowl to earn MVP honors. Overall, Flacco completed 11 touchdown passes without throwing a single interception during the postseason. Not bad for a guy about to negotiate a new contract. "He's taken a lot of criticism over his career, for whatever reason," said Ravens tight end Dennis Pitta. "But we've always believed in him. We've known the kind of player that he is. He's showed up on the biggest stage and performed."

THE HAR BOWL

Sports can be just as much a family business as anything else. So it wasn't unusual when Jack Harbaugh, a football coach at the high school and collegiate levels, wound up with two sons coaching the same sport. It was surprising, however, to see them both coaching in the same Super Bowl game. The story of San Francisco's Jim and Baltimore's John was woven throughout Super Bowl week, but the brothers seemed to enjoy coaching against one another in the championship game. At the end of the day, only one could win, and in this case it was older brother John and his Ravens. "I never thought you could feel 100 percent elation and 100 percent devastation at the same time," John said in regard to his victory and his brother's loss. "But I learned tonight you can."

SUPER BOWL | FORTY-EIGHT

XLVIII

FEBRUARY 2, 2014

SEATTLE SEAHAWKS 43 — 8 DENVER BRONCOS

PATH TO THE SUPER BOWL

NFC: DIVISION – SEATTLE 23 VS. NEW ORLEANS 15
CONFERENCE CHAMPIONSHIP – SEATTLE 23 VS. SAN FRANCISCO 17

AFC: DIVISION – DENVER 24 VS. SAN DIEGO 17
CONFERENCE CHAMPIONSHIP – DENVER 26 VS. NEW ENGLAND 16

WHERE
METLIFE STADIUM, EAST RUTHERFORD, NEW JERSEY

ATTENDANCE
82,529

TV AUDIENCE
112.2 MILLION

HALFTIME
BRUNO MARS AND THE RED HOT CHILI PEPPERS

The Super Bowl is where a player's legacy can be either made or broken. For Denver Broncos quarterback Peyton Manning, making his third Super Bowl appearance and the first on his new team, Super Bowl XLVIII figured to be one of those games.

Manning had been fantastic since he'd come back from missing the entire 2011 season while recovering from neck surgery. Released by the Indianapolis Colts postsurgery, Manning joined the Broncos and had two straight 13-3 seasons. In 2013 he led the NFL in touchdown passes and passing yards. Those who'd doubted he could maintain his elite status were made to eat their words. But whispers about his playoff shortcomings had started to reemerge; Manning had been to the playoffs 12 times but had only one Super Bowl ring.

Russell Wilson, Manning's Seattle Seahawks counterpart, was playing in his second season and had transformed the club from 7-9 the year before his arrival to 13-3 in 2013. He threw 26 touchdowns and only nine interceptions, plus rushed 539 yards. Would Wilson and his defense be enough to beat the experienced Manning and his offense?

It was a bad omen when a shotgun snap floated past Manning into the end zone for a safety on Denver's first possession of the game. But that was only the beginning. Manning looked overwhelmed each time he dropped back to pass. By halftime he had thrown a pair of interceptions, and the season's highest-scoring team was down 22–0 to a Seahawks club that showed their defense was worthy of some all-time recognition.

If Denver was hoping for a fresh start to begin the second half, they didn't get it. Seattle returned the opening kickoff for an 87-yard touchdown and later recovered a fumble to make it 36–0. The Broncos managed a touchdown and two-point conversion just before the end of the third quarter, but it was impossible to catch up.

"I don't know if you ever get over it," Manning said afterward. "It's a difficult pill to swallow. You have to find a way to deal with it and process it, and if you can, you try and fuel it to make yourself a better team next year."

NOT OUT IN THE COLD

Super Bowl XLVIII was the first to be held in the northern United States in an outdoor stadium. It may sound like a small consideration, but for decades the Super Bowl was contested in domes or open-air stadiums where sunshine was typically on the forecast. A game played in snow, as entertaining as it may be, isn't football at its best. That the game went off without a hitch was a relief for organizers, who certainly counted themselves lucky. Sleet started falling roughly two hours after the game, and by morning the New York–New Jersey area was a mess — traffic was snarled and flights were delayed or canceled. Had that weather arrived just a few hours earlier, the lasting images of Super Bowl XLVIII would have been very different.

LISTEN UP

BRONCOS PEYTON MANNING AND DEMARYIUS THOMAS SET THE SUPER BOWL RECORDS FOR MOST COMPLETED PASSES AND MOST RECEPTIONS, RESPECTIVELY, DESPITE LOSING. MANNING'S RECORD FELL THE NEXT YEAR TO TOM BRADY.

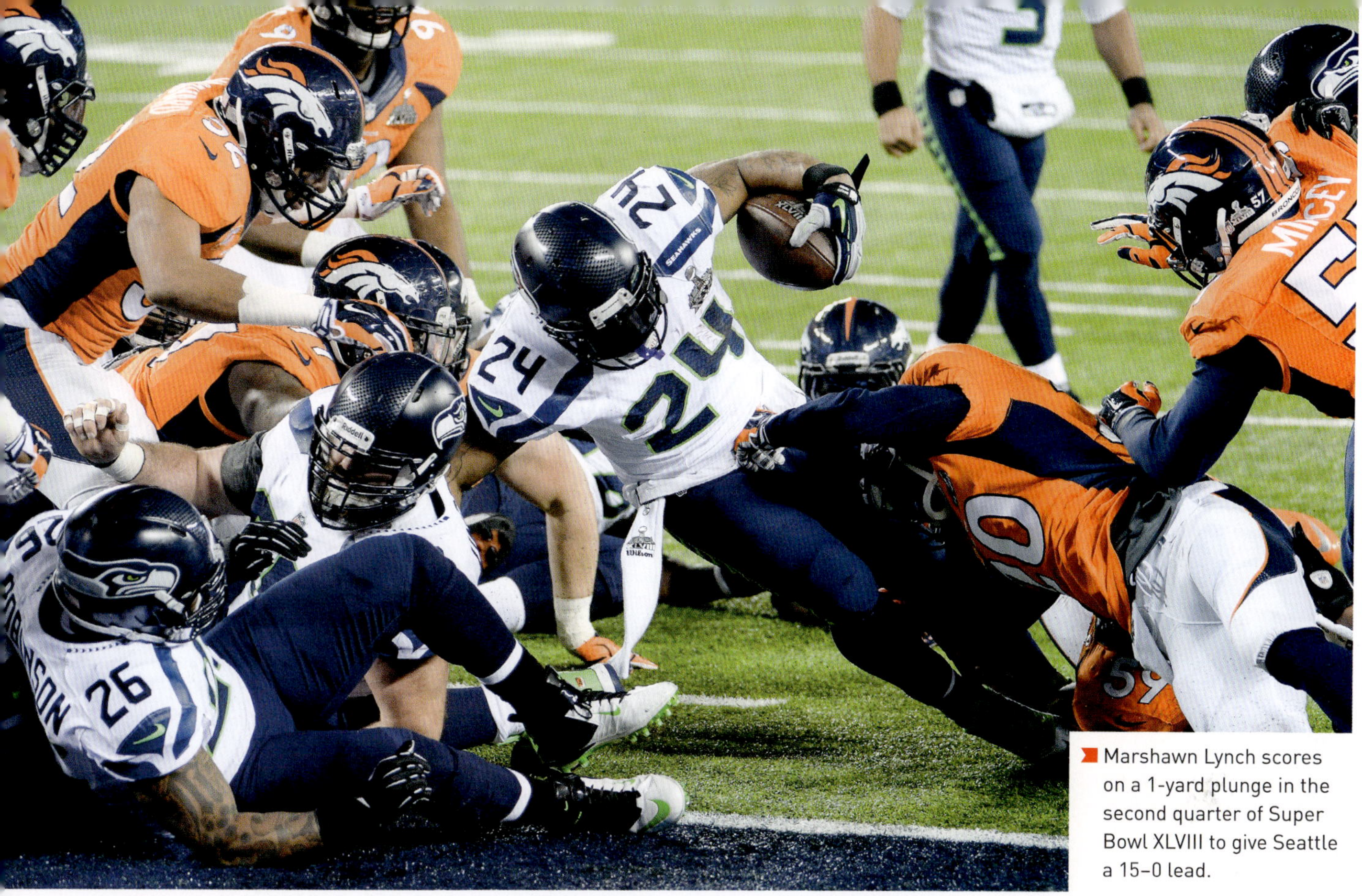

Marshawn Lynch scores on a 1-yard plunge in the second quarter of Super Bowl XLVIII to give Seattle a 15–0 lead.

MVP

MALCOLM SMITH | LB

It was one of those times when the MVP award could have gone to the entire defense. But Seattle Seahawks linebacker Malcolm Smith was the perfect player to represent them all because he symbolized not just the way the Seahawks played in Super Bowl XLVIII but also the manner in which the defensive players had grown together, the majority of whom had been drafted between 2010 and 2012. A seventh-round pick in 2011, Smith's draft stock had plummeted because of a rare condition that causes the esophagus to shut down. Despite his stellar college career, NFL teams remained unsure. Smith, who had earned a starting role during the 2013 season, made the most significant play of the game by picking off Manning and returning the ball for a 69-yard touchdown, turning an opportunity for Denver to get back into the game into a 22-point lead. His third-quarter fumble recovery solidified his position as MVP.

SUPER BOWL | FORTY-NINE

XLIX

FEBRUARY 1, 2015

NEW ENGLAND **PATRIOTS** **28** | **24** SEATTLE **SEAHAWKS**

PATH TO THE SUPER BOWL

NFC: DIVISION – SEATTLE 31 VS. CAROLINA 17
CONFERENCE CHAMPIONSHIP – SEATTLE 28 VS. GREEN BAY 22

AFC: DIVISION – NEW ENGLAND 35 VS. BALTIMORE 31
CONFERENCE CHAMPIONSHIP – NEW ENGLAND 45 VS. INDIANAPOLIS 7

WHERE
UNIVERSITY OF PHOENIX STADIUM, GLENDALE, ARIZONA

ATTENDANCE
70,288

TV AUDIENCE
114.4 MILLION

HALFTIME
KATY PERRY, LENNY KRAVITZ AND MISSY ELLIOT

Malcolm Butler intercepts a goal-line pass intended for Seattle's Ricardo Lockette. The interception sealed the win for New England.

During the opening month of the 2014 NFL season, a debate raged about the team that had reigned supreme over the AFC for much of the last decade and a half: was the New England Patriots' remarkable run of success over?

Between 2001 and 2014, the Patriots had won 11 AFC East titles, appeared in the AFC Championship Game eight times, and won the Super Bowl three times in five appearances. But when New England opened the regular season with a 2-2 record, they sure didn't look like a force to be reckoned with.

The Seahawks came into the game as the NFL's rising power; they were the defending NFL titleholders and still had the number one rated defense in the league. Their win over the Green Bay Packers in the NFC Championship Game, during which they trailed 19–7 with just under four minutes remaining, said everything about their resolve.

In the Super Bowl, the Seahawks took the lead for the first time in the third quarter with a field goal to make the score 17–14. Gaining some momentum, Seattle quarterback Russell Wilson threw a touchdown to receiver Doug Baldwin for a 10-point lead. The Patriots, however, engineered a comeback of their own, making it 28–24 after scoring two touchdowns in the fourth quarter, the second one with just two minutes left. The four-point lead also meant Seattle needed a touchdown — a field goal wouldn't do.

So they marched, and with 26 seconds left, Seattle had the ball on New England's 1-yard line. "I didn't have any doubt," receiver Doug Baldwin said about how certain he was the Seahawks would score.

But instead of handing the ball to pro-bowl running back Marshawn Lynch, the called play was a pass to Ricardo Lockette. Up stepped undrafted Patriots defensive back Malcolm Butler, who intercepted the throw and instantly became part of Super Bowl lore. "We thought we had them," said Wilson. "I thought it was going to be a touchdown when I threw it. When I let it go, I thought it was going to be game over."

Turns out it was. Only it was the Patriots who were celebrating.

MVP

TOM BRADY | QB

New England's win in Super Bowl XLIX added to the debate over whether Tom Brady might be the greatest quarterback in NFL history. He not only set the Super Bowl record for completions, going 37 of 50 for 328 yards, but also threw four touchdowns to four different receivers, indicating his ability to read the field for the best possible outcome. His performance was also remarkable in that he led his team against the Seahawks defense that had dismantled Peyton Manning and the Denver Broncos one year earlier. With four Super Bowl wins and three Super Bowl MVP awards, Brady had matched his boyhood idol, Joe Montana. "I'm a big Joe Montana fan — I love him to death, I thought he was the best and everything," said Patriots receiver Julian Edelman. "Tom Brady came out here, he's been to six Super Bowls, he's won four with the salary cap. It's hard to argue against that."

LISTEN UP

TOM BRADY BECAME THE FIRST PLAYER TO START IN SIX SUPER BOWLS AT ANY POSITION. HE ALSO TIED JOE MONTANA WITH THREE SUPER BOWL MVP AWARDS.

DEFLATEGATE

The week between the NFL's conference championship games and Super Bowl week is usually a quiet one, the calm before the storm so to speak. But the storm came early for the New England Patriots when they were accused of altering the inflation of their footballs during their rout of the Indianapolis Colts in the AFC Championship Game. Supposedly underinflated balls would mean a better grip for Tom Brady. The NFL began an investigation, leaving the world to wonder about the legitimacy of the claims. Although the episode did not affect the Super Bowl in any way, Brady was later suspended for the first four games of the 2015 season, but because of a lack of substantial evidence and due process, that punishment was overturned. A year later, the Second Circuit Court of Appeals overturned that ruling, meaning Brady's suspension was reinstated.

★ ★ ★

SUPER BOWL | FIFTY

50

FEBRUARY 7, 2016

DENVER **BRONCOS 24** | **10** CAROLINA **PANTHERS**

PATH TO THE SUPER BOWL

AFC: DIVISION – DENVER 23 VS. PITTSBURGH 16
CONFERENCE CHAMPIONSHIP – DENVER 20 VS. NEW ENGLAND 18

NFC: DIVISION – CAROLINA 31 VS. SEATTLE 24
CONFERENCE CHAMPIONSHIP – CAROLINA 49 VS. ARIZONA 15

WHERE	ATTENDANCE	TV AUDIENCE	HALFTIME
LEVI'S STADIUM, SANTA CLARA, CALIFORNIA	71,088	111.9 MILLION	COLDPLAY, BRUNO MARS AND BEYONCÉ

Throughout most of his illustrious career, quarterback Peyton Manning was the player who could light up a scoreboard like no other. Manning would pick apart opposing defenses and leave the opposition in catch-up mode before they knew what hit them.

But by the time he reached Super Bowl 50 at age 39, Manning had become more of a game manager, no longer simply capable of outgunning the opposition with his arm. Fortunately, the 2015 Denver Broncos had an all-world defense and a strong running game to complement him.

It wasn't clear, though, whether Manning had enough left to hold down the starting job for the 2015 season. In fact, for roughly two months, it appeared Manning's NFL career might be over — his team was off to a hot 7-0 start, but Manning had 11 interceptions and only seven touchdowns. After a foot injury in Week 10, Manning was replaced by 25-year-old Brock Osweiler. With Osweiler at the controls, the Broncos went 4-2 over his first six starts. But when Denver struggled during its final regular-season game against the San Diego Chargers, Manning came off the bench and helped rally his team to a win, regaining the starting job for the postseason.

It was storybook stuff, to be sure. But so were the Carolina Panthers, a team that rattled off a 15-1 record in 2015 before crushing both the Seattle Seahawks and Arizona Cardinals to get to the Super Bowl. Quarterback Cam Newton had an incredible season, with 35 touchdowns and 636 rushing yards for an additional 10 touchdowns.

So, could Newton be stopped by the league's number one defense? Would Manning hold things together against a defense that led the league in forced turnovers? The answer to both those questions was a definitive Y-E-S! The Broncos got on the board first with a field goal and never trailed the Panthers. Newton was besieged by the Broncos' defense. He was sacked six times and fumbled the ball twice — both drops leading to Bronco scores.

And that age-old adage of defense being a team's best offense? Turns out that one's true too.

NEWTON'S POSTGAME SESSION

During the 2015 season, Carolina quarterback Cam Newton showed a zest for celebration. After the Super Bowl, he showed he had a thing or two to learn about how to be a gracious loser. Following a humiliating loss that included Newton deciding not to pounce on a fumble on Carolina's final possession (that was instead recovered by the Broncos), the NFL MVP was at a loss for words. So he grunted out a series of short answers after the game and then abruptly left his perch after a few minutes. Newton was called a sore loser because of his conduct. On that, even he didn't argue. "Who likes to lose? You show me a good loser and I'm going to show you a loser. It's not a popularity contest. I'm here to win football games."

LISTEN UP

PEYTON MANNING BECAME THE FIRST STARTING QUARTERBACK IN HISTORY TO WIN THE SUPER BOWL WITH TWO DIFFERENT FRANCHISES.

Denver's C.J. Anderson collects a few of his 90 rushing yards during Super Bowl 50. Anderson scored Denver's only offensive touchdown in the win.

MVP

VON MILLER | LB

Without a doubt the MVP of Super Bowl 50 had to come from the Denver Broncos' defense. And the fact that linebacker Von Miller made the two definitive plays of the game made him an easy choice for the honors. Halfway through the first quarter and toward the end of the fourth, Miller sacked Cam Newton, forcing fumbles that both led to Denver's only touchdowns of the game. It was a sweet result for a player who'd missed Denver's Super Bowl appearance two years earlier because of an injury. "Who would have ever thought?" Miller asked. "Like coach [Gary] Kubiak always says, 'Life is 90 percent fair and the other 10 percent you've got to roll with it.'"

★ ★ ★

SUPER BOWL | FIFTY-ONE

LI

FEBRUARY 5, 2017

OT	NEW ENGLAND **PATRIOTS** **34**	**28** ATLANTA **FALCONS**

PATH TO THE SUPER BOWL

AFC: DIVISION – NEW ENGLAND 22 VS. CLEVELAND 17
CONFERENCE CHAMPIONSHIP – NEW ENGLAND 38 VS. BUFFALO 24

NFC: DIVISION – ATLANTA 36 VS. SEATTLE 20
CONFERENCE CHAMPIONSHIP – ATLANTA 44 VS. GREEN BAY 21

WHERE	ATTENDANCE	TV AUDIENCE	HALFTIME
NRG STADIUM, HOUSTON, TEXAS	70,807	111.3 MILLION	LADY GAGA

New England's Julian Edelman makes an improbable catch while covered by three Atlanta defenders during the second half of Super Bowl LI.

Super Bowl LI wasn't just a football game, it was a surgical procedure, a clinical dismembering that saw Tom Brady take apart the Atlanta Falcons as if they were med school cadavers. And what made his performance even more impressive was how precise Brady's handiwork was after suffering through a nightmarish start.

Led by quarterback Matt Ryan, the NFC Champion Falcons scored first and often. A Patriots' fumble was recovered by the Falcons' Robert Alford and sparked a 71-yard drive capped off by running back Devonta Freeman's 5-yard touchdown scamper. That was followed by a 19-yard touchdown completion to tight end Austin Hooper and soon after, an 82-yard interception return for a touchdown by the ball-hawking Alford. When Atlanta's Tevin Coleman reached the end zone on a 6-yard pass play, the score was 28–3 well into the third quarter.

That was when Brady transformed into the Chief of Surgery. He dissected the Falcons' defense with razor-sharp passes, expertly moving his offense downfield before finding James White with a 5-yard TD pass. Brady was just getting warmed up for a fourth-quarter assault that saw receiver Danny Amendola score on a 6-yard pass. White made good on the two-point conversion. Then it was White scoring on a 1-yard run and Amendola counting the two-point convert. The tying touchdown was set up by Julian Edelman's mind-blowing catch. Despite being covered by three defenders, including Alford, Edelman outmaneuvered his attackers, followed the ball that bounced off a leg and managed to make sure he had secured it before crash landing on the turf. It represented a 23-yard gain and earned *Sports Illustrated*'s recognition as "the greatest catch in Super Bowl history."

With the game deadlocked at 28–28, the stage was set for first overtime in Super Bowl history. The most critical play in OT was arguably the coin toss. New England correctly called heads and opted to receive the kickoff. That put Brady & Co. right back on the field knowing a touchdown on the opening possession would give New England the win.

With Atlanta still reeling from having blown a 25-point lead, the Patriots fashioned a nine-play, 75-yard drive that ended with White scoring his third touchdown of the day. It was New England's fifth Super Bowl championship in seven appearances with Bill Belichick as coach and Brady as QB. There was more to come.

LISTEN UP

THE PATRIOTS BECAME THE FIRST TEAM TO WIN A SUPER BOWL WITHOUT LEADING THE GAME AT ANY POINT IN REGULATION TIME.

MVP

TOM BRADY | QB

Who else but Tom Brady? And yet the QB, hailed as the "Greatest Of All Time," was adamant that the Patriot most crucial to his team's stunning win over Atlanta should have been James White, who ran for 29 yards, caught 14 passes for 110 yards and scored three touchdowns along with a two-point conversion. That added up to 20 points, a Super Bowl record. Brady was so convinced White was the star of the show he announced he would have given the Patriots' running back the new pick-up truck awarded to the MVP. One problem, though. The award's sponsor (Ford) had stopped giving away vehicles the year before. That didn't stop Brady from singing White's praises. "White is like my oldest son," Brady said the day after the win. "He just does everything right and you can never get mad at him because even if he doesn't make the play, he feels worse about it than you do." Late-night TV host Conan O'Brien solved matters by presenting White with a new truck, which White later gifted.

A RECORD PERFORMANCE FOR SUPER BOWL RECORDS

There were more than 30 team and individual records set by the Patriots and Falcons, with New England earning most of them, starting with Brady. The 39-year-old QB completed 43 of 62 passes for 466 yards (all record bests), two touchdowns and an interception that was returned for a TD. It marked the first time Brady had tossed a quick-six pick in his playoff career. Undaunted, the Patriots totaled the most offensive plays in a Super Bowl (93), clinched the most first downs (37), and overcame the largest deficit faced by the winning team after three quarters (19 points). As for Belichick, the win put him ahead of Pittsburgh's Chuck Noll for most Super Bowl rings as a head coach.

★ ★ ★

SUPER BOWL | FIFTY-TWO

LII

FEBRUARY 4, 2018

PHILADELPHIA **EAGLES 41** | **33** NEW ENGLAND **PATRIOTS**

PATH TO THE SUPER BOWL

NFC: DIVISION – PHILADELPHIA 15 VS. ATLANTA 10
CONFERENCE CHAMPIONSHIP – PHILADELPHIA 38 VS. MINNESOTA 7

AFC: DIVISION – NEW ENGLAND 35 VS. TENNESSEE 14
CONFERENCE CHAMPIONSHIP – NEW ENGLAND 24 VS. JACKSONVILLE 20

WHERE	ATTENDANCE	TV AUDIENCE	HALFTIME
U.S. BANK STADIUM, MINNEAPOLIS, MINNESOTA	67,612	103.4 MILLION	JUSTIN TIMBERLAKE

It was one thing for the Philadelphia Eagles to forgo an easy field goal and increase their lead to 18–12 just before the half. It was a whole other level of daring to run a play on fourth and goal against the defending Super Bowl champion New England Patriots.

That's what the Eagles chose to do after a brief sideline meeting between head coach Doug Pederson and his quarterback Nick Foles.

"You want Philly Philly?" Foles asked.

Pederson gave it a moment's thought then replied, "Yeah, let's do it."

They did it so perfectly, it resulted in a touchdown that caught the Patriots flat-footed and injected new confidence into the Eagles.

Here's how the play known as the Philly Special worked: Instead of lining up directly behind the center, Foles moved to his right and positioned himself as a receiver. The ball was a direct snap to running back Corey Clement, who then pitched it to reserve tight end Trey Burton, who passed it to an uncovered Foles for a slice of football history. Foles became the first player to catch and throw for a touchdown in a Super Bowl. Oddly enough, Foles could have been beaten to the punch by QB Tom Brady, who ran a pass pattern earlier in the game only to drop a perfectly thrown ball.

The rest of the game featured back and forth offensive excellence with both teams fashioning long drives with key plays from key players. Trailing 41–33 and in need of a touchdown and a two-point conversion to tie the score and produce overtime, Brady's last-play Hail Mary to Rob Gronkowski fell incomplete giving Philadelphia its first Super Bowl triumph. It had been 58 years between championships for the beleaguered Eagles, whose one and only other title came in the NFL's pre–Super Bowl era. Philadelphia defeated the Green Bay Packers in 1960, paced by the legendary Concrete Charlie (Chuck) Bednarik, the last of the two-way players.

For the Patriots, there was no comeback magic akin to the previous Super Bowl. That said, Brady put up some amazing numbers against Philadelphia, completing 28 of 48 passes for 505 yards and three TDs. Combined with Foles' statistics, the opposing pivots threw for a monumental 878 yards and unleashed 1,151 yards of total offense.

SUPER FOOD FIGHT

By football standards, Philadelphia versus New England provided next to no pre-game hype or mass hysteria. Yes, the two teams had met in a previous Super Bowl, but that was 13 years prior, an eon in professional sports. So, when Dottie's Donuts in Philadelphia made the bold decision to scrap its Boston cream donuts and clam chowder specials for a local favorite, a green pistachio matcha number, it became the most widely reported feud leading up to Super Bowl LII. According to CBS Philadelphia, New England fans took notice of the slight and the oven mitts came off. Boston's Charles River Esplanade issued a ban of its own, dictating there would be no Philadelphia cream cheese, Philly cheese steaks or soft pretzels sold or consumed in the park. The two sides carried on the prank confrontation until the big game was in the record books (and the cookbooks, too).

LISTEN UP

THE EAGLES ARE ONE OF FOUR TEAMS WITH WHOM THE PATRIOTS HAVE HAD A SUPER BOWL REMATCH, ALONG WITH THE GIANTS, RAMS AND SEAHAWKS.

Philadelphia's Nick Foles catches a touchdown pass from tight end Trey Burton in Super Bowl LII versus the New England Patriots.

MVP

NICK FOLES | QB

Before he was crowned the MVP of Super Bowl LII, Nick Foles was drafted by Philadelphia in 2012, traded to the St. Louis Rams, released so he could sign with the Kansas City Chiefs then released again only to end up back where he started, with the Eagles. Well on his way to being the journeyman's journeyman, Foles' luck changed in 2017 when Carson Wentz was sidelined by a knee injury, making Foles the No. 1 QB for the balance of the regular season and playoffs. He made good on that opportunity by defeating the Atlanta Falcons and Minnesota Vikings to advance to the Super Bowl. It was after receiving MVP honors that he spoke openly of his stumbles and setbacks on his way to the top.

"Failure is a part of life. I wouldn't be up here if I hadn't fallen thousands of times, made mistakes. We all are human, we all have weaknesses," he said at his post-game media conference. "I'm not perfect. I'm not Superman. I might be in the NFL and we might have just won the Super Bowl, but hey, we still have daily struggles."

Soon after his rise to glory, Foles signed with the Jacksonville Jaguars, was traded to the Chicago Bears and released, then signed with the Indianapolis Colts and was released, this time for good. He retired September 16, 2024, at the age of 35.

★ ★ ★

SUPER BOWL | FIFTY-THREE

LIII

FEBRUARY 3, 2019

NEW ENGLAND **PATRIOTS** **13** / **3** LOS ANGELES **RAMS**

PATH TO THE SUPER BOWL

AFC: DIVISION – NEW ENGLAND 41 VS. LOS ANGELES CHARGERS 28
CONFERENCE CHAMPIONSHIP – NEW ENGLAND 37 VS. KANSAS CITY 31

NFC: DIVISION – LOS ANGELES RAMS 30 VS. DALLAS 22
CONFERENCE CHAMPIONSHIP – LOS ANGELES RAMS 26 VS. NEW ORLEAN

WHERE	ATTENDANCE	TV AUDIENCE	HALFTIME
MERCEDES-BENZ STADIUM, ATLANTA, GEORGIA	70,081	98.2 MILLION	MAROON 5, BIG BOI AND TRAVIS SCOTT

Little did anyone know that this was the grand finale of the greatest partnership in NFL history, the final big game for New England Patriots' head coach Bill Belichick and his unsinkable quarterback Tom Brady.

Facing the Los Angeles Rams in Super Bowl LIII, Belichick's Patriots executed a gem of a defensive game plan that harassed L.A. QB Jared Goff and prevented the second-year starter from finding the end zone. A 53-yard field goal by Greg Zuerlein was all the Rams could squeeze out of their offense.

The Super Bowl entrants were set with the Patriots listed as two-and-a-half-point favorites. Through the first half it was clear this was not going to be a high scoring affair. The Patriots' opening possession saw Brady's first pass intercepted. On New England's second possession, Stephen Gostkowski missed a 46-yard field goal attempt. On his second try, this time from 42 yards out, Gostkowski gave New England a seemingly insurmountable 3–0 lead at the half.

Things got a little better in the third quarter but not much. The Rams set a Super Bowl record with eight consecutive drives ending in a punt. They eventually got on the scoreboard when Zuerlein nailed a 53-yard field goal, which, at the time, was the second longest kick in Super Bowl history. That tied the game at 3–3. It marked the first time the competing teams had failed to score a touchdown through three quarters. Thankfully, the Patriots woke up in time to march downfield on the strength of Rob Gronkowski's two pass receptions for 47 yards. From the Rams' two-yard line, running back Sony Michel took the hand-off and crashed his way into the end zone. Gostkowski added a 41-yard field goal to close out the scoring with little over a minute remaining in the game. Sticking with the script for this dramaless non-classic, the Rams attempted a 48-yard field goal hoping it would give them a shot at an on-side kick and one last go for a touchdown. Zuerlein misfired, leaving the Patriots to celebrate their sixth and final NFL championship with Belichick and Brady as their dynamic duo.

THE SUPER BORE

This was not a ratings buster of a televised sporting event. In fact, it experienced a 5 percent drop in viewership compared to the previous big game, Super Bowl LII. New England and the Rams managed a Nielsen national ratings number of 44.9 and attracted 98.2 million watchers, low by Super Bowl standards. Then there was the on-the-field action, which was dominated by both teams' defensive units. Take away Tom Brady going 4 for 4 for 67 yards on the one and only touchdown march, and the rest of the game was decidedly pedestrian. Leave it to the game's MVP to put things into perspective: "It was an ugly win," said Julian Edelman. "But I'd rather win ugly than lose pretty."

LISTEN UP

AT 40 YEARS AND 185 DAYS, TOM BRADY BECAME THE OLDEST NON KICKER-PUNTER TO PLAY IN A SUPER BOWL. JERRY RICE HAD PREVIOUSLY HELD THE RECORD AT 40 YEARS AND 105 DAYS.

Patriots running back Sony Michel crashes into the end zone with the ball for a 2-yard touchdown during Super Bowl LIII.

MVP

JULIAN EDELMAN | WR

Considering everything he had been through — the injury, the suspension, the comeback from a full season lost — New England's Julian Edelman was as much an inspirational source as he was a clutch receiver. He didn't score a touchdown in Super Bowl LIII, but he had the game of his career, making 10 catches for 141 yards. It was enough for him to be named MVP, an award usually reserved for QB Tom Brady. For the likeable Edelman, it was payback for all the hard work he had put into rehabilitating a torn knee ligament. He suffered the injury in the Patriots' third preseason game in 2017, and it forced him to miss the entire regular season. To ensure he'd be ready for the opening of training camp in 2018, Edelman used a banned substance to maximize his physical revival, only to fail a drug test administered by the NFL. The league listened to Edelman's plea but ended up suspending him for four games. By the time he started in Super Bowl LIII, he was back to full form. Five of his first six catches resulted in first downs.

SUPER BOWL | FIFTY-FOUR

LIV

FEBRUARY 2, 2020

KANSAS CITY **CHIEFS 31** / **20** SAN FRANCISCO **49ers**

PATH TO THE SUPER BOWL

AFC: DIVISION – KANSAS CITY 51 VS. HOUSTON 31
CONFERENCE CHAMPIONSHIP – KANSAS CITY 35 VS. TENNESSEE 24

NFC: DIVISION – SAN FRANCISCO 27 VS. MINNESOTA 10
CONFERENCE CHAMPIONSHIP – SAN FRANCISCO 37 VS. GREEN BAY 20

WHERE	ATTENDANCE	TV AUDIENCE	HALFTIME
HARD ROCK STADIUM, MIAMI GARDENS, FLORIDA	62,417	102.1 MILLION	JENNIFER LOPEZ, SHAKIRA, J BALVIN AND BAD BUNNY

Kansas City's Damien Williams runs toward the end zone and a touchdown during the second half of Super Bowl LIV.

This was where it all began. The Andy Reid era, the emergence of quarterback Patrick Mahomes and the confirmation of the Kansas City Chiefs as a championship organization. Their 31–20 Super Bowl win legitimized them as a team that could make a habit of playing meaningful games now and in the future.

For Reid, the mustachioed head coach known for making the right call at the right time, this was his first Super Bowl win with the Chiefs. He had come this far before as coach of the Philadelphia Eagles, only to lose to the New England Patriots. The difference in Kansas City was the 2017 arrival of Mahomes, who didn't play much his first season as Alex Smith's backup. When named the starter, Mahomes got right down to business, throwing for 5,097 yards and a staggering 50 touchdowns. For that, Mahomes was voted the NFL's Offensive Player of the Year as well as the league's MVP.

Kansas City went 12-4 during the 2019 season with Mahomes running and gunning with pitch outs and no-look passes that left defenders unsure of how to stop the 23-year-old marvel. In Super Bowl LIV, San Francisco's offense was head-manned by QB Jimmy Garoppolo, who helped the 49ers win 13 of 16 games that season.

In the big game, the 49ers built a 10-point lead with less than three minutes left in the third quarter. That was when Mahomes took command. Faced with a third-and-15 situation, he found receiver Tyreek Hill for a 44-yard gain. That led to a 1-yard TD toss to tight end Travis Kelce, pulling the Chiefs to within a field goal of San Francisco with less than seven minutes left in the game. Mahomes was just getting warmed up.

He crafted a seven play, 65-yard drive that included a 38-yard pass to Sammy Watkins, who got the better of cornerback Richard Sherman.

That drive ended with Mahomes throwing a 5-yard TD pass to Damien Williams, who cemented the win minutes later with a 38-yard scoring run. The victory was especially sweet for Reid. He had held the most dubious distinction of posting the most wins by a head coach without winning a Super Bowl (221). Turned out he, like his quarterback, was just getting warmed up.

LISTEN UP

AT 50 YEARS, THE CHIEFS HELD THE LONGEST TIME GAP BETWEEN SUPER BOWL WINS FOR AN NFL FRANCHISE.

MVP

PATRICK MAHOMES | QB

Against San Francisco, Mahomes shook off a pair of interceptions and passed for 286 yards and two TDs. He also ran five times for 29 yards and a touchdown. Heading into the 2025 NFL season, Mahomes had quarterbacked the Chiefs to three Super Bowl wins in five appearances. Only Tom Brady, Joe Montana and Terry Bradshaw have won more NFL championships. Mahomes won his three Super Bowl rings before he turned 30. He is also the most recent QB to be named the regular-season MVP and the Super Bowl MVP in the same season.

FOOTBALL WASN'T EVEN HIS DREAM SPORT

When he was a kid, Patrick Mahomes didn't think as much about competing in a Super Bowl as he did playing in the World Series. It was only natural given that his dad, Pat Mahomes Sr., was a major league relief pitcher for 11 seasons from 1992 to 2003. Mahomes Jr. used his post-Super Bowl LIV media conference to talk about his family, their love for him and his love of baseball. Asked what winning a Super Bowl meant to his family, Mahomes answered, "I think it means the world. Being a little kid and running around baseball fields.... My dream was to become a professional athlete, and I thought it was going to be in baseball, not football. But now to be here and winning it, it's amazing."

Mahomes played baseball at Texas Tech and was drafted by the Detroit Tigers in 2014, but by then he was committed to football. Head coach Andy Reid praised Mahomes' development into a championship QB and offered a word of warning to all of Kansas City's NFL rivals. "The scary part is he's going to get even better with time." That he has, most assuredly.

★ ★ ★

SUPER BOWL | FIFTY-FIVE

LV

FEBRUARY 7, 2021

TAMPA BAY **BUCCANEERS** **31** | **9** KANSAS CITY **CHIEFS**

PATH TO THE SUPER BOWL

NFC: WILD CARD – TAMPA BAY 31 VS. WASHINGTON 23
DIVISION – TAMPA BAY 30 VS. NEW ORLEANS 20
CONFERENCE CHAMPIONSHIP – TAMPA BAY 31 VS. GREEN BAY 26

AFC: DIVISION – KANSAS CITY 22 VS. CLEVELAND 17
CONFERENCE CHAMPIONSHIP – KANSAS CITY 38 VS. BUFFALO 24

WHERE	ATTENDANCE	TV AUDIENCE	HALFTIME
RAYMOND JAMES STADIUM, TAMPA BAY, FLORIDA	24,825	91.6 MILLION	THE WEEKND

Buccaneers tight end Rob Gronkowski runs with the ball during Super Bowl LV against the Kansas City Chiefs.

MVP

TOM BRADY | QB

Even though he would play two more seasons, Super Bowl LV marked the end of Brady's championship run. The final tally included 10 Super Bowl appearances, seven wins, five MVP awards while setting a wealth of Super Bowl records, from most passing attempts (421) to most completions (277) to most yards (3,039) and TD passes (21), along with engineering the greatest comeback in Super Bowl history (Super Bowl LI against the Atlanta Falcons.) About the only thing he didn't do well was retire. On February 1, 2022, Brady announced he was leaving the NFL only to change his mind and un-retire 40 days later. On February 1, 2023, Brady announced once again he was quitting, only this time he meant it.

As send-offs go, Tom Brady's last Super Bowl appearance couldn't have been any better. In his first season in a new city, in a new uniform, in a different conference, Brady directed the Tampa Bay Buccaneers to their second NFL title in franchise history and his seventh. He did it in true Brady fashion, with pinpoint passing and a knack for taking advantage of his opponents when they were most vulnerable.

There were no assurances Brady would step away from the New England Patriots and maintain his greatness in Florida, but that he did exactly that surprised some. At the age of 43, Brady looked invigorated when he took to the field in Buccaneer colors. Being free from Bill Belichick, the only coach he had played for as a professional quarterback, played a huge role in that. The two men had pushed each other to their limits. It created what Brady acknowledged as "natural tension."

So it was that Brady signed as a free agent with the Buccaneers, a team that had Jameis Winston at QB and was in search of a catalyst to take it to a higher level. Brady's influence was immediate. Tampa Bay won six of its first eight games only to hit the skids in November, losing three of its next four. Brady rallied his team to an 11-5 record that was good enough to lock up a wild card berth in the playoffs. From there, he and the Bucs knocked off the Washington Football Team, the New Orleans Saints and the Green Bay Packers. That landed Brady in what was his 10th and final Super Bowl.

Against the Kansas City Chiefs, Brady threw three TD passes, two of them to tight end Rob Gronkowski, who had retired from the Patriots shortly after Brady jumped to Tampa. It took a phone call from Brady to convince Gronk to unretire and sign with the Bucs. In the Super Bowl, the two were at the top of their games. Gronk made six catches for 67 yards and made it look easy. Kansas City was unable to keep up with Brady and the Bucs' offense. It also didn't help that the Chiefs were often their own worst enemy. They were penalized 11 times for 120 yards. Tampa was flagged only four times for 39 yards.

LISTEN UP

PATRICK MAHOMES WAS PRESSURED ON 52 PERCENT OF HIS DROPBACKS — THE MOST EVER RECORDED IN A SUPER BOWL.

NFL STARES DOWN COVID-19

The Bucs earned another distinction while ousting Kansas City: They became the first team to win a Super Bowl on home turf. They accomplished that in a convincing way, but instead of showing their mastery to a full house of more than 65,000, the crowd at Raymond James Stadium was less than half of that. It had to do with the NFL sanitizing its fan-friendly annual gala to prevent mass transmission of the COVID-19 virus. To do that, the NFL canceled some pre-Super Bowl events while cutting back on others. Those who actually sat in the stands were given masks and hand sanitizer. It helped prevent the Super Bowl from becoming a super-spreader event.

The league also instituted a no-cannon decree at the Super Bowl. Even though it was a Tampa Bay tradition to fire off a cannon after every Bucs' touchdown, the NFL brass ruled against it. The Super Bowl was meant to be held at a neutral site, and for the most part that's how it has gone, with these exceptions: the 1979 Los Angeles Rams, who played and lost at the Rose Bowl in Pasadena, California, instead of their home field, the L.A. Memorial Coliseum; and the 1984 San Francisco 49ers, who played at Stanford University Stadium instead of Candlestick Park and won. Aside from the Bucs, the only other team to win on its true home field was the 2021 Los Angeles Rams, who won Super Bowl LVI at SoFi Stadium.

SUPER BOWL | FIFTY-SIX

LVI

FEBRUARY 13, 2022

LOS ANGELES RAMS 23 / 20 CINCINNATI BENGALS

PATH TO THE SUPER BOWL

NFC: WILD CARD – LOS ANGELES RAMS 34 VS. ARIZONA 11
DIVISION – LOS ANGELES RAMS 30 VS. TAMPA BAY 27
CONFERENCE CHAMPIONSHIP – LOS ANGELES RAMS 20 VS. SAN FRANCISCO 17

AFC: WILD CARD – CINCINNATI 26 VS. LAS VEGAS 19
DIVISION – CINCINNATI 19 VS. TENNESSEE 16
CONFERENCE CHAMPIONSHIP – CINCINNATI 27 VS. KANSAS CITY 24

WHERE
SOFI STADIUM, INGLEWOOD, CALIFORNIA

ATTENDANCE
70,048

TV AUDIENCE
112.3 MILLION

HALFTIME
DR. DRE, SNOOP DOGG, 50 CENT, MARY J. BLIGE, KENDRICK LAMAR AND EMINEM

The climb from the bottom of the NFL standings to reaching a Super Bowl can be grueling, sometimes spanning decades. But every once in a while, it happens virtually overnight.

Which was the case for the Cincinnati Bengals who showed up at Super Bowl LVI in Southern California to face the home-city Rams just two years removed from a 2-14 season.

But by virtue of two first round draft picks — quarterback Joe Burrow in 2020 and Ja'Marr Chase a year later — the Bengals had improved to 10-7, then won their first two playoff games in almost 30 years before shocking the defending AFC champion Kansas City Chiefs in a conference championship game in which they had trailed 21–3 on the road.

The Los Angeles Rams, meanwhile, were making the franchise's fourth Super Bowl appearance. And like the Bengals, their climb to the Super Bowl had been built on a new quarterback, Matthew Stafford.

Ten months earlier, the Rams had pulled off one of the biggest trades in recent NFL history by dealing Jared Goff and a handful of draft picks to Detroit for Stafford, who hadn't won a playoff game in 12 seasons with Detroit. The Rams then pushed their chips to the center of the table mid-season by trading two more draft picks to Denver for linebacker Von Miller.

The Bengals trailed 13–10 at halftime but the game changed dramatically after each quarterback made their first throws of the third quarter. First Burrow hit Tee Higgins for a 75-yard catch-and-run touchdown that gave the Bengals their first lead of the game with 17–13. Then Stafford's first pass of the second half was intercepted by corner Chidobe Awuzie, which the Bengals converted into a field goal and a 20–13 lead.

With less than half a quarter to play, the Rams were trailing 20–16 when they took over at their own 21-yard-line, with Stafford engineering a 79-yard drive that ended with a 1-yard pass to Super Bowl MVP Cooper Kupp.

COACHING YOUTH

Super Bowl LVI illustrated the NFL's trend at the time of leaning toward younger head coaches. The Rams' Sean McVay had turned 36 just two weeks before the big game, while Cincinnati's Zac Taylor was just 38. McVay became the youngest head coach to win a Super Bowl while the game marked the first time two head coaches under the age of 40 had faced one another on the NFL's biggest stage. Both men had experience from other pro leagues on their résumés. McVay had been the receivers coach of the UFL's Florida Tuskers in 2009, while Taylor spent 2007 as a backup quarterback with the CFL's Winnipeg Blue Bombers.

LISTEN UP

THE RAMS' VICTORY MARKED THE SECOND TIME IN TWO YEARS — AND THE SECOND TIME EVER — THAT A TEAM HAS PLAYED A SUPER BOWL GAME IN ITS OWN STADIUM.

Rams quarterback Matthew Stafford passes against the Cincinnati Bengals during Super Bowl LVI.

MVP

COOPER KUPP | WR

Cooper Kupp was among the most accomplished receivers in NCAA college football history, playing at Eastern Washington at the FCS level, away from the bright lights of network TV and bowl games. But as a third-generation NFL player, he adapted quickly to the pro game, catching more than 100 passes in his first two seasons, despite missing half of one to injury. The 2021 season saw him break-out with 145 catches for 1,947 yards and 16 touchdowns. But Kupp's most important imprint on the season came on the Rams' final drive of the Super Bowl, in which he caught four passes, ran for 7 yards on a fourth-down play and hauled in the game's winning score.

★ ★ ★

SUPER BOWL | FIFTY-SEVEN

LVII

FEBRUARY 12, 2023

KANSAS CITY **CHIEFS 38** | **35** PHILADELPHIA **EAGLES**

PATH TO THE SUPER BOWL

AFC: DIVISION – KANSAS CITY 27, JACKSONVILLE 20
CONFERENCE CHAMPIONSHIP – KANSAS CITY 23, CINCINNATI 20

NFC: DIVISION – PHILADELPHIA 38 VS. NEW YORK 7
NFC CONFERENCE CHAMPIONSHIP – PHILADELPHIA 31, SAN FRANCISCO

WHERE	ATTENDANCE	TV AUDIENCE	HALFTIME
STATE FARM STADIUM, GLENDALE, ARIZONA	67,827	115.1 MILLION	RIHANNA

Kansas City's tight end Travis Kelce runs against Philadelphia's linebacker T.J. Edwards during the first half of Super Bowl LVII.

There was no surprise in the two teams that wound-up facing one another in the 57th Super Bowl game.

The Philadelphia Eagles, under second-year head coach Nick Sirianni, began the season with eight consecutive wins, exhibiting an ultra-confident style of play on all sides of the ball. And the Kansas City Chiefs … well, they were at their third Super Bowl game in four years. Both teams entered the playoffs as their respective conference's No. 1 seed.

The game featured two starting quarterbacks still in their 20s, coming off career years during the 2022 regular season. Kansas City's Patrick Mahomes was already widely considered the NFL's greatest quarterback of his generation. While Philadelphia's Jalen Hurts was demonstrating a higher ceiling than many had projected for him.

The Chiefs trailed through most of the first three quarters, taking their first lead of the game early in the fourth on a 5-yard pass from Mahomes to Kadarius Toney. With that the score was 28–27 with just over 12 minutes to play.

Throughout the game on offense, both teams leaned on their best players. Philadelphia receivers DeVonta Smith and A.J. Brown combined for 13 catches, 196 yards and one touchdown, while for the Chiefs, it was the unstoppable Travis Kelce who caught all six passes directed his way for 81 yards and a touchdown.

The Eagles were victimized by two fourth-quarter mistakes.

The first came immediately after surrendering the lead, when a line-drive punt by Arryn Siposs allowed Toney to return the ball 65 yards to the Philadelphia 5-yard line, where three plays later the Chiefs increased their lead to 35–27.

After the Eagles tied the game with a touchdown and two-point convert, Kansas City took over the ball at their own 25-yard-line with just over five minutes to play.

That's when defensive back James Bradbury committed the second mistake with a holding penalty on third-and-eight that gave the Chiefs a first down on the 11. That allowed the Chiefs to bleed the clock before a game-winning 27-yard Harrison Butker field goal with just eight seconds remaining.

LISTEN UP

FOX'S BROADCAST BECAME THE MOST-WATCHED PROGRAM IN U.S. TELEVISION HISTORY AT THE TIME, WITH OVER 115 MILLION VIEWERS.

MVP

PATRICK MAHOMES | QB

The list of accomplishments belonging to Patrick Mahomes by the end of Super Bowl LVII is simply astounding, high-lighted by two NFL MVP Awards and two Super Bowl MVP Awards as well.

But there was a historic aspect to Mahomes appearance in this game as well, since he and Philadelphia's Jalen Hurts represented the first time a Super Bowl had featured two starting quarter-backs who are Black. (It should be noted this was more than 40 years after the CFL had its first championship game with two Black starting quarterbacks.)

Mahomes won the MVP for Super Bowl LVII for a performance in which he played through an injured ankle, throwing two fourth-quarter touchdowns while com-pleting 21 of 27 passes for 182 yards, three touchdown passes and no interceptions.

Had the Chiefs not won the game, the MVP would have most certainly gone to Hurts who'd completed 27 of 38 passes for 304 yards, one touchdown through the air and three along the ground.

THE TUSH PUSH

Innovations have always been a part of NFL team success.

And the Philadelphia Eagles showed up at Super Bowl LVII with one that was sparking plenty of debate.

The "Tush Push" (also known as "The Brotherly Shove"), is a variation of the traditional quarterback sneak where one or more players line-up behind the quarterback and attempt to help shove-him forward for a short-yardage game.

The Eagles used it for the first time in 2021 and increased its use the next season, taking advantage of its offensive line plus the mobility of quarterback Jalen Hurts to a high rate of success and producing two Super Bowl touchdowns against the Chiefs.

Though the play remains controver-sial, a proposal for its ban was rejected during the NFL off-season. It remained a legal play through the 2025 season.

★ ★ ★

SUPER BOWL | FIFTY-EIGHT

LVIII

FEBRUARY 11, 2024

OT KANSAS CITY **CHIEFS 25** / **22** SAN FRANCISCO **49ers**

PATH TO THE SUPER BOWL

AFC: WILDCARD – KANSAS CITY 26 VS. MIAMI 7
DIVISION – KANSAS CITY 27 VS. BUFFALO 24
CONFERENCE CHAMPIONSHIP – KANSAS CITY 17 VS. BALTIMORE 10

NFC: DIVISION – SAN FRANCISCO 24 VS. GREEN BAY 21
CONFERENCE CHAMPIONSHIP – SAN FRANCISCO 34 VS. DETROIT 31

WHERE
ALLEGIANT STADIUM, LAS VEGAS, NEVADA

ATTENDANCE
61,629

TV AUDIENCE
123.4 MILLION

HALFTIME
USHER, ALICIA KEYS, JERMAINE DUPRI, H.E.R., WILL.I.AM, LIL JON AND LUDACRIS

It's not often that the NFL gets upstaged at its biggest event. But it felt like the most talked-about person leading up to the 58th Super Bowl wasn't a football player or coach, but pop superstar Taylor Swift.

Swift, the public had learned six months earlier, was in a relationship with Kansas City Chiefs future-hall-of-fame tight end Travis Kelce. Was their relationship real or just a publicity stunt? Was the NFL rigging games in favor of the Chiefs so that they could get a ratings boost from Swift's presence at the Super Bowl?

These were the kinds of questions that were swirling leading up to and during the very first Super Bowl ever held in Las Vegas.

The backbone of both teams was on defense, with the Chiefs and 49ers ranked second and third, respectively, in terms of yards surrendered per play during the regular season.

And it was the defenses that set the tone early for this game, with the 49ers taking a 10–3 lead at halftime, the only touchdown coming with less than five minutes to play in the second quarter on a trick play. Receiver Jauan Jennings took a backward throw from 49ers QB Brock Purdy and delivered the ball across the field to running back Christian McCaffrey, who ran it in for a 21-yard score.

The Chiefs had a red zone turnover during the first half but took one away in the second, leading to a one-play touchdown drive on a 16-yard pass to Marquez Valdes-Scantling with two and a half minutes left in the third quarter to give KC its first lead of the game at 13–10.

The margin between the two teams would not exceed three points the rest of the game.

And it was the 49ers settling for a three-point lead on their first possession of overtime, that opened the door for Patrick Mahomes to play the hero, which he did right on schedule, engineering a touchdown drive on the Chiefs only possession of extra time to win their second Super Bowl in a row.

THE END OF NFL KICKOFFS

By the end of the 2023 season, there was a general unhappiness about the state of NFL kickoffs due to the high percentage of touchbacks

The improving range of NFL kickers meant that nearly three in four kickoffs weren't being returned at all, making it often a dead play that simply set-up the receiving team to scrimmage at their own 25-yard line.

Nowhere was the silliness of what NFL kickoffs had become more evident than in the Super Bowl, with zero returns of the 13 kickoffs during the game.

It turned out to be the last game ever played with a standard kickoff rule. Less than two months later, the NFL adopted the kickoff model created by the XFL, in which teams kickoff from their own 35-yard line, with coverage teams lining up on the opposing 40-yard line but not moving until the ball hits the ground or is touched by a member of the receiving team.

LISTEN UP

THE CHIEFS BECAME THE EIGHTH TEAM TO WIN BACK-TO-BACK SUPER BOWLS. NO TEAM HAS EVER WON THREE IN A ROW.

49ers running back Christian McCaffrey runs into the end zone for a 21-yard touchdown at Super Bowl LVIII.

MVP

PATRICK MAHOMES | QB

Forty-six pass attempts tells part of the story of Patrick Mahomes' third Super Bowl MVP award. So does 333 passing yards for a team that was not an aerial juggernaut during the regular season, despite the skill of its quarterback.

The real story of Patrick Mahomes' Super Bowl LVIII MVP honor is found in two drives where the Chiefs absolutely had to score.

The first was their final possession of regulation time, an 11-play field goal drive that went 64 yards in one minute and 50 seconds and left just three seconds on the clock. The other was in overtime when, with the Chiefs trailing by three, Mahomes took the offense 75 yards in 13 plays and finished the game with a touchdown pass to Mecole Hardman Jr. to end it.

SUPER BOWL | FIFTY-NINE

LIX

FEBRUARY 9, 2025

PHILADELPHIA **EAGLES** **40**

22 KANSAS CITY **CHIEFS**

PATH TO THE SUPER BOWL

NFC: WILDCARD – PHILADELPHIA 22 VS. GREEN BAY 10
DIVISION – PHILADELPHIA 28 VS. LOS ANGELES RAMS 22
CONFERENCE CHAMPIONSHIP – PHILADELPHIA 55 VS. WASHINGTON 23

AFC: DIVISION – KANSAS CITY 23 VS. HOUSTON 14
CONFERENCE CHAMPIONSHIP – KANSAS CITY 32 VS. BUFFALO 29

WHERE	ATTENDANCE	TV AUDIENCE	HALFTIME
CEASARS SUPERDOME, NEW ORLEANS, LOUISIANA	65,719	127.7 MILLION	KENDRICK LAMAR AND SZA

Chiefs wide receiver Xavier Worthy is wrapped up by Philadelphia's smothering defense after a catch during Super Bowl LIX.

By the start of the 59th Super Bowl Week in New Orleans, there was a palpable feeling of "Kansas City Chiefs fatigue" in the air.

That's what happens when you've played in seven consecutive AFC Championship games and are playing in your fifth Super Bowl in six years. Contributing to that fatigue was how the Chiefs seemed to win by the slimmest of margins and in the most serendipitous of ways. And occasionally — at least in the eyes of some — with the assistance of the officials.

No doubt their margins of victory had been slim throughout the season, winning 11 of their 15 victories during the regular season by a single score, with seven requiring game-winning drives in the fourth quarter or overtime.

Still, these were the Kansas City Chiefs who could rise to the occasion in the biggest moments of the biggest games like no other. And while no NFL team had ever won three consecutive Super Bowls, few doubted the Chiefs could pull it off.

All of which made what unfolded that Sunday night in New Orleans so shocking.

Here is a summary of Kansas City's seven possessions during the first half versus Philadelphia's top-ranked defense: punt-punt-punt-interception-punt-interception-punt. Their total offense consisted of 23 yards, 20 through the air, 3 along the ground.

It was nearly unfathomable that a Patrick Mahomes offense could be held in check to such a degree, but the Eagles' ability to pressure the Chiefs quarterback without having to employ blitzes proved devastating to Kansas City.

The Chiefs trailed 24–0 at the half, didn't score at all until late in the third quarter and found themselves down 34 with less than five minutes to play before a pair of touchdowns at garbage time balanced the scoring slightly.

One of the biggest questions heading into the game was whether the Chiefs would be able to slow Eagles running back Saquon Barkley, who'd become just the ninth player in NFL history to rush for more than 2,000 yards in a season. The Chiefs held him to just 57 yards on 25 carries, but it didn't matter.

Without a doubt, Super Bowl LIX goes down as one of the most shocking results in the game's history.

JALEN HURTS | QB

While the true MVP of this game was the Philadelphia defense, quarterback Jalen Hurts was very much deserving of the game's top individual honor.

During his five regular seasons in the NFL, Hurts had established himself as one of the most dangerous dual-threat quarterbacks in the game, with 85 touchdown throws and 55 scored along the ground. In 2024 he had the highest completion percentage of his career (68.7), the best touchdown-to-interception ratio (18:5) and had scored the second-most rushing touchdowns of his career (14).

The skills behind those numbers were evident in the 59th Super Bowl game, in which he completed more than 77 percent of his pass attempts, threw two touchdown passes and ran for another. His 72 yards rushing on 11 carries established a new Super Bowl record for a quarterback.

LISTEN UP

THE 24–0 EAGLES HALFTIME LEAD WAS THE GREATEST HALFTIME DEFICIT OF PATRICK MAHOMES' CAREER.

THE FIX WAS NOT IN

Grumbling that the NFL and its officials were doing all they could to get the Chiefs back to the Super Bowl reached such fervor that both NFL Commissioner Roger Goodell and NFL Referees Association president Scott Green had to address it during Super Bowl week.

Goodell called it a "ridiculous theory" during his Tuesday state-of-the-league address, backing his league's officials by stating "the men and women that officiate the NFL are outstanding. They have the highest possible standards."

The next day Green went further.

"It is insulting and preposterous to hear conspiracy theories that somehow 17 officiating crews consisting of 138 officials are colluding to assist one team."

SUPER BOWL | SIXTY

LX

FEBRUARY 8, 2026

SEATTLE SEAHAWKS 29 | **13 NEW ENGLAND PATRIOTS**

PATH TO THE SUPER BOWL

NFC: DIVISION – SEATTLE 41 VS. SAN FRANCISCO 6
CONFERENCE CHAMPIONSHIP – SEATTLE 31 VS. LOS ANGELES RAMS 27

AFC: WILDCARD – NEW ENGLAND 16 VS. LOS ANGELES CHARGERS 3
DIVISION – NEW ENGLAND 28 VS. HOUSTON 16
CONFERENCE CHAMPIONSHIP – NEW ENGLAND 10 VS. DENVER 7

WHERE	ATTENDANCE	TV AUDIENCE	HALFTIME
LEVI'S STADIUM, SANTA CLARA, CALIFORNIA	70,823	125.6 MILLION	BAD BUNNY FEATURING LADY GAGA AND RICKY MARTIN

Seahawks kicker Jason Myers scores with a 39-yard field goal to put the Seahawks up 6–0 in the second quarter of Super Bowl LX.

Just seven years removed from the last Super Bowl title of the Tom Brady/Bill Belichick era, the New England Patriots were back for Super Bowl LX. And few saw it coming.

The Seattle Seahawks had also made it from outside the playoffs all the way to the Super Bowl in one season. But the Patriots' climb was historic: their back-to-back four-win seasons in 2023 and '24 were the lowest win totals of an NFL team over those two seasons.

After a 1-2 start, the Patriots lost just a single game after September 21, demonstrating consistency on both sides of the ball and riding the upside of 23-year-old quarterback Drake Maye to their first AFC East title in six years. There was a caveat to all this, however. New England had played the softest regular season schedule of any NFL team this century, facing just three opponents that finished with winning records. All of which fueled debate over whether they could stand-up to playoff competition.

The answer got no clearer when New England's three playoff wins included historically strong performances on defense and historically futile performances on offense, scoring just 54 points while surrendering just 26.

So it wasn't a complete surprise when Seattle's No. 1 scoring defense threw a blanket over the Patriots, keeping them off the scoreboard until early in the fourth, when the Pats trailed 19–0.

On football's biggest stage, the Seahawks controlled the game where it is often won — at the line of scrimmage, dominating the run game and sacking Maye six times while forcing three turnovers.

The New England quarterback had just 48 passing yards at halftime, collecting most of his 295 that day after the result was out of doubt.

Seattle was 11 years removed from its last Super Bowl appearance and three years removed from the playoffs. But a series of strong draft classes and signing the right quarterback, Sam Darnold, in free agency had them hoisting the Vince Lombardi Trophy for a second time.

LISTEN UP

SEATTLE RUNNING BACK KENNETH WALKER III BECAME THE FIRST PLAYER AT HIS POSITION TO WIN SUPER BOWL MVP IN 28 YEARS.

MVP

KENNETH WALKER III | RB

It had been 28 years since a running back was named the Super Bowl MVP, a trend very much reflective of the NFL's direction over that time, which has prioritized throwing the football over running it.

But in a game largely marked by first-half offensive gridlock and fourth-down punts, Kenneth Walker III was one of the few players able to move the needle offensively, carrying 14 times for 94 yards during the first half, including runs of 30 and 29 yards.

It was a modest performance by Super Bowl MVP standards, or when measured against the best rushing performances in the game's history. And while many felt the MVP award truly belonged to the Seattle defense, on a day when the Seahawks didn't need much on offense to win the Super Bowl, Walker gave them more than enough.

SAM DARNOLD'S LONG AND WINDING ROAD TO THE SUPER BOWL

Sam Darnold's Super Bowl performance won't be one fans will be talking about for ages, but the story of his road to hoisting the Vince Lombardi Trophy certainly is.

Darnold was the third player and second quarterback selected in the 2018 NFL Draft, going to the New York Jets.

He quickly wound-up in the "bust category" for a high-first-round pick, throwing almost as many interceptions as touchdown passes during his first three seasons with the Jets before stops in Carolina and San Francisco.

The Minnesota Vikings signed him before immediately selecting a new franchise quarterback, J.J. McCarthy, but when McCarthy tore his meniscus during training camp, they handed the full-season job to Darnold, who made the most of it, leading the Vikings to a 14-win season.

When Minnesota recommitted to McCarthy over Darnold, Seattle signed him to a three-year, $100.5 million contract. He immediately delivered, setting career highs in completion percentage and yards per pass, while cutting his sack total nearly in half from the year before.

With Darnold, Seattle had the NFL's third-highest scoring offense during the regular season. But in a Super Bowl dominated by the Seahawks' defense, Darnold's job that day was not so much to win the game for Seattle but to ensure that the offense didn't lose it.

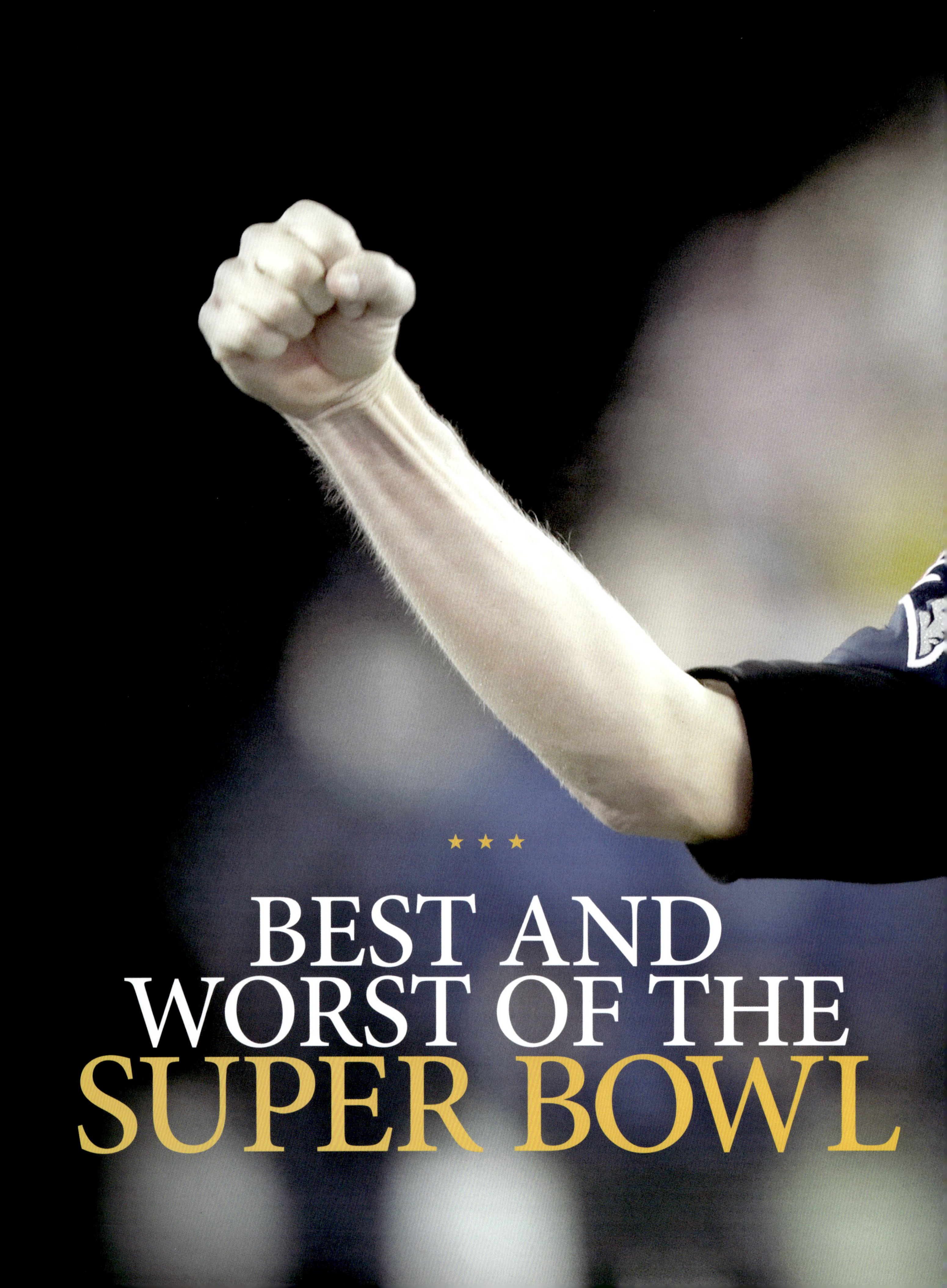

BEST AND WORST OF THE SUPER BOWL

TOM BRADY
GREATEST SUPER BOWL
QUARTERBACK

Joe Montana celebrates with lineman Guy McIntyre during his record-setting performance in Super Bowl XXIV.

GREATEST SUPER BOWL QUARTERBACKS

★ ★ ★

Sports agent Leigh Steinberg aptly said that "the Super Bowl is like a movie, and the quarterback is the leading man." It is his job to guide his team to victory in the NFL's most important game. A combination of talent and calmness under pressure is required to get the job done, which is what you'll find in abundance among the following five quarterbacks.

1. TOM BRADY

Brady's brilliance can be found in the numbers. Start with most Super Bowl wins: Brady has seven (six with the New England Patriots, one with the Tampa Bay Buccaneers). How about being hailed Super Bowl MVP? Brady has been so honored five times and was the first QB to be named MVP with two different teams. What about his passing totals? Brady completed 277 of 421 passes for 3,039 yards and 21 touchdowns — all Super Bowl records. He also passed 466 yards in Super Bowl LI against the Atlanta Falcons, then followed that the next Super Bowl by throwing for 505 yards against the Philadelphia Eagles — the two highest single-game passing totals in Super Bowl history. That he passed for close to 1,000 yards in just two games is almost unthinkable. Then again, we are talking about the QB who began his NFL career as the 199th pick in the 2000 NFL Draft.

2. JOE MONTANA

Joe Montana of the San Francisco 49ers amassed the highest passer rating (127.83) in Super Bowl history during his four appearances, all of them victories. Montana ranks seventh in Super Bowl passes attempted (122) and fourth in completions (83). His completion percentage is second best among quarterbacks who have started in at least three Super Bowls at 68.0, just slightly behind Troy Aikman. Montana's 11 touchdowns in four Super Bowls puts him in second behind Brady, and his five-touchdown performance in Super Bowl XXIV was bested only once by the six that were thrown by former San Francisco teammate Steve Young. At the time of his retirement, Montana owned most of the Super Bowl passing records, many of which have fallen as the NFL game trends toward passing.

3. PATRICK MAHOMES

Their first encounter took place in the Kansas City dressing room after Tom Brady's Patriots had defeated Mahomes' Kansas City Chiefs in the 2018 AFC Championship game. Brady didn't make a habit of crashing the opposition's dressing room, but he was so impressed by Mahomes that he convinced security to let him in. Once inside, Brady praised Mahomes and, according to Mahomes, said, "'Man, you had a heck of a season.' He knows what it's like to win a lot of big games and what it's like go lose some big games, but not many. He said to keep grinding. He loved the way I played." What's not to love? In his first season as a starter (2018) he threw for 5,097 yards and 50 touchdowns. Since then, he has played in five Super Bowls, won three of them, was the MVP in all three victories and was twice named NFL MVP.

4. KURT WARNER

Kurt Warner has a 1-2 record in Super Bowl games, but it's awfully tough to pin either of those losses on him. One of just four quarterbacks to take two franchises to the Super Bowl (St. Louis and Arizona), Warner has three of the top six highest single-game passing yards totals in Super Bowl history (414, 377 and 365). He ranks third in all-time Super Bowl passing yards (1,156) and is the only quarterback among the top nine in that category with three or fewer appearances in the game.

5. TERRY BRADSHAW

Pittsburgh Steelers quarterback Terry Bradshaw lacks the gaudy statistics of the greatest players at his position, but it's hard to ignore the four Vince Lombardi Trophies he won in four Super Bowl appearances. In only one of these four appearances did Bradshaw attempt more than 21 passes, thanks to a Steelers team built largely on defense and running the football. Still, Bradshaw ranks fourth all-time in Super Bowl passer rating (112.8), seventh in passing yards (932) and fourth in Super Bowl touchdown passes (9), and he has the second-highest average yards per pass in a Super Bowl, including the highest average of a single game (14.7) in Super Bowl XIV.

Travis Kelce catches the ball during Super Bowl LV versus the Tampa Bay Buccaneers. He caught 10 passes for 133 yards in a 31–9 loss for the Chiefs.

GREATEST SUPER BOWL RECEIVERS

★ ★ ★

There's nothing quite like watching a football sail through the air into the arms of a receiver, especially when the game is on the line. Receivers need to have an incredible awareness of the field, so when a great receiver comes along, it's pure magic. Here are five of the greatest Super Bowl receivers in history.

1. JERRY RICE

There's hardly any doubt about the greatest receiver in Super Bowl history. Jerry Rice is the Super Bowl's No. 2 leader in receptions (33) and the all-time leader in yards receiving (589), and his eight touchdown receptions are three more than any other player. Rice's 215 yards receiving in Super Bowl XXIII is a record, as are his three receiving touchdowns in a single game, a feat he accomplished twice. Throw in the fact that he was on the winning side of the game in each of his four appearances with the San Francisco 49ers, with two different quarterbacks, and there is no doubt about Rice's place in Super Bowl history.

2. TRAVIS KELCE

The evolution of the tight end position has given these players a much more prominent role in the NFL's offenses. And no player illustrates that as much as Kansas City's Travis Kelce, who has been the Chiefs' most important offensive player — besides quarterback Patrick Mahomes — throughout their latest run of success. Kelce has averaged seven catches and 77.8 receiving yards over five Super Bowl appearances, including Super Bowl LV, in which he caught 10 passes (tied for fourth most in a game all-time) for 133 yards. Three years later, at Super Bowl LVIII, he was targeted 10 times and caught nine passes for 93 yards. Kelce's 35 Super Bowl catches are the most all-time, two ahead of Jerry Rice. His 389 yards receiving in Super Bowls is behind only Rice.

3. LYNN SWANN

Lynn Swann failed to make a catch in Super Bowl IX, and in fact had one carry for a loss of 7 yards. But that was hardly an indication of his Super Bowl future since Swann became a huge part of the Pittsburgh Steelers' next three Super Bowl wins. His four catches for 161 yards in the Steelers' Super Bowl X win over the Dallas Cowboys earned him MVP honors, as he made two of the most acrobatic catches in the game's history. His total receiving yards in that game remains the fourth highest single-game total in Super Bowl history, and his 364 total Super Bowl yardage ranks fourth all-time. Swann ranks third in career yards per catch (22.75) and is tied for third in touchdown receptions (three).

4. ROB GRONKOWSKI

Tom Brady did not enjoy a plethora of all-time great offensive players around him during his years with the New England Patriots, but he did have the luxury of an all-time great tight end. And Rob Gronkowski had a way of showing up for the biggest moments. In five Super Bowl appearances (four with New England, one with Tampa Bay) Gronkowski's 29 catches rank third all-time behind Travis Kelce and Jerry Rice, while his 364 receiving yards trail the same two, only in reverse. Gronkowski's five touchdown receptions trail only Rice. During his final two Super Bowl appearances, Gronkowski hauled in 12 of 14 passes directed his way for 154 yards and two touchdowns.

5. JULIAN EDELMAN

For a player who was a college football quarterback, Julian Edelman became a stalwart NFL receiver and a key piece of the New England Patriots' dynasty. So often, when Tom Brady absolutely had to make a play, it was Edelman on the receiving end. Edelman was a role player on the Patriots early in his career, catching just 69 passes during his first four seasons and having no passes thrown his way during his first Super Bowl appearance (XLVI) when they faced the New York Giants. But by the time the Patriots reached Super Bowl XLIX two seasons later, Edelman had broken out. In his final three Super Bowl games with New England, he averaged eight catches and over 112 yards per game. His 337 receiving yards in the Super Bowl rank fifth all-time, while his 24 receptions rank sixth.

GREATEST SUPER BOWL RUNNING BACKS

★ ★ ★

Franco Harris, the Super Bowl career leader in rushing attempts, carries the ball in Super Bowl XIII.

Some of the most famous professional football players have been running backs: Walter Payton, Franco Harris, Larry Csonka and Emmitt Smith are just a few who have terrified opposition defenses. While other position players avoid the pack of opposing linebackers, running backs charge right through them. So it takes a special kind of athlete to be the best in his role in the most important game of the season. Here are the five best running backs in Super Bowl history.

Emmitt Smith celebrates scoring a touchdown during Dallas' dominant 52–17 victory over Buffalo in Super Bowl XXVII.

1. FRANCO HARRIS

Franco Harris was the workhorse of the great Pittsburgh Steelers teams of the 1970s. Harris' 101 Super Bowl carries put him 31 ahead of any other player in the game's history. This is a record unlikely to be surpassed given the modern game's emphasis on passing and the use of multiple running backs to share the load. His total of 354 rushing yards is the most ever, and his four rushing touchdowns trail only Emmitt Smith. Harris' 158 yards rushing in Super Bowl IX is the fourth highest in a single Super Bowl. He earned MVP honors for that performance, as only the second running back to receive the award.

2. EMMITT SMITH

The Dallas Cowboys' great running back Emmitt Smith was part of the trio known as "the Triplets," which also included quarterback Troy Aikman and wide receiver Michael Irvin. Together they led America's Team to three NFL titles, and Smith was named MVP of Super Bowl XXVIII. He earned the award for his 30-carry, 132-yard performance that included a pair of touchdowns as his team defeated the Buffalo Bills. Smith scored an additional three touchdowns in two other Super Bowl appearances, giving him an all-time best of five. His 70 Super Bowl carries are the second most of any running back, and he sits third for all-time rushing yards with 289.

3. LARRY CSONKA

Larry Csonka was an absolute powerhouse running back for the Miami Dolphins for seven seasons, making the playoffs six times. They won two Super Bowls with Csonka, who amassed over 100 yards in each back-to-back victory (VII and VIII). His total of 297 rushing yards puts him second all-time, and his 33 rushing attempts in Super Bowl VIII are the third most in any one Super Bowl game.

4. TERRELL DAVIS

The Denver Broncos struck gold when they drafted running back Terrell Davis in 1995. He was a mighty force in both of Denver's Super Bowl victories in the 1997 and 1998 seasons, rushing a combined 55 times for 259 yards. He earned MVP honors for Super Bowl XXXII when the Broncos' passing game struggled, so they relied on Davis to rumble through the Green Bay defense. Throw in his three touchdowns and 157 total yards and the award was easily his.

5. TIMMY SMITH

Timmy Smith of the Washington Redskins is the only player in Super Bowl history to have over 200 rushing yards in a single game — 204 to be exact. This is even more remarkable when you consider that he had been drafted in the fifth round only nine months before and had only 29 carries during his rookie regular season. Somewhere in those 204 yards he also scored two touchdowns. Smith never made it back to the championship game, but based on that one performance, he is tied for sixth on the Super Bowl's all-time rushing list with Buffalo's Thurman Thomas, who played in four games.

Denver's Derek Wolfe celebrates a sack — one of seven for the Broncos defense — against the Carolina Panthers during Super Bowl 50.

GREATEST SUPER BOWL DEFENSES

★ ★ ★

What wins championships, offense or defense? History shows it is the latter, as several teams have shut down powerful offenses with their defensive lines on their way to glory. Here are five of the best examples.

1. 2015 DENVER BRONCOS

Of all the great defenses that have led teams to a Super Bowl, none were more accomplished than the 2015 Denver Broncos. The league's top-rated regular-season defense went up against the Pittsburgh offense led by Ben Roethlisberger and the New England offense led by Tom Brady during the playoffs — two quarterbacks who'd been to nine Super Bowls between them. During the championship game, Denver's defense destroyed the offensive-best Carolina Panthers and quarterback Cam Newton. Carolina had put up at least 30 points in eight of their 15 regular-season wins and combined for 80 points in their two playoff wins. But it wasn't enough when facing Denver's defense. They not only held Carolina to just 10 points but also were responsible for the two plays that led directly to Denver's only two touchdowns: a pair of strip sacks by linebacker Von Miller, who claimed the Super Bowl MVP award for his superb efforts.

2. 2000 BALTIMORE RAVENS

The Baltimore Ravens of 2000 were another team that could win games almost entirely on defense alone — an ability they put on display in their 34–7 win over the New York Giants in Super Bowl XXXV. Middle linebacker Ray Lewis was the star, becoming just the fifth defensive player up to that time to be named Super Bowl MVP. The Ravens prevented the Giants from scrimmaging inside their 29-yard line and left quarterback Kerry Collins with one of the saddest quarterback stat lines in the game's history: 15 of 39 passes for 112 yards and four interceptions. Baltimore's strategy was simple: they completely took away their opponents' running game, limiting teams to just 2.7 yards per rush.

3. 1974 PITTSBURGH STEELERS

The Pittsburgh Steelers crushed the Minnesota Vikings by a score of 16–6 during Super Bowl IX. Pittsburgh's defense allowed a Super Bowl-record low of 119 yards. They also produced five turnovers and a safety, earning them the nickname "the Steel Curtain." The Steelers had eight players from that defense go to the Pro Bowl and four who wound up in the Pro Football Hall of Fame. During the 1974 season, Pittsburgh's defense led the NFL in takeaways, sacks, opponent passer rating and fewest yards allowed.

4. 1985 CHICAGO BEARS

The only Super Bowl–winning team in Chicago Bears history is best remembered for a defense that took aggressiveness to new heights. Under defensive coordinator Buddy Ryan and his 46 defensive scheme, the Bears brought relentless pressure on quarterbacks. At the Super Bowl they quickly snuffed out the hopes of the New England Patriots by completely limiting the efforts of quarterback Tony Eason, who was pulled before halftime. Chicago amassed seven sacks in the Super Bowl, a mark that wouldn't be equaled for 30 years, and allowed New England just 7 yards of rushing.

5. 2024 PHILADELPHIA EAGLES

The Philadelphia Eagles' defense was good but not elite during the 2024 regular season. But in the Super Bowl game against the Kansas City Chiefs they had a historic performance against a quarterback considered unstoppable in big games. Patrick Mahomes' stat line through the first half of the 59th Super Bowl game is hard to fathom: 6 of 14 passing for 33 yards with two sacks for minus-13 yards and two interceptions. On the three occasions during the first half when Mahomes handed the ball off, the Chiefs gained 3 yards on three carries. The Eagles were able to shut-down Kansas City's offense by putting pressure on Mahomes without having to blitz, forcing the quarterback to make hurried throws into coverage. Halfway through the final quarter the score was 40–6 in an eventual 40–22 Eagles' victory.

GREATEST SUPER BOWL TEAMS

★ ★ ★

Jerry Rice celebrates the San Francisco 49ers' fifth Super Bowl victory. He was an integral part of all five championships.

Trying to decide which franchise is the greatest in Super Bowl history is a tough choice. Is it the team with the most wins or with the higher percentage of winning? What about the team with some incredible comebacks? There isn't really a right answer, but here are five franchises that should definitely be in the conversation.

1. NEW ENGLAND PATRIOTS

There is no denying that for two decades the road to the Super Bowl went through Foxborough, Massachusetts — home of the New England Patriots. That meant getting past the most decorated quarterback in NFL history. What made Tom Brady so successful was how he elevated the play of those around him. When Randy Moss joined the Patriots in 2007, he caught 98 passes for 1,493 yards and 23 touchdowns, a record for wide receivers. Deion Branch came within 2 yards of a 1,000-yard season with New England. He was at his best in Super Bowl XXXIX against the Philadelphia Eagles, ruffling their secondary with 11 catches for 133 yards. On that day, he was voted the game's MVP. With the likes of Danny Amendola, Julian Edelman and Rob Gronkowski on his go-to list, Brady shredded defensive backfields. And in 2004, the Patriots latched onto running back Corey Dillon, who carved out a career-best 1,635 yards and 12 TDs. Unfortunately, injuries and inconsistencies undid Dillon's career after that. He was out of football within two years.

2. PITTSBURGH STEELERS

For a franchise that was a near disaster in the years leading up to the Super Bowl era, the Pittsburgh Steelers have been a model of consistency and success over the past five decades. Pittsburgh co-owns the most Vince Lombardi Trophies with six (tied with the Patriots). Remarkably, the Steelers' success has been achieved with just three head coaches in the Super Bowl era: Chuck Noll, Bill Cowher and Mike Tomlin. And only two quarterbacks in that time have lifted the Vince Lombardi Trophy: Terry Bradshaw (four) and Ben Roethlisberger (two). The Steelers' Super Bowl success has been built on a consistent foundation of hard-nosed defense, a solid running game, and calm and efficient play at quarterback.

3. SAN FRANCISCO 49ers

The first 14 years of the Super Bowl era were not kind to the San Francisco 49ers, who managed just three playoff appearances over that span. They then rocketed to the top of the 1981 season with a 13-3 record and their first Super Bowl win. That was Joe Montana's first season as the full-time starting quarterback and it proved to be the beginning of an era of dominance. The strike-shortened year of 1982 aside, the 49ers reached the postseason in 15 of the next 16 seasons, winning the Super Bowl four more times. The only championship game they lost was Super Bowl XLVII to the Baltimore Ravens by a heartbreaking three points.

4. DALLAS COWBOYS

The Dallas Cowboys have enjoyed two distinct Super Bowl periods in their history. They won their first Super Bowl at the end of the 1971 season, the same year that Roger Staubach took over as the team's starting quarterback. Staubach guided the Cowboys through a period of prosperity that included three more Super Bowl appearances and one more win. By the time the Cowboys next emerged as Super Bowl competitors, a new cast of future Hall of Famers was wearing the star on their helmets. The Cowboys of the 1990s rattled off six consecutive regular seasons of double-digit wins and three Super Bowl victories. In total, Dallas has five trophies in eight appearances.

5. KANSAS CITY CHIEFS

The Kansas City Chiefs were at center stage in the very first Super Bowl game, where they fell 35–10 to Green Bay in the first of the Packers' back-to-back championships. Three years later it was the Chiefs' turn, winning Super Bowl IV to the Minnesota Vikings 23–7. But it would be half-a-century before they would get back to the big game. And some might even suggest it was worth the wait. Andy Reid was already a highly successful coach from his years in Philadelphia when the Chiefs hired him in 2013. Four years later they drafted quarterback Patrick Mahomes 10th overall, pairing him with tight end Travis Kelce to create one of the most unstoppable combinations in NFL history. A third sure-fire Hall of Famer, Chris Jones, anchored the defense, which in some seasons outperformed Mahomes and the offense. The Chiefs played in five Super Bowl games in six seasons, winning their first, their third and their fourth. Kansas City was denied becoming the first team to win three consecutive Super Bowls by their 40–22 loss to the Philadelphia Eagles in Super Bowl LIX.

Terry Bradshaw and Pittsburgh coach Chuck Noll celebrate the Steelers' 1975 championship.

BEST SUPER BOWL CATCHES

★ ★ ★

Santonio Holmes drags his toes through the back corner of the end zone after catching a pinpoint Ben Roethlisberger pass to win Pittsburgh's sixth title.

It's amazing to watch tight ends and wide receivers blast off the line, run their route as hard as a rookie runs the 40-yard dash at the scouting combine, and then turn on a dime or leap in the air in time to make a phenomenal catch. That skill level has led to some incredible receptions during the past 50 Super Bowls, and here are our top five.

1. TYREE'S HELMET CATCH

Without a doubt, New York Giants receiver David Tyree's helmet catch during Super Bowl XLII is heads above the rest. It was such a sweet catch that it could rank No. 1 in several Super Bowl categories — best play, best passing play, best play to set up a Super Bowl win. It wasn't just the 32-yard gain by a guy holding the football against his helmet; it was the importance of the catch, made late in the fourth quarter on third and five at the Giants' 44-yard line. It was the kind of play that sparked the team and helped Eli Manning throw the game-winning ball to Plaxico Burress, clinching the Giants' victory over the New England Patriots, 17–14. NFL Films deservingly called the Tyree catch "the play of the decade (2000s)."

2. EDELMAN'S GRAVITY DEFIER

In a second half that saw the Patriots erase a 25-point deficit, there was one play in Super Bowl LI that resisted all logic. Facing a first-and-10 from his own 35-yard line late in the fourth quarter, Tom Brady found Julian Edelman open over the middle. But by the time the ball arrived, three Atlanta Falcons had descended upon Edelman, who somehow was able to track the ball as it bounced off one set of hands then off a leg right into his grasp without touching the turf. It resulted in a 19-yard gain to set up the tying touchdown in regulation time. Edelman added another critical catch in overtime to help New England win its fifth Super Bowl crown.

3. SWANN'S JUMP

In Super Bowl X, Pittsburgh Steelers receiver Lynn Swann may have made the play of the 1970s. He timed his jump perfectly over a defender to get his hands on a pass from quarterback Terry Bradshaw. When he failed to make the catch on his first try, Swann kept his eyes glued to the ball and was able to grab it as he fell to the ground, earning a 53-yard gain. The Steelers defeated the Dallas Cowboys, 21–17, on the strength of Swann's record 161 yards receiving. He was the first receiver to be named Super Bowl MVP.

4. HOLMES' CORNER

Santonio Holmes of the Pittsburgh Steelers had the game of his career during Super Bowl XLIII. He made nine receptions for

Lynn Swann dives to catch a pass in Super Bowl X against the Dallas Cowboys,

131 yards, but it was his one touchdown catch that gets him on this list. Covered by three defenders in the deep corner of the Arizona Cardinals' end zone, Holmes jumped high for a pass and managed to drag his toes in the turf before falling out of bounds. On-field officials called it a touchdown and video replays confirmed. Holmes had four catches for 73 yards in that drive alone. It was the game-winning touchdown, earning Holmes MVP honors and giving the Steelers their sixth Super Bowl victory — the most for any NFL franchise.

5. JONES' CATCH AND RUN

Sometimes the run after the catch is as important as the catch itself. During Super Bowl XLVII, Baltimore Ravens quarterback Joe Flacco threw a deep ball to his receiver Jacoby Jones, who had to slow down to snag the ball. Jones then fell backwards, rolled over and got on his feet. His loss of momentum should have ended the play there, as two San Francisco 49ers went after him to make the tackle. But Jones was determined and spun away to avoid them before running the last few yards into the end zone. Baltimore went on to beat San Francisco to claim its second Super Bowl title.

BEST SUPER BOWL RUNNING PLAYS

A pack of Seahawks chases Pittsburgh's Willie Parker as he sprints ahead of all comers to record the Super Bowl's longest rushing touchdown at Super Bowl XL.

Defenses in the NFL can be terrifying, populated by monster-sized men whose sole job is to stop people from passing them. So when a running back manages to not only plow through opposing defenders but evade them as well, it's truly a spectacle to see. Here are five of the best Super Bowl running plays.

1. ALLEN'S 74-YARDER

Marcus Allen's freelance, spin-around 74-yard touchdown run in Super Bowl XVIII won the Los Angeles Raiders an NFL championship and raised Allen's status to otherworldly. It was more than just a signature play for the veteran running back; many have rated it the greatest play in Super Bowl history. It happened against the defending-champion Washington Redskins, and it tore a hole right through their defense. "It was beautiful," said Allen, whose speed and shimmy-shake moves ravaged Washington's defense in yet another big run in the same game. That 39-yard gain led to a field goal, a Raiders' 38–9 runaway victory and MVP honors for Allen.

2. SMITH'S 58-YARDER

With the Washington Redskins clinging to a 14–10 lead during Super Bowl XXII, Timmy Smith showed his strength, quickness and determination all in one play. He took the ball and ran it around the Denver Broncos' tacklers on his way to the end zone. The 58-yard touchdown run was Smith's first scoring play of the day. In the fourth quarter, he added another touchdown on a 4-yard run, making Smith the first NFL rookie to score two touchdowns in a Super Bowl. His rushing count was a remarkable 204 yards, a performance that still reigns as a single-game Super Bowl record.

Marcus Allen reads his blocks and races to a 74-yard touchdown romp.

3. RIGGINS' 43-YARDER

John Riggins was a smash-mouth running back, as big as a linebacker and faster than most of them. The proof came in Super Bowl XVII between Riggins' Washington Redskins and the Miami Dolphins. In the fourth quarter of a close game, the Washington offense lined up for a fourth-and-inches play at the Miami 43-yard line. Riggins got the ball, blew off one tackle, and then out-legged the Dolphins all the way to their end zone. Through the postseason, Riggins thrived on getting the ball — the longer the game went on, the better he played. As he told Washington head coach Joe Gibbs, "Just give me the ball." Against Miami, Riggins gained 166 yards (third all-time) and was named the Super Bowl's MVP.

4. PARKER'S 75-YARDER

This was the scene during Super Bowl XL's third quarter: the Pittsburgh Steelers' offense was on its 25-yard line for a critical third down against the Seattle Seahawks. The ball was handed off to running back Willie Parker and just like that, he was off and running all the way to the end zone. His 75-yard touchdown run is the longest in Super Bowl history, edging Marcus Allen's 74-yard score. For the game, Parker had 10 carries and 93 yards.

5. CSONKA'S SMASH-MOUTH TDS

Larry Csonka of the Miami Dolphins, another smash-mouth, straight-ahead runner, wasted no time avoiding defenders, especially those belonging to the Minnesota Vikings during Super Bowl VIII. He just crashed into the closest pile of them he could find and shook off the ones who had the gall to grab hold of him. For that championship game, Csonka had 33 carries, 145 yards and two touchdowns. The Vikings were plundered by a score of 24–7.

Philadelphia Eagles cornerback Cooper DeJean runs the ball after making an interception during Super Bowl LIX.

BEST SUPER BOWL INTERCEPTIONS

★ ★ ★

Nothing makes a football fan jump out of their seat like a well-timed interception. The nature of the play — more than almost any other in football — has fans and players alike experiencing immediate and contrasting emotions; the joy of an interception is rivaled in its extreme pleasure only by the pain of being intercepted. Not all interceptions are game breakers, but when one is, it's a wild ride. Here are the best interceptions of the Super Bowl.

1. BUTLER'S GAME SAVER

In terms of drama, nothing comes close to how New England Patriots cornerback Malcolm Butler became part of Super Bowl lore during the 49th championship game. The Seattle Seahawks were sitting on the Patriots' 1-yard line with 26 seconds remaining, trailing by a score of 28–24. The only thing less expected than Seattle attempting to throw the ball was the possibility that it could be picked off. But that's exactly what happened. Butler coolly cut under the intended receiver and intercepted what was to be the game-winning score. It was one of the most stunning moments in NFL history and his play deprived Seattle of back-to-back titles. Instead, the Patriots were on top of the football world once again. As for Butler, his play was undoubtedly the greatest end to an NFL season for an undrafted rookie free agent.

2. HARRISON'S RECORD ROMP

It's often said that giving up points right before halftime is a wound that can sit with a team for the remainder of the game. The Pittsburgh Steelers were facing that undesirable possibility in Super Bowl XLIII. With 18 seconds left in the first half, the Arizona Cardinals looked to punch the ball in from the Steelers' 1-yard line in order to take the lead. But a pass intended for Anquan Boldin wound up instead in the arms of Pittsburgh's James Harrison — a bruising linebacker not renowned for his open-field speed. Harrison somehow weaved his way all the way down the field, crossing the Arizona goal line after time had expired and giving his team a 10-point lead in an eventual 27–23 win.

3. PORTER'S PERFECT PICK

The Indianapolis Colts and New Orleans Saints were locked in a shootout featuring two of the best passers in football — Peyton Manning and Drew Brees, respectively. Between them they threw 84 passes, completing 63, all but one to their intended targets. The lone exception took place late in the game with the Colts marching down the field, trailing 24–17. Manning made a mistake, hurrying his throw to Reggie Wayne; the ball was picked off by Saints cornerback Tracy Porter at the New Orleans 26-yard line. The crowd in Miami watched helplessly as Porter streaked 74 yards toward the end zone for a game-changing score that put the Saints up 31–17 with 3:24 to play. Essentially, game over.

4. DEJEAN'S PICK-SIX

Super Bowl LIX was still very much up for grabs — and then rookie cornerback Cooper DeJean took matters into his hands and shook the two-time defending Super Bowl champions to their core. It happened in the second quarter with the Philadelphia Eagles leading the Kansas City Chiefs by a score of 10–0. Chiefs' QB Patrick Mahomes was chased out of the pocket and threw while on the run. DeJean stepped in front of the pass and made a clean interception. He returned it 38 yards for a touchdown that increased the Eagles' lead and cast Kansas City into a serious funk. What made the DeJean pick-six extra special was that it was the first of his pro career and it came on his 22nd birthday.

5. WOOD IS THE FIRST

The first interception in Super Bowl history still stands out as one of the greatest. The Kansas City Chiefs trailed the Green Bay Packers by a score of 14–10 in the third quarter of Super Bowl I. Facing third and five near midfield, Chiefs quarterback Len Dawson fired a pass to his left intended for tight end Fred Arbanas. The ball fluttered long enough for Green Bay safety Willie Wood to snatch it. He took off downfield from his own 45-yard line and was downed at the Chiefs' five. Green Bay's Elijah Pitts scored on the next play, and the Packers went on to a convincing 35–10 victory.

BEST SUPER BOWL COACHES

★ ★ ★

Bill Walsh is hoisted by his San Francisco 49ers following his team's victory at Super Bowl XIX.

A team is only as good as the man calling the plays. Head coaches are integral to the winning process, and here are five of the best from Super Bowl history.

1. BILL BELICHICK

Before becoming New England's head coach in 2000, Bill Belichick had five years of head coaching experience in the early 1990s with the Cleveland Browns. He worked as an assistant coach with several teams, including the Patriots, before replacing Pete Carroll as the field boss in New England. They missed the playoffs his first season but came back strong in his second to win the franchise's first Super Bowl. With Tom Brady at quarterback and Belichick in command, the Patriots went to nine Super Bowls and won six. Belichick's reputation paints him as a coach who will do anything to win, even if it's questionable. From "Spygate" in 2007 (a supposed illegal recording of the New York Jets' defensive signals) to "Deflategate" in 2015 (the alleged deflating of footballs to make them easier for the Patriots to handle), Belichick has had his share of controversy. Even so, his career playoff record of 31–13 makes it hard to deny his abilities.

2. BILL WALSH

Two seasons was all it took for Bill Walsh to transform the San Francisco 49ers from long-time losers into Super Bowl champions. In his decade as head coach, Walsh guided the 49ers to three Super Bowl championships (XVI, XIX, XXIII) and was twice named NFL Coach of the Year. Known as an innovator, Walsh designed the West Coast Offense — an attack that spread out defenses and made them vulnerable to short passes. When San Francisco drafted quarterback Joe Montana and receiver Jerry Rice, Walsh had the right players at the right positions to elevate the West Coast Offense to a new level of effectiveness. It is telling that several of Walsh's assistant coaches went on to become successful NFL head coaches.

3. VINCE LOMBARDI

Vince Lombardi cared about the basics: blocking, tackling, conditioning. His Green Bay Packers were as efficient in the fourth quarter as they were in the first, helping them win the first two Super Bowls. Add those to the three championships they won in 1961, 1962 and 1965, and their record was an incredible five NFL titles in seven years. Lombardi left Green Bay to coach the Washington Redskins in 1969, taking them to their first winning record in 14 years. Following his death in 1970, the NFL chose to name its Super Bowl trophy after him. It was first presented to the Baltimore Colts when they won Super Bowl V.

4. CHUCK NOLL

The Pittsburgh Steelers share the honor as the most successful NFL franchise with the New England Patriots, with six Super Bowl victories apiece. The Steelers' success is due in large part to Chuck Noll, who was head coach from 1969 to 1991 and helped the team win four of those championships. Noll also oversaw Pittsburgh's draft selections, since he had a great eye for great talent. During the 1974 NFL Draft, the Steelers took receivers Lynn Swann and John Stallworth, linebacker Jack Lambert and center Mike Webster — all four are now in the Hall of Fame.

5. ANDY REID

During his 14 seasons as head coach of the Philadelphia Eagles, Andy Reid was often labeled a guy who couldn't get the best out of his team in big games. Three consecutive years his team got to the NFC Championship Game, and all three times they lost. The fourth year proved to be the charm, but being erased by the New England Patriots without much fight in Super Bowl XXXIX did nothing to appease his critics. Reid's next stop, however, would change everything. Getting his Kansas City Chiefs to five Super Bowl games in six seasons is an amazing feat in today's NFL, where team's fortunes often vary from one season to the next, based on parody. He now has a 3-3 record in six total Super Bowl appearances. Known for his offensive innovation and influence on the coaching profession overall, Reid is considered among the great NFL head coaches of all time.

Vince Lombardi is carried off the field after Green Bay won Super Bowl II.

Arizona Cardinals wide receiver Larry Fitzgerald celebrates his 64-yard touchdown during the fourth quarter of Super Bowl XLIII.

BEST PERFORMANCE BY A PLAYER ON A LOSING TEAM

★ ★ ★

Football can be a cruel game when it comes time to play for all the marbles. Sometimes a player will outplay his opposition so thoroughly it seems unfair that his team must lose. Such is the way things go in team sports. But, when the pain finally subsides, those players know they excelled on the sport's biggest stage. It doesn't replace winning, but for these five players, let the record show that they pulled out all the stops, even if they lost.

1. TOM BRADY

It doesn't seem fair that a player who won seven Super Bowl games should have the distinction of owning the best performance by a player on a losing team. But that's exactly the case for Tom Brady, the losing quarterback in Super Bowl LII, a 41–33 victory for the Philadelphia Eagles. Brady's 505 yards passing still stands as a Super Bowl record, and three of his Super Bowl record 21 touchdown passes came in that game as well. Three New England players finished the game with more than 100 yards receiving: Danny Amendola (152), Chris Hogan (128) and Rob Gronkowski (116). Brady either set or tied seven Super Bowl records with his performance in a losing cause.

2. JALEN HURTS

Jalen Hurts led his Philadelphia Eagles to Super Bowl LVII with a dual-threat style of play at quarterback that was unlike most others. Especially in the way he scored touchdowns, throwing for 22 of them and rushing for another 13. That style served Hurts well against the Kansas City Chiefs in a game in which he threw for 304 yards and a touchdown, while adding 70 yards and three touchdowns along the ground. His 70-yard rushing performance is a Super Bowl record for a quarterback, and his three touchdowns tie him with several others for the most times crossing the goal line in a Super Bowl game.The 35 points scored by the Eagles that day is the 15th highest point total for a team in the Super Bowl. Hurts would get his chance to taste the winning side two years later, when his Eagles avenged their loss to the Chiefs at Super Bowl LIX.

3. LARRY FITZGERALD

In Super Bowl XLIII against the Pittsburgh Steelers, Larry Fitzgerald showed the world exactly why he's such a dangerous force. He scored two touchdowns that game, both at critical times. The first was a 1-yard catch from quarterback Kurt Warner to bring the Arizona Cardinals within one touchdown of taking the lead. On his second notable play, Fitzgerald caught a pass from Warner and completely took off, leaving three tacklers in his dust on a 64-yard touchdown burst to take the lead. Pittsburgh ended up winning 27–23, but Fitzgerald went above and beyond what any receiver has done in the postseason. In four games, he gained 546 yards, caught 30 receptions and scored seven touchdowns — records that may never be broken.

4. MARSHAWN LYNCH

It's the play that should have happened but never did that has landed Marshawn Lynch on this list. In Super Bowl XLIX, Lynch had already produced 102 yards rushing and a touchdown for the Seattle Seahawks when, trailing 28–24, his club had the ball and was on the New England Patriots' 1-yard line with 26 seconds on the clock. Everyone expected Lynch to get the call to romp into the end zone and win the game (and quite possibly be named Super Bowl MVP). But coach Pete Carroll called a pass, the ball was intercepted and two seasons later Lynch retired, never getting another Super Bowl chance.

5. CHUCK HOWLEY

You have to go all the way back to 1971 to find the only player on the losing team to have won the Super Bowl MVP award. Dallas Cowboys linebacker Chuck Howley didn't just stop running backs and receivers, he could also run with them and make plays downfield. Against the Baltimore Colts in Super Bowl V, Howley had an incredible showing, recording two interceptions and a forced fumble to win MVP honors over Baltimore players who actually won the Super Bowl.

Dan Marino of the Miami Dolphins in the early 1990s.

BEST PLAYERS TO NEVER WIN A SUPER BOWL

★ ★ ★

They're all in the Pro Football Hall of fame — a huge honor for any NFL player. Yet their trophy shelves are missing the big one. These five players broke records and established themselves as some of the best, but they never won a Super Bowl.

1. DAN MARINO

Dan Marino and his exploits with the Miami Dolphins were a joy to watch. And yet for all that greatness, Marino retired without winning an NFL title. His one and only chance was during Super Bowl XIX against a San Francisco 49ers team at its best. Fans and media were looking forward to a showdown between Marino and his San Francisco counterpart Joe Montana, but it turned out to be a one-sided game. The 49ers' defense sacked Marino four times and intercepted him twice. Worse than that was Miami's running game, which produced just 25 yards on nine rushes. Marino would go on to play another 14 seasons but never got back to the Super Bowl.

2. BARRY SANDERS

Barry Sanders had 15,269 rushing yards, 109 total touchdowns in 10 seasons with the Detroit Lions and plenty left in the tank. Yet he suddenly retired in 1999, leaving many to wonder why he was quitting. The answer, in part, was five playoff appearances in 10 seasons with little more than a sniff of the Super Bowl. Sanders said he was tired of the team's losing attitude and it was draining his competitive spirit. The Lions demanded that he return half of his $11 million signing bonus, which an arbitrator upheld. Sanders asked to be traded to another team; the Lions refused. Such was the inglorious end for one of football's greatest players.

3. DICK BUTKUS

Everything about Dick Butkus, from his bone-crunching tackles to his ferocious attitude was made for playing middle linebacker. An NFL general manager called Butkus "an annihilating SOB" — and meant it as a compliment. Accused of biting, scratching and mauling his rivals, the All-Pro Chicago Bear insisted that he "never set out to hurt anybody, unless it was, you know, important — like a league game or something." He played nine years in the NFL without once making the playoffs. No wonder he was so mad on the field.

4. EARL CAMPBELL

From 1978 to 1984, Earl Campbell was the Houston Oilers' one-man ground game. He played in five Pro Bowls, led the league in rushing three years in a row and was named a first-team all-star three years in a row. Campbell could roll through even the best defenses. In his 1978 *Monday Night Football* debut, he quashed the Miami Dolphins with 199 yards running and four touchdowns. He would go on to win the NFL's top rookie honors and MVP. Campbell finished his career with 9,407 yards rushing and 74 touchdowns, but no Super Bowl appearances.

5. DEACON JONES

NFL players are credited for what they do during games, but strange as it sounds, Deacon Jones earned his praise for doing something the NFL didn't acknowledge at the time — sacking quarterbacks. A terror at defensive end, Jones was a founding father of the Los Angeles Rams' Fearsome Foursome. He hunted down and attacked quarterbacks, but it was all unofficial because the league didn't keep tabs on sacks until 1982. Even without an official sack count, Jones made it to the Pro Football Hall of Fame because of his supreme pass-rushing skills. The league banned Jones' patented head slap for being too dangerous a play, but they couldn't banish his speed or ferocity, which he used in equal measure to get the job done. After his death in 2013, the NFL named a trophy in his honor for the player who gets the most sacks.

WORST SUPER BOWL QUARTERBACKS

★ ★ ★

Rich Gannon suffers one of his five sacks during Super Bowl XXXVII.

Quarterbacks tend to face the most pressure and scrutiny during the NFL's biggest game of the year. The Super Bowl can break the team leader just as quickly as it can make him (just ask Cam Newton). Whether they faced a tough defense or choked under pressure, here are five quarterbacks whose Super Bowl appearance was memorable for all the wrong reasons.

1. TONY EASON

Tony Eason of the New England Patriots had the misfortune of facing one of the NFL's all-time great defenses in the 1985 Chicago Bears. It's hard to actually imagine things going any worse for the Patriots, who were completely dominated throughout the entire game. Eason's first quarter was a nightmare — he threw incomplete passes on his first five times dropping back before being sacked on the next three. He went 0 for 6 in passing before mercifully being replaced by backup Steve Grogan with five minutes remaining in the half. The Bears won 46–10 for the biggest Super Bowl blowout at the time.

Chicago Bears linebacker Otis Wilson hits New England Patriots quarterback Tony Eason in Super Bowl XX in New Orleans.

2. KERRY COLLINS

Like Tony Eason, Kerry Collins ran into one of the most dominant defenses in NFL history when his New York Giants faced the Baltimore Ravens in January of 2001. Collins completed just 15 of 39 passes for 112 yards and four interceptions. He was also sacked four times for 26 yards, giving the Giants just 86 yards net passing. The Giants never scrimmaged from inside the Ravens' 29-yard line, and only a kick return touchdown prevented the shutout. His passer rating was a woeful 7.1 for the game (compared to his Ravens counterpart Trent Dilfer's 80.9).

3. RICH GANNON

Oakland Raiders quarterback Rich Gannon was the NFL's Most Valuable Player of the 2002 season, having led in attempted and completed passes. He also finished in second with a 97.3 quarterback rating, but none of that magic showed up in Super Bowl XXXVII against the Tampa Bay Buccaneers. Gannon threw more touchdowns for his opponents (three interceptions returned) than for his own team, who got to the end zone only twice. It was an easy 48–21 blowout.

4. CRAIG MORTON

Craig Morton was one of three quarterbacks to lead two franchises to the Super Bowl, although it's hard to say which team had more reason to be disappointed with his championship performance. With the Dallas Cowboys in Super Bowl V, Morton's three interceptions sealed a loss against the Baltimore Colts. Seven years later in Super Bowl XII with the Denver Broncos, Morton tossed four interceptions against his former team, Dallas. His combined Super Bowl stats are 16 for 41 passing for 166 yards, one touchdown, seven interceptions and a measly rating of 20.0.

5. JIM KELLY

Jim Kelly stands out from the other quarterbacks on this list because he still made it to the Pro Football Hall of Fame, despite his Super Bowl failings. He managed to guide the Buffalo Bills to four consecutive Super Bowl appearances from 1991 to 1994, although all of them were losses. Kelly was far from his best on the big stage. He had led the NFL in touchdown percentage for two straight years but failed to throw a touchdown pass in three of four appearances in the big show. In the one game where Kelly managed two touchdown passes against the Washington Redskins, he also threw four interceptions. Overall, Kelly's losing Super Bowl resume will be more memorable than his regular-season successes.

BIGGEST SUPER BOWL BLUNDERS

★ ★ ★

Dallas Cowboys tight end Jackie Smith is on the ground after he dropped a pass in the end zone during Super Bowl XIII.

Every once in a while, an athlete will make a horrible mistake that can cost his team the win, or even cost the athlete his job. Those are the kinds of plays that follow athletes around for the rest of their careers. Here are five of the biggest blunders in Super Bowl history.

1. CARROLL'S CLUELESS CALL

Many would say Super Bowl XLIX's blunder belongs not to quarterback Russell Wilson of the Seattle Seahawks, but rather to head coach Pete Carroll or offensive coordinator Darrell Bevell. Seattle was trailing by four points in the fourth quarter and had the ball at the New England Patriots' 1-yard line with 26 seconds left on the clock. The sensible play would have been a handoff to running back Marshawn Lynch, but the call was a pass to low-level receiver Ricardo Lockette. Patriots rookie defensive back Malcolm Butler, however, ended up making one of the most critical interceptions in Super Bowl history. The coaching staff bore the brunt of the criticism, but Wilson took his share as well. The most dramatic blunder in Super Bowl history preserved a 28–24 win for New England and robbed the Seahawks of back-to-back titles.

2. KASAY'S ERRANT KICK

The Carolina Panthers' John Kasay is known for one of the most stunningly critical errors in Super Bowl history. It was Super Bowl XXXVIII and the Panthers had just scored a touchdown to tie the New England Patriots 29–29 with just over a minute to play in regulation. Understanding the need to put Tom Brady and the Patriots' offense on a long field, Kasay whiffed the kickoff out of bounds, giving New England the ball at their own 40-yard line. A few plays later, Patriots kicker Adam Vinatieri made the second Super Bowl–winning kick of his career, and Kasay was left with the loss on his shoulders.

3. SMITH'S DROP

The Pittsburgh Steelers led the Dallas Cowboys 21–14 early in the second half of Super Bowl XIII when the Cowboys marched down the field in pursuit of the tying score. Facing third down deep in Steelers territory, quarterback Roger Staubach found tight end Jackie Smith alone in the end zone. Smith attempted a very makeable sliding catch, but he bobbled the ball and it fell incomplete. Dallas settled for a field goal and Smith's drop became infamous, as the Cowboys suffered an eventual 35–31 loss.

4. WARNER'S TERRIBLE TOSS

Kurt Warner, quarterback of the Arizona Cardinals during Super Bowl XLIII, had his highest passer rating of three Super Bowl appearances against the Pittsburgh Steelers, completing 31 passes for 377 yards and three touchdowns. But it was the one Super Bowl pass Warner threw to the opposition that proved to be the Cardinals' undoing. Trailing Pittsburgh by a score of 10–7, the Cardinals had the ball on the Steelers' 1-yard line with 18 seconds to play in the first half when Warner tried to find receiver Anquan Boldin in the end zone. Instead, he found Steelers linebacker James Harrison, who somehow rumbled all the way down the field for a touchdown. The Steelers ended up winning 27–23.

5. YEPREMIAN'S YIPS

It's one of the most indelible images in Super Bowl memory: a picture of futility from the only team in NFL history to complete an undefeated season. When Miami Dolphins kicker Garo Yepremian lined up for a field goal that would have given his team a 17–0 lead over the Washington Redskins, he never imagined his next move would become infamous. Yepremian's kick was blocked, and the ball bounded back to him. Instead of just pouncing on it to kill the play, the former professional soccer player made a vain attempt to throw the ball. His attempt slipped through his hands, bounced away from him, and ended up in the hands of Washington's Mike Bass, who returned it for a touchdown. Much to Yepremian's relief, the Dolphins held on to win 14–7.

Garo Yepremian, seconds before his fateful throw, after his blocked field goal bounced back toward him.

MOST MEMORABLE SUPER BOWL DRIVES

★ ★ ★

The New Orleans Saints recover an on-side kick during the third quarter of Super Bowl XLIV to start their second-half comeback.

Some moments are still talked about years after they're over — times when the game was on the line and a team managed to pull out the win or fall just short. Here are five of the most memorable Super Bowl drives in history.

1. JOE'S 92-YARD MARCH

San Francisco 49ers quarterback Joe Montana had the touch of a surgeon in the fading minutes of the fourth quarter of Super Bowl XXIII. He completed seven of eight passes for 86 of the 92 yards that San Francisco needed to defeat the Cincinnati Bengals. He then passed the winning touchdown to receiver John Taylor. After the game, some of the 49ers were still laughing over what had happened during the final drive. It turned out Montana, who had a knack for remaining calm under pressure, had pointed to the stands and asked, "Isn't that John Candy?"

2. VINATIERI CAPS IT

From the New England Patriots' 17-yard line with no time-outs left during Super Bowl XXXVI, second-year quarterback Tom Brady hit on five of seven passes. One was to Troy Brown for a 23-yard gain to put the Patriots in game-winning position. Adam Vinatieri kicked a 48-yard field goal to seal a 20–17 win over the St. Louis Rams. It was the first time in Super Bowl history that a game was settled by a last-play score. It was also New England's first Super Bowl victory.

Adam Vinatieri kicks a game-winning 48-yard field goal for a 20–17 victory over the St. Louis Rams in Super Bow XXXVI.

3. THE CHIEFS KILL THE CLOCK, WIN THE GAME

Part of the art of a winning drive is knowing how to make sure there's not enough time for the other team to rally with a tying or go-ahead score. There were five minutes and 15 seconds remaining in the fourth quarter of a 35–25 game when the Kansas City Chiefs took over the ball on their own 25-yard-line and got set to drive against the Philadelphia Eagles defense. What followed was a work of art — 12 plays, 66 yards, eight runs and four pass plays of which Patrick Mahomes completed three. Harrison Butker's 27-yard field goal made it 38–35 for the Chiefs. And as it sailed between the uprights, the clock showed 8 seconds, snuffing-out any chance the Eagles had of rallying a comeback at Super Bowl LVII.

4. IT STARTED WITH AN ON-SIDE KICK

With his New Orleans Saints trailing the Indianapolis Colts 10–6 at halftime during Super Bowl XLIV, head coach Sean Payton needed something to jump-start his players. The call was to open the third quarter with a risky on-side kick in the hopes of generating a quick strike. Rookie punter Thomas Morstead delivered the short kick, and after players from both sides piled on top of one another, the officials indicated the Saints had possession. New Orleans' quarterback Drew Brees then marched his team to the end zone with 51 yards passing to put the Saints back in it. Defensive back Tracy Porter's fourth-quarter interception sealed the deal on the Saints' first Super Bowl win.

5. DYSON DIES SHORT

The St. Louis Rams were ahead 23–16, but Tennessee Titans quarterback Steve McNair wasn't about to go away quietly. He dashed and passed his way from his own 12-yard line to the Rams' 10-yard line. Receiver Kevin Dyson caught two passes for 23 yards to set up the big finish with six seconds left in the game. On the final play, McNair went back to Dyson, who was running a slant route through the middle of the field. Rams linebacker Mike Jones saw Dyson make the catch and moved to tackle him. As Jones wrapped up Dyson's legs, the Tennessee receiver reached out with the football but failed to cross the goal line. The play was given a telling tagline: "One yard short."

Buffalo's Scott Norwood seconds before missing a 47-yard field goal that would have represented the winning points in Super Bowl XXV.

MOST MEMORABLE SUPER BOWL FIELD GOALS

★ ★ ★

Often put in a position to win the game for his team, the field-goal kicker has a lot of pressure on his shoulders. When a crucial kick is attempted, the game virtually stops in anticipation of whether the ball will sail through the uprights or agonizingly miss. Through the uprights and he's a hero. A miss and his career might as well be over. Here are the five most memorable field goals in Super Bowl history.

1. VINATIERI'S GOOD FOR TWO

The only thing better than kicking a last-second field goal to win a Super Bowl is to kick two last-second field goals to win two Super Bowls. Such is the success of Adam Vinatieri. His first dramatic game-winner was on the last play of Super Bowl XXXVI against the St. Louis Rams, when he made a 48-yard field goal to give the New England Patriots their first-ever Super Bowl. Two years later, during Super Bowl XXXVIII, virtually the same thing happened — Vinatieri kicked a 41-yard field goal to seal the victory over the Carolina Panthers.

2. STENERUD'S BIG BOOTS

In Super Bowl IV, Jan Stenerud announced the Kansas City Chiefs' winning intentions by booming a first-quarter 48-yard field goal against the Minnesota Vikings. Stenerud was good on all three of his field goals, giving Kansas City a 9–0 lead en route to a 23–7 outcome. The Norwegian-born Stenerud was among the first place-kickers to use a soccer-style approach to the ball rather than hit it straight on. As proof of his importance to the Chiefs, he is one of only four kickers in the Pro Football Hall of Fame.

3. O'BRIEN FINALLY NAILS IT

It was one kick in one game, but Jim O'Brien sure picked the right time to nail it. The Baltimore Colts' backup receiver proved to be more valuable as their kicker, earning him a starting role in Super Bowl V. In what ended up as a poorly played championship game, with the Colts and Dallas Cowboys trading fumbles and interceptions, the two teams were tied 13–13 with six seconds left. O'Brien, who had completed only three of eight field goals until that point in the playoffs, lined up for a 32-yard kick. It was no surprise, then, that after the ball sailed through the uprights, he jumped up and down in jubilation. It turned out to be the one shining moment in O'Brien's NFL career.

4. NORWOOD IS WIDE RIGHT

Any discussion about memorable Super Bowl field goals inevitably mentions Scott Norwood, the kicker for the Buffalo Bills whose game-winning field goal attempt went wide right. It was Super Bowl XXV and Buffalo's first appearance in a championship game. Down 20–19 against the New York Giants, the Bills managed to get Norwood to the 47-yard line so he could win them the game. But Norwood lost his chance to be remembered as a hero, and his infamous kick plagued the Bills, who went to four consecutive Super Bowls only to come up empty handed.

5. YEPREMIAN'S BOTCHED BOOT

Garo Yepremian's flub in Super Bowl VII was as much slapstick as it was near disastrous. He lined up for a 42-yard field goal that would have given his Miami Dolphins a 17–0 advantage late in the fourth quarter over the Washington Redskins. The kick, however, was blocked. Yepremian chased down the bouncing ball, caught it, and attempted to throw it. The ball fell comically out of Yepremian's hand during the throw, bounced off his head and was intercepted by Washington's Mike Bass, who returned it for a touchdown. The Dolphins hung on for a 14–7 victory despite Yepremian's poorly timed case of the yips.

"Mean" Joe Greene of the Pittsburgh Steelers during the 1972 season.

MOST MEMORABLE SUPER BOWL COMMERCIALS

★ ★ ★

Forget about Joe Namath getting prepped for a shave by Farrah Fawcett (1973), or even Cindy Crawford in shorts slugging back Pepsi from a new can in 1992. These are the five most memorable Super Bowl TV commercials.

1. APPLE'S *NINETEEN EIGHTY-FOUR*

In 1984, Apple computers paid tribute to George Orwell's futuristic novel *Nineteen Eighty-Four*. Men in drab prison-like uniforms march toward a screen where "Big Brother" is speaking. A single female athlete runs toward the screen and throws a hammer, destroying the image. A light shines through and a voice says, "On January 24th, Apple will introduce Macintosh. And you'll see why 1984 won't be like '1984.'" The ad cost $900,000 and was directed by Ridley Scott, who had completed *Alien* and *Blade Runner* before taking on 1984, the commercial. Scott's offering proved to be so visually stunning and thought provoking that in 2007 it was voted the best Super Bowl spot in the game's 40 years by several media outlets, and *TV Guide* called it the greatest TV commercial of all-time.

2. SNICKERS AND BETTY WHITE

Snickers' 2010 commercial kicked off their "You're not *you* when you're hungry" campaign. Actress Betty White is playing football in the park with a bunch of guys and gets flattened in a mud puddle after going for a pass. She's told she's playing like Betty White, which prompts her to say, "That's not what your girlfriend said." After a bite of Snickers, "Mike" returns to normal and doesn't play like Betty White anymore. However 89-year-old actor Abe Vigoda is now at quarterback and gets sacked. Snickers did a similar ad with Willem Dafoe as Marilyn Monroe in 2016.

3. MEAN JOE'S SOFTER SIDE

In a 1979 commercial, a young fan offers Mean Joe Greene a Coke. The Pittsburgh Steelers' defensive lineman takes it, downs it, and then tosses his game-worn jersey to the kid and says, "Hey kid, catch." The ad was so well received, it was redone in other countries with other athletes. Greene later commented, "I have been told over the years that it was a pivotal point in bringing Black athletes to the national forum . . . and if that's so, I think that's a good thing."

4. ALEXA LOST HER VOICE

Super Bowl commercials featuring celebrities are usually part of the annual mix, and that was the case with the most popular Super Bowl ad of Super Bowl LII between the New England Patriots and Philadelphia Eagles. In the ad, the popular virtual assistant Alexa loses her voice and isn't able to perform her duties. Jeff Bezos, the Amazon CEO and one of the wealthiest people on earth, demands to be reassured by his staff that they have a solution. That's when the comedy begins. Among those who try in vain to fill-in for Alexa's voice are Gordon Ramsay, Rebel Wilson, Cardi B and Sir Anthony Hopkins. Alexa returns, presumably virtually, to reclaim her job in the final scene.

5. THE SHUFFLE WAS FINE IN 1985

In 2010, Boost Mobile decided to redo the Chicago Bears' Super Bowl Shuffle from 1985, which was a terrible idea. The original featured the vocal styling of William "the Refrigerator" Perry, quarterback Jim McMahon, running back Walter Payton, receiver Willie Gault and many others, and it came out just before the Bears clobbered the New England Patriots 46–10 in Super Bowl XX. The iconic video was nominated for a Grammy Award and even repackaged for its 20th anniversary and sold for a cause — more than $300,000 was donated to Chicago families in need of help. As for the 2010 version, it was awkward, not funny and in need of a Snickers bar.

The Boss belts out his hits on February 1, 2009, at Super Bowl XLIII.

MOST MEMORABLE SUPER BOWL HALFTIME SHOWS

★ ★ ★

From its humble beginnings when university marching bands played and cheerleaders cheered, the Super Bowl's halftime show has risen to starry heights. Now there are big-name entertainers wowing fans and shocking crowds, making for some unforgettable moments.

1. MALFUNCTION

The most memorable Super Bowl halftime show of all time can be summed up in two words: wardrobe malfunction. There was something off the wall about the 2004 show right from the start, mostly because its musical cast was very eclectic. Included in the mix were Jessica Simpson, P. Diddy, Nelly and Kid Rock. The two biggest names were Justin Timberlake and Janet Jackson, who teamed up to perform Timberlake's "Rock Your Body." At the end of the song, Timberlake reached over and ripped off a piece of Jackson's outfit, exposing her right breast (and nipple cover) before the cameras moved away. This was met with a huge outcry over whether it was done on purpose or by accident. Jackson and her handlers said it was a "wardrobe malfunction," which quickly became a popular catch phrase. The halftime show now airs with a five-second broadcast delay to protect viewers from further "malfunctions."

2. M.J.'S ROSE BOWL

Moving from one Jackson to another, Michael Jackson took to the Super Bowl stage in 1993 at Pasadena's Rose Bowl. There were no other artists, just Michael, who did five songs including "Jam" and "Heal the World." This was very much a strategic move by the NFL, who wanted to highlight the best acts available. Jackson's performance opened the door for the likes of Diana Ross, U2, Paul McCartney and The Who. They came, they played, and the TV viewership for the Super Bowl went higher and higher. Conveniently the revenues did too.

3. THE BOSS

Bruce Springsteen got the Michael Jackson treatment at the 2009 Super Bowl in Tampa, when he and the E Street Band got to play the entire show on their own. The show was nominated for four Emmys, including the award for Outstanding Special Class Live-Action Entertainment Program. It was the first time a performer had been nominated, upping the prestige value of the Super Bowl halftime show.

4. BAD BUNNY, GOOD SHOW

As the first Super Bowl halftime entertainer to sing and rap entirely in Spanish, the artist also known as Benito Antonio Martínez Ocasio waved the Puerto Rican flag in an elaborate 13-minute show laced with acknowledgments to the history of his island country and its culture. It was a planned follow-up to his comments made a week earlier after winning a Grammy Award for Album of the Year. "Before I say thanks to God, I want to say ICE out. We are not savage, we are not animals, we are not aliens, we are humans and we are Americans," Ocasio said when accepting the award. The rebuke was aimed at the Trump administration's heavy-handed immigration practices. With guest appearances by Lady Gaga and Ricky Martin, Bad Bunny had a viewership of 128.2 million. That made it the fourth most-watched halftime show in Super Bowl history

5. DETROIT ROCK CITY

The Rolling Stones were another solo act when they did the 2006 Super Bowl at Detroit's Ford Field. They turned in a three-song set that included their huge hits "Start Me Up," "Rough Justice" and "[I Can't Get No] Satisfaction." Still rattled by the Janet Jackson clothing incident, the NFL turned off Mick Jagger's microphone for words deemed too offensive. The recently implemented five-second delay ensured the NFL was in complete control of things, which must have given them great satisfaction.

MOST FREQUENT SUPER BOWL CITIES

★ ★ ★

A crowd of nearly 80,000 fills Miami's Orange Bowl for Super Bowl XIII on January 21, 1979.

Back when the idea for an AFL–NFL title game first surfaced in the mid-1960s, no one could have anticipated what the Super Bowl would become. Companies spend millions on commercial spots, and cities swoon at the chance to host the game. Here are the five most frequent Super Bowl hosts.

1. NEW ORLEANS

New Orleans has hosted 11 Super Bowls, including five of the first 15. Three took place outdoors at the now defunct Tulane Stadium, and two were held indoors at the Louisiana Superdome (now Caesars Superdome). It's the perfect Super Bowl city — a mild climate and everything within walking distance. And of course the party never stops. Plus, unlike most Super Bowl sites where the teams stay many miles out of town away from the fans and hoopla, the lack of high-end hotel space outside of New Orleans means Super Bowl participants stay right in the middle of the football atmosphere.

2. MIAMI

The state of Florida takes the cake when it comes to hosting Super Bowls. Miami co-leads with 11, including five of the first 13 championship games. Those took place at the Orange Bowl (demolished in 2008), the last being played in January of 1979. By the 1980s, however, a stadium that opened in 1937 could no longer compete with modern venues bidding for the Super Bowl, and Miami went nine years without. The game returned in 1989 at Joe Robbie Stadium (now Hard Rock Stadium), the first of six games played in a facility that has operated under nine different names. A $350-million renovation job launched in 2015 addressed the NFL's demand for a canopy over the stadium, after a steady drizzle fell during Super Bowl XLIV.

3. LOS ANGELES

Los Angeles hosted the very first Super Bowl game, known officially then as the AFL–NFL World Championship Game. While hosting rights are now handed out years in advance, Los Angeles wasn't awarded the initial game until six weeks before kickoff. The Los Angeles area has played host to seven other Super Bowls, including five at the Rose Bowl in Pasadena between 1977 and 1993. The departure of both the Raiders and the Rams to Oakland and St. Louis, respectively, cut L.A. out of the Super Bowl rotation after 1993. The game returned to Los Angeles for the first time in 29 years in February 2022, when the newly-built SoFi Stadium played host to the Cincinnati Bengals and the Los Angeles Rams, who became the second team ever — and the second team in two years — to play the big game in their home stadium.

4. TAMPA BAY

The central Florida city of Tampa Bay has played host to five Super Bowls: two at Tampa Stadium and three at the newer Raymond James Stadium. Two of those games stand out because of the larger world context in which they were staged. The 1991 Super Bowl was held 11 days after the start of Operation Desert Storm during the Gulf War. The 2009 game took place after the crash of the U.S. real estate market and became known as the Recession Bowl. None of the big automakers bought television advertisements, Playboy canceled its customary party and about 200 fewer journalists covered the game. In February 2021, the Tampa Bay Buccaneers became the first team to play a Super Bowl game in their home stadium.

Chiefs and Eagles fans arrive at Caesars Superdome for Super Bowl LIX on February 9, 2025, in New Orleans.

5. PHOENIX

The Phoenix area has hosted four Super Bowl games, the first at the Sun Devil Stadium in January 1996, in Tempe, just east of the city. The three most recent have been played in Glendale at the State Farm Stadium. Phoenix's most recent Super Bowl was hosted in February 2023 between the Philadelphia Eagles and Kansas City Chiefs. The Phoenix area provides a less-than-ideal Super Bowl setting, thanks to its massive geographical sprawl and the fact that the stadium is located 17 miles from downtown.

Snow and ice outside of AT&T Stadium in Arlington, Texas, in the lead up to Super Bowl XLV.

SUPER BOWL ONE-HIT WONDERS

★ ★ ★

The rotation of Super Bowl cities used to be simple: if you were Miami, New Orleans or somewhere in Southern California, you could host the game. And if you weren't . . . better luck next year. That, however, began to change as the NFL came to appreciate the economic impact of hosting a Super Bowl, and how awarding the game to a city could serve as leverage to secure public funds for a new stadium. So here are the one-hit wonders among hosts of the first 60 Super Bowls.

1. JACKSONVILLE

When sub-zero Minnesota hosted Super Bowl XXVI in 1992, the actual football game took place indoors. Players were probably wishing they had the same option for Super Bowl XXXIX in Jacksonville, Florida, where the weather was cool and wet. Accommodations were sprawled around Northern Florida, forcing fans to book rooms on docked cruise ships. Mostly due to the lack of suitable hotel space and appropriate infrastructure, it doesn't look like Jacksonville will host another Super Bowl anytime soon.

2. ARLINGTON

Giving the Super Bowl to Arlington, Texas, sounded like a great idea for the weather alone. Unfortunately, a freak ice storm hit the Dallas area on Monday night of Super Bowl week, followed by frigid wind-chill temperatures, making travel around the city nearly impossible. For part of Super Bowl week, it was colder in Dallas than in Wisconsin. Sadly, up until the day before the game, most of downtown Dallas was a ghost town as locals stayed home and visitors tried to stay warm.

3. INDIANAPOLIS

The week of Super Bowl XLVI will be remembered for unseasonably warm Indianapolis weather and the uncertainty of Peyton Manning's future with the Colts. On top of that, limited hotel space forced some visitors to stay in small rural towns, far from Indianapolis, and a labor dispute threatened the championship game. Fortunately all was resolved well before the Super Bowl took place, but Indianapolis has never hosted again.

4. EAST RUTHERFORD

While northern cities had hosted championship games before, Super Bowl XLVIII was the first to be held outdoors in a cold climate. East Rutherford, New Jersey, had bone-chilling temperatures during Super Bowl week, making many wonder how the actual game would go off. However, by kickoff, the temperature had warmed to 49 degrees, making it feel more like a *Monday Night Football* game in mid-November. Shortly after the game wet snow began to fall, turning the New York/New Jersey area into a mess by morning. Flights were canceled and delayed as Super Bowl travelers scrambled to get home amid the slop and snow.

A view of the outdoor MetLife Stadium prior to Super Bowl XLVIII, hosted in East Rutherford, New Jersey.

TEAMS SHUT OUT OF THE SUPER BOWL

★ ★ ★

The Detroit Lions offense huddles during the NFC Championship on January 28, 2024, which they lost to the San Francisco 49ers. As of printing, the Detroit Lions have yet to reach a Super Bowl.

The NFL is an incredibly competitive league, making it difficult to get all the way to the Super Bowl. But with the salary cap and free agency, it makes sense that nearly every NFL franchise should have had its turn on pro football's biggest stage. However, there are four cities with franchises whose Super Bowl number has never come up, and they are still waiting for their chance at the Vince Lombardi Trophy.

Cleveland Browns fans mock the franchise with signs about playoff football during the club's miserable 2014 season.

1. CLEVELAND BROWNS

The Cleveland Browns actually have eight NFL championships to their credit, although all were won before the Super Bowl era began. Things got tougher for the Browns once the AFL and NFL decided to play each other for all the marbles, and the Cleveland team has never made it past the conference championship. The franchise moved to Baltimore following the 1995 season and, in a weird twist, was reborn as an expansion team, retaining the name, colors and history of the original club, in 1999. The Browns have made it into the playoffs only three times since that time and have just a single playoff win since being reborn. The Browns-turned-Ravens, meanwhile, have gone on to win two Super Bowls in Baltimore.

2. DETROIT LIONS

The Detroit Lions have made the NFL playoffs just 14 times during the Super Bowl era, meaning most times they don't even get a ticket to the dance. Twice they've come just one win away from the Super Bowl by reaching the NFC Championship Game, and both those chances ended in losses. The first was a 41–10 drubbing at the hands of the Washington Redskins at the end of the 1992 season. The other was pure heartbreak, as the Lions blew a 24–7 halftime lead over the San Francisco 49ers in the NFC Championship Game played at the end of the 2023 season. The result set-off a fierce debate about Detroit head coach Dan Campbell twice passing-up field goal opportunities during the second half for what turned out to be failed fourth-down gambles.

3. HOUSTON OILERS/TEXANS

A charter member of the AFL, the Houston Oilers won championships in their first two seasons. Houston had a chance to play in Super Bowl II but got thumped by the Oakland Raiders in the conference championship game. Eleven years later, the Oilers ran headlong into the Pittsburgh Steelers, losing to them in both the 1978 and 1979 conference finals. The era of quarterback Warren Moon saw the Oilers reach the playoffs for seven consecutive seasons, but they never made it to the conference championship game. In 1997, the Oilers relocated to Nashville, Tennessee, and two years later were in the Super Bowl as the Tennessee Titans, losing to the St. Louis Rams. By 2002, Houston was back in the NFL as the Texans but has not appeared in a Super Bowl or conference championship game.

4. JACKSONVILLE JAGUARS

When the NFL expanded to Jacksonville and Carolina in 1995, both teams were playing in their respective conference championship games the very next season. The Jaguars lost to the New England Patriots in the conference championship at the end of the 1996 season but were back in the playoffs in each of the next three seasons, reaching the conference championship for the second time at the conclusion of the 1999 season. There they lost to the Tennessee Titans after a franchise-best regular-season record of 14-2. The Jaguars have never reached that period of greatness again, having reached the playoffs five times since then.

5. THE NO-LUCK CLUB

Eight teams have gone to the Super Bowl but never won it: Carolina Panthers, Los Angeles (formerly San Diego) Chargers, Arizona Cardinals, Buffalo Bills, Minnesota Vikings, Atlanta Falcons, Cincinnati Bengals and Tennessee Titans.

15
HOMES

Philadelphia Eagles quarterback Jalen Hurts talks with Kansas City Chiefs quarterback Patrick Mahomes after Super Bowl LIX. Hurts and Mahomes were the first Black quarterbacks to face each other at the Super Bowl when their teams went head-to-head two years earlier at Super Bowl LVII.

SUPER BOWL
SUMMARY

SUPER BOWL I — Jan. 15, 1967
Memorial Coliseum, Los Angeles, California
Green Bay Packers 35
Kansas City Chiefs 10
MVP: Bart Starr, QB, Green Bay

SUPER BOWL II — Jan. 14, 1968
Orange Bowl, Miami, Florida
Green Bay Packers 33
Oakland Raiders 14
MVP: Bart Starr, QB, Green Bay

SUPER BOWL III — Jan. 12, 1969
Orange Bowl, Miami, Florida
New York Jets 16
Baltimore Colts 7
MVP: Joe Namath, QB, New York

SUPER BOWL IV — Jan. 11, 1970
Tulane Stadium, New Orleans, Louisiana
Kansas City Chiefs 23
Minnesota Vikings 7
MVP: Len Dawson, QB, Kansas City

SUPER BOWL V — Jan. 17, 1971
Orange Bowl, Miami, Florida
Baltimore Colts 16
Dallas Cowboys 13
MVP: Chuck Howley, LB, Dallas

SUPER BOWL VI — Jan. 16, 1972
Tulane Stadium, New Orleans, Louisiana
Dallas Cowboys 24
Miami Dolphins 3
MVP: Roger Staubach, QB, Dallas

SUPER BOWL VII — Jan. 14, 1973
Memorial Coliseum, Los Angeles, California
Miami Dolphins 14
Washington Redskins 7
MVP: Jake Scott, S, Miami

SUPER BOWL VIII — Jan. 13, 1974
Rice Stadium, Houston, Texas
Miami Dolphins 24
Minnesota Vikings 7
MVP: Larry Csonka, RB, Miami

SUPER BOWL IX — Jan. 12, 1975
Tulane Stadium, New Orleans, Louisiana
Pittsburgh Steelers 16
Minnesota Vikings 6
MVP: Franco Harris, RB, Pittsburgh

SUPER BOWL X — Jan. 18, 1976
Orange Bowl, Miami, Florida
Pittsburgh Steelers 21
Dallas Cowboys 17
MVP: Lynn Swann, WR, Pittsburgh

SUPER BOWL XI — Jan. 9, 1977
Rose Bowl, Pasadena, California
Oakland Raiders 32
Minnesota Vikings 14
MVP: Fred Biletnikoff, WR, Oakland

SUPER BOWL XII — Jan. 15, 1978
Superdome, New Orleans, Louisiana
Dallas Cowboys 27
Denver Broncos 10
co-MVP: Harvey Martin, DE, Dallas
Randy White, DT, Dallas

SUPER BOWL XIII — Jan. 21, 1979
Orange Bowl, Miami, Florida
Pittsburgh Steelers 35
Dallas Cowboys 31
MVP: Terry Bradshaw, QB, Pittsburgh

SUPER BOWL XIV — Jan. 20, 1980
Rose Bowl, Pasadena, California
Pittsburgh Steelers 31
Los Angeles Rams 19
MVP: Terry Bradshaw, QB, Pittsburgh

SUPER BOWL XV — Jan. 25, 1981
Louisiana Superdome,
New Orleans, Louisiana
Oakland Raiders 27
Philadelphia Eagles 10
MVP: Jim Plunkett, QB, Oakland

SUPER BOWL XVI — Jan. 24, 1982
Pontiac Silverdome, Pontiac, Michigan
San Francisco 49ers 26
Cincinnati Bengals 21
MVP: Joe Montana, QB, San Francisco

SUPER BOWL XVII — Jan. 30, 1983
Rose Bowl, Pasadena, California
Washington Redskins 27
Miami Dolphins 17
MVP: John Riggins, RB, Washington

SUPER BOWL XVIII — Jan. 22, 1984
Tampa Stadium, Tampa, Florida
Los Angeles Raiders 38
Washington Redskins 9
MVP: Marcus Allen, RB, Los Angeles

SUPER BOWL XIX — Jan. 20, 1985
Stanford Stadium, Stanford, California
San Francisco 49ers 38
Miami Dolphins 16
MVP: Joe Montana, QB, San Francisco

SUPER BOWL XX — Jan. 26, 1986
Louisiana Superdome,
New Orleans, Louisiana
Chicago Bears 46
New England Patriots 10
MVP: Richard Dent, DE, Chicago

SUPER BOWL XXI — Jan. 25, 1987
Rose Bowl, Pasadena, California
New York Giants 39
Denver Broncos 20
MVP: Phil Simms, QB, New York

SUPER BOWL XXII — Jan. 31, 1988
Jack Murphy Stadium, San Diego, California
Washington Redskins 42
Denver Broncos 10
MVP: Doug Williams, QB, Washington

SUPER BOWL XXIII — Jan. 22, 1989
Joe Robbie Stadium, Miami, Florida
San Francisco 49ers 20
Cincinnati Bengals 16
MVP: Jerry Rice, WR, San Francisco

SUPER BOWL XXIV — Jan. 28, 1990
Louisiana Superdome,
New Orleans, Louisiana
San Francisco 49ers 55
Denver Broncos 10
MVP: Joe Montana, QB, San Francisco

SUPER BOWL XXV — Jan. 27, 1991
Tampa Stadium, Tampa, Florida
New York Giants 20
Buffalo Bills 19
MVP: Ottis Anderson, RB, New York

SUPER BOWL XXVI — Jan. 26, 1992
Metrodome, Minneapolis, Minnesota
Washington Redskins 37
Buffalo Bills 24
MVP: Mark Rypien, QB, Washington

SUPER BOWL XXVII — Jan. 31, 1993
Rose Bowl, Pasadena, California
Dallas Cowboys 52
Buffalo Bills 17
MVP: Troy Aikman, QB, Dallas

SUPER BOWL XXVIII — Jan. 30, 1994
Georgia Dome, Atlanta, Georgia
Dallas Cowboys 30
Buffalo Bills 13
MVP: Emmitt Smith, RB, Dallas

SUPER BOWL XXIX — Jan. 29, 1995
Joe Robbie Stadium, Miami, Florida
San Francisco 49ers 49
San Diego Chargers 26
MVP: Steve Young, QB, San Francisco

SUPER BOWL XXX — Jan. 28, 1996
Sun Devil Stadium, Tempe, Arizona
Dallas Cowboys 27
Pittsburgh Steelers 17
MVP: Larry Brown, CB, Dallas

SUPER BOWL XXXI — Jan. 26, 1997
Louisiana Superdome,
New Orleans, Louisiana
Green Bay Packers 35
New England Patriots 21
MVP: Desmond Howard, KR/PR, Green Bay

SUPER BOWL XXXII — Jan. 25, 1998
Qualcomm Stadium, San Diego, California
Denver Broncos 31
Green Bay Packers 24
MVP: Terrell Davis, RB, Denver

SUPER BOWL XXXIII — Jan. 31, 1999
Pro Player Stadium, Miami, Florida
Denver Broncos 34
Atlanta Falcons 19
MVP: John Elway, QB, Denver

SUPER BOWL XXXIV — Jan. 30, 2000
Georgia Dome, Atlanta, Georgia
St. Louis Rams 23
Tennessee Titans 16
MVP: Kurt Warner, QB, St. Louis

SUPER BOWL XXXV — Jan. 28, 2001
Raymond James Stadium, Tampa, Florida
Baltimore Ravens 34
New York Giants 7
MVP: Ray Lewis, LB, Baltimore

SUPER BOWL XXXVI — Feb. 3, 2002
Louisiana Superdome,
New Orleans, Louisiana
New England Patriots 20
St. Louis Rams 17
MVP: Tom Brady, QB, New England

SUPER BOWL XXXVII — Jan. 26, 2003
Qualcomm Stadium, San Diego, California
Tampa Bay Buccaneers 48
Oakland Raiders 21
MVP: Dexter Jackson, FS, Tampa Bay

SUPER BOWL XXXVIII — Feb. 1, 2004
Reliant Stadium, Houston, Texas
New England Patriots 32
Carolina Panthers 29
MVP: Tom Brady, QB, New England

SUPER BOWL XXXIX — Feb. 6, 2005
Alltel Stadium, Jacksonville, Florida
New England Patriots 24
Philadelphia Eagles 21
MVP: Deion Branch, WR, New England

SUPER BOWL XL — Feb. 5, 2006
Ford Field, Detroit, Michigan
Pittsburgh Steelers 21
Seattle Seahawks 10
MVP: Hines Ward, WR, Pittsburgh

SUPER BOWL XLI — Feb. 4, 2007
Dolphin Stadium, Miami, Florida
Indianapolis Colts 29
Chicago Bears 17
MVP: Peyton Manning, QB, Indianapolis

SUPER BOWL XLII — Feb. 3, 2008
University of Phoenix Stadium,
Glendale, Arizona
New York Giants 17
New England Patriots 14
MVP: Eli Manning, QB, New York

SUPER BOWL XLIII — Feb. 1, 2009
Raymond James Stadium, Tampa, Florida
Pittsburgh Steelers 27
Arizona Cardinals 23
MVP: Santonio Holmes, WR, Pittsburgh

SUPER BOWL XLIV — Feb. 7, 2010
Miami Gardens, Miami, Florida
New Orleans Saints 31
Indianapolis Colts 17
MVP: Drew Brees, QB, New Orleans

SUPER BOWL XLV — Feb. 6, 2011
Cowboys Stadium, Arlington, Texas
Green Bay Packers 31
Pittsburgh Steelers 25
MVP: Aaron Rodgers, QB, Green Bay

SUPER BOWL XLVI — Feb. 5, 2012
Lucas Oil Stadium, Indianapolis, Indiana
New York Giants 21
New England Patriots 17
MVP: Eli Manning, QB, New York

SUPER BOWL XLVII — Feb. 3, 2013
Mercedes-Benz Superdome,
New Orleans, Louisiana
Baltimore Ravens 34
San Francisco 49ers 31
MVP: Joe Flacco, QB, Baltimore

SUPER BOWL XLVIII — Feb. 2, 2014
MetLife Stadium, East Rutherford, New Jersey
Seattle Seahawks 43
Denver Broncos 8
MVP: Malcolm Smith, LB, Seattle

SUPER BOWL XLIX — Feb. 1, 2015
University of Phoenix Stadium,
Glendale, Arizona
New England Patriots 28
Seattle Seahawks 24
MVP: Tom Brady, QB, New England

SUPER BOWL 50 — Feb. 7, 2016
Levis' Stadium, Santa Clara, California
Denver Broncos 24
Carolina Panthers 10
MVP: Von Miller, LB, Denver

SUPER BOWL LI — Feb. 5, 2017
NRG Stadium, Houston, Texas
New England Patriots 34
Atlanta Falcons 28
MVP: Tom Brady, QB, New England

SUPER BOWL LII — Feb. 4, 2018
U.S. Bank Stadium, Minneapolis, Minnesota
Philadelphia Eagles 41
New England Patriots 38
MVP: Nick Foles, QB, Philadelphia

SUPER BOWL LIII — Feb. 3, 2019
Mercedes-Benz Stadium, Atlanta, Georgia
New England Patriots 13
Los Angeles Rams 3
MVP: Julian Edelman, WR, New England

SUPER BOWL LIV — Feb. 2, 2020
Hard Rock Stadium, Miami Gardens, Florida
Kansas City Chiefs 31
San Francisco 49ers 20
MVP: Patrick Mahomes, QB, Kansas City

SUPER BOWL LV — Feb. 13, 2021
Raymond James Stadium,
Tampa Bay, Florida
Tampa Bay Buccaneers 31
Kansas City Chiefs 9
MVP: Tom Brady, QB, Tampa Bay

SUPER BOWL LVI — Feb. 7, 2022
SoFi Stadium, Inglewood, California
Los Angeles Rams 23
Cincinnati Bengals 20
MVP: Cooper Kupp, WR, Los Angeles

SUPER BOWL LVII — Feb. 12, 2023
State Farm Stadium, Glendale, Arizona
Kansas City Chiefs 38
Philadelphia Eagles 35
MVP: Patrick Mahomes, QB, Kansas City

SUPER BOWL LVIII — Feb. 11, 2024
Allegiant Stadium, Las Vegas, Nevada
Kansas City Chiefs 25
San Francisco 49ers 22
MVP: Patrick Mahomes, QB, Kansas City

SUPER BOWL LIX — Feb. 9, 2025
Caesars Superdome, New Orleans,
Louisiana
Philadelphia Eagles 40
Kansas City Chiefs 22
MVP: Jalen Hurts, QB, Philadelphia

SUPER BOWL LX — Feb. 8, 2026
Levi's Stadium, Santa Clara, California
Seattle Seahawks 29
New England Patriots 13
MVP: Kenneth Walker III, RB, Seattle

INDEX

A
Adderley, Herb 16, 25
Aikman, Troy 66–68, 73, 141
Alford, Robert 115
Allen, George 25
Allen, Marcus 48–49, 149
Alworth, Lance 25
Amendola, Danny 115, 145, 155
Anderson, C.J. 113
Anderson, Dick 27
Anderson, Donny 16
Anderson, Ken 44
Anderson, Ottis 62–63
Arbanas, Fred 151
Arnsparger, Bill 27
Atkinson, George 34
Awuzie, Chidobe 124

B
Baldwin, Doug 111
Banaszak, Pete 34
Banks, Carl 55
Barkley, Saquon 131
Bass, Mike 27, 161, 165
Bavaro, Mark 55
Beebe, Don 65–67
Belichick, Bill 85, 89, 104, 115, 118, 153
Bengtson, Phil 16
Benson, Tom 101
Bettis, Jerome 93
Bevell, Darrell 161
Biletnikoff, Fred 34–35
Billick, Brian 83
Bledsoe, Drew 75, 85
Bleier, Rocky 39
Blount, Mel 30, 33
Boldin, Anquan 151, 161
Bostic, Jeff 65
Bradbury, James 127
Bradshaw, Ahmad 105
Bradshaw, Terry 30–31, 33, 39–41, 137, 145, 147
Brady, Tom 11, 75, 85, 89–91, 96, 104, 108, 111, 114–115, 116, 118, 123, 134–135, 137, 143, 145, 153, 155, 161, 163
Branch, Cliff 43
Branch, Deion 88–89, 91, 145
Bratkowski, Zeke 17
Brees, Drew 101, 151, 163
Brown, A.J. 127
Brown, Charlie 47
Brown, Larry 30, 73
Brown, Terry 30
Brown, Troy 163
Brown, Willie 16, 34
Bruce, Isaac 81
Bulaich, Norm 22–23
Bulger, Marc 98
Bullitt, Melvin 101
Buoniconti, Nick 27
Burress, Plaxico 147
Burrow, Joe 124
Burton, Trey 116–117
Butker, Harrison 127, 163
Butkus, Dick 157
Butler, LeRoy 76–77
Butler, Malcolm 110–111, 151, 161
Byner, Earnest 64

C
Callahan, Bill 86
Campbell, Dan 175
Campbell, Earl 157
Carroll, Pete 153, 155, 161
Carson, Harry 55
Casper, Dave 34
Cefalo, Jimmy 47
Chatham, Matt 89
Clark, Dwight 44–45
Clark, Gary 56
Clayton, Mark 51
Clement, Corey 116
Coleman, Andre 70
Coleman, Tevin 115
Collins, Kerry 82, 143, 159
Collins, Nick 103
Conners, Dan 16
Cooper, Earl 44
Coughlin, Tom 104
Cowher, Bill 73, 93, 145
Crabtree, Michael 107
Craig, Roger 50–51, 59
Csonka, Larry 25, 28–29, 141, 149

D
Darnold, Sam 133
Davidson, Ben 16–17
Davis, Al 34, 43, 86
Davis, Clarence 34–35
Davis, Terrell 76–77, 79, 141
Dawson, Donald 21
Dawson, Len 20–21
DeJean, Cooper 150–151
Delhomme, Jake 89
Dent, Richard 52–53
Dickerson, Chuck 65
Didier, Clint 56
Dilfer, Trent 82–83, 159
Dillon, Corey 145
Ditka, Mike 25, 52
Dorsett, Tony 36–37
Dowler, Boyd 15
Duerson, Dave 52
Dungy, Tony 95
DuPree, Billy Joe 39
Dyson, Kevin 80–81, 163

E
Eason, Tony 52, 143, 159
Edelman, Julian 111, 114–115, 118–119, 139, 145, 147
Edwards, Glen 33
Edwards, T.J. 126
Eller, Carl 21
Elway, John 55, 56, 60–61, 76–77

F
Faulk, Marshall 81
Favre, Brett 74–75, 101, 103
Fernandez, Manny 27
Ferragamo, Vince 40
Fitzgerald, Larry 98, 154–155
Flacco, Joe 107, 147
Foles, Nick 116–117
Foreman, Chuck 28, 34
Foster, DeShaun 89
Frank, John 59
Frazier, Leslie 52
Freeman, Antonio 75
Freeman, Devonta 115
Freeney, Dwight 95
Fuqua, John 31

G
Gannon, Rich 86, 158–159
Garoppolo, Jimmy 121
Garrett, Mike 20–21
Gault, Willie 52, 167
Gbaja-Biamila, Kabeer 75
George, Eddie 81
Gibbs, Joe 47–48, 55, 149
Gilliam, John 28
Goff, Jared 118
Goodell, Roger 131
Gordon, Darrien 79, 87
Gore, Frank 107
Gostkowski, Stephen 118
Green, Cornell 25
Green, Scott 131
Green, Trent 81
Greene, "Mean" Joe 30, 166–167
Griese, Bob 25–29
Griffin, Archie 45
Grogan, Steve 52–53, 159
Gronkowski, Rob 116, 118, 122–123, 139, 145, 155
Grossman, Rex 95
Gruden, Jon 86

H
Haden, Pat 40
Hampton, Dan "Danimal" 52–53
Harbaugh, Jack 107
Harbaugh, Jim 107
Harbaugh, John 107
Harper, Nick 95
Harris, Cliff 25
Harris, Franco 30–32, 38–40, 140–141
Harrison, James 98–99, 151, 161
Harrison, Rodney 96–97
Hasselbeck, Matt 82, 93
Hayden, Kelvin 94–95
Hegman, Mike 39
Henderson, Thomas "Hollywood" 39
Hester, Devin 95
Higgins, Tee 124
Hill, Jerry 18
Hill, Kenny 54
Hill, Tony 39
Hill, Tyreek 121
Hinton, Eddie 22
Hogan, Chris 155
Holmes, Santonio 99, 146–147
Holub, E.J. 14
Hooper, Austin 115
Hostetler, Jeff 63
Howard, Desmond 75
Howard, Percy 33
Howell, John 87
Howley, Chuck 22–23, 25, 63, 155
Hurts, Jalen 127, 131, 155

I
Irsay, Jim 104
Irvin, Michael 73, 141

J
Jackson, Bo 48
Jackson, Dexter 87
Jacoby, Joe 65
Jaworski, Ron 43
Jefferson, Roy 25
Jennings, Greg 103
Jennings, Jauan 128
Jennings, Stanford 59
Jensen, Derrick 48
Johnson, Butch 36, 39

Johnson, Dan 51
Johnson, Jimmy 66
Johnson, Pete 44
Johnson, Vance 54
Johnston, Daryl 72
Jones, Brent 60
Jones, Chris 145
Jones, Deacon 157
Jones, Jacoby 107, 147
Jones, James 102
Jones, Jerry 69
Jones, Mike 81, 163
Jordan, Lee Roy 25

K
Kaepernick, Colin 107
Kapp, Joe 21
Karlis, Rich 56
Kasay, John 89, 161
Kelce, Travis 121, 126–127, 128, 138–139, 145
Kelly, Jim 62–63, 65–66, 69, 159
Kiick, Jim 25, 27–29
Kraft, Robert 75
Kramer, Jerry 15
Kroenke, Stan 40
Kubiak, Gary 113
Kupp, Cooper 124–125

L
Lachey, Jim 65
Lambert, Jack 30, 153
Lamonica, Daryle 16
Landry, Tom 25, 33, 36
Larsen, Gary 21
Lett, Leon 66–67
Levy, Marv 65
Lewis, Jamal 83
Lewis, Ray 82–83, 107, 143
Lilly, Bob 22, 25
Lockette, Ricardo 110, 161
Lombardi, Vince 15–17, 75, 153
Loomis, Mickey 101
Lott, Ronnie 51, 59
Luck, Andrew 104
Lynch, John 86
Lynch, Marshawn 109, 111, 155, 161
Lytle, Rob 36

M
Mackey, John 22
Madden, John 85
Mahomes, Patrick 121, 127, 128–129, 131, 137, 143, 145, 151, 163
Manning, Eli 96–98, 104–105, 147
Manning, Peyton 85, 95, 101, 104, 108–109, 111–112, 151, 173
Marino, Dan 51, 156–157
Marshall, Jim 21
Marshall, Leonard 55
Martin, Harvey 37
Martin, Rod 43
Matthews, Clay 103
Maye, Drake 133
McCaffrey, Christian 128–129
McCaffrey, Ed 78
McCarthy, J.J. 133
McConkey, Phil 55
McGee, Max 15–16
McIntyre, Guy 136
McMahon, Jim 52, 167
McNabb, Donovan 90
McNair, Steve 81, 163
McNoll, Milt 45
McVay, Sean 124
Mendenhall, Rashard 103
Metzelaars, Pete 65
Michel, Sonny 118–119
Millen, Matt 48
Miller, Von 113, 143
Monroe, Carl 51
Montana, Joe 5, 44–45, 51, 58–61, 70–71, 82, 111, 136–137, 145, 153, 157, 163
Moon, Warren 175
Moore, Lance 100
Morrall, Earl 18, 22
Morris, Bam 73
Morris, Mercury 28–29
Morstead, Thomas 163
Morton, Craig 22, 36, 159
Moss, Randy 145
Muhammad, Muhsin 89
Myers, Jason 132

N
Namath, Joe 18–19, 167
Nattiel, Ricky 56
Newhouse, Robert 36
Newton, Cam 112–113, 143, 159
Noll, Chuck 33, 40, 115, 145, 153
Norwood, Scott 62, 65, 164–165

O
O'Brien, Jim 22, 165
O'Donnell, Neil 73
Orr, Jimmy 18
Osweiler, Brock 112
Owens, Terrell 90

P
Page, Alan 21
Parcells, Bill 55, 75
Parilli, Babe 15
Parker, Willie 93, 148–149
Pastorini, Dan 43
Payton, Sean 101, 163
Payton, Walter 52–53, 82, 141, 167
Pederson, Doug 116
Perry, William "the Refrigerator" 52, 167
Pitta, Dennis 107
Pitts, Elijah 151
Plunkett, Jim 43
Porter, Tracy 101, 151, 163
Prior, Mike 76–77
Purdy, Brock 128

R
Randle El, Antwaan 92–93
Reeves, Dan 60, 79
Reich, Frank 66
Reid, Andy 121, 145, 153
Renfro, Mel 22, 25
Rice, Jerry 51, 59–61, 70–71, 82, 86, 91, 139, 144, 153
Rice, Ray 107
Richards, Golden 36
Riggins, John 47–48, 149
Robbins, Barret 86
Robinson, Eugene 79
Rodgers, Aaron 75, 103
Roethlisberger, Ben 93, 98–99, 103, 143, 145, 146
Rooney, Art 33
Rooney, Dan 33
Ross, Dan 44, 91
Rote, Tobin 15
Rozelle, Pete 21, 43, 52
Rutledge, Jeff 55
Ryan, Buddy 52, 143
Ryan, Matt 115
Rypien, Mark 65

S
Sanders, Barry 157
Sanders, Deion "Neon" 73
Sanders, Ricky 56
Scott, Herbert 37
Scott, Jake 27
Seifert, George 44
Shanahan, Mike 79
Sharpe, Shannon 76
Shell, Art 95
Shula, Don 25, 29
Simms, Phil 55
Singletary, Mike 52–53
Siposs, Arryn 127
Sirianni, Nick 127
Smith, Antowain 89
Smith, DeVonta 127
Smith, Emmitt 66, 68–69, 73, 82, 141
Smith, Jackie 160–161
Smith, Lovie 95
Smith, Malcolm 109
Smith, Rod 79
Smith, Timmy 56, 141, 149
Snell, Matt 18–19
Spagnuolo, Steve 96
Squirek, Jack 48
Stabler, Ken 34–35
Stafford, Matthew 124–125
Stallworth, John 39–40
Starr, Bart 15, 17
Staubach, Roger 25, 33, 36, 39, 145, 161
Stenerud, Jan 165
Strahan, Michael 96
Stram, Hank 21
Stubbs, Danny 61
Sumner, Charlie 48
Swann, Lynn 30, 33, 39–40, 139, 147, 153
Swift, Doug 24
Switzer, Barry 73

T
Tagliabue, Paul 101
Tarkenton, Fran 28, 30–31, 34
Tasker, Steve 66
Tatum, Jack 31, 34
Taylor, Ike 102
Taylor, Jim 14
Taylor, John 59, 163
Taylor, Lawrence 55
Taylor, Otis 21
Taylor, Zac 124
Theismann, Joe 46–48
Thigpen, Yancey 73
Thomas, Demaryius 108
Thomas, Duane 22, 24–25
Thomas, J.T. 41
Thomas, Thurman 62–63, 65, 69, 141
Tomlin, Mike 98, 145
Toney, Kadarius 127
Treu, Adam 86
Tuck, Justin 96
Tuggle, Jessie 79
Turner, Jim 18
Twilley, Howard 27
Tyler, Wendell 40–41
Tyree, David 9, 96–97, 105, 147

INDEX

U

Umenyiora, Osi 96
Unitas, Johnny 18, 22–23
Upshaw, Gene 42

V

Valdes-Scantling, Marquez 128
Van Brocklin, Norm 18
Vermeil, Dick 81
Vinatieri, Adam 84–85, 89, 161, 163, 165
Vitt, Joe 101

W

Walker III, Kenneth 12–13, 133
Walsh, Bill 44, 59, 152–153
Ward, Hines 92–93
Warfield, Paul 25
Warner, Kurt 81, 98, 137, 155, 161
Washington, James 69
Washington, Mark 33
Watkins, Sammy 121
Watters, Ricky 70
Wayne, Reggie 151
Webster, Mike 33, 153
Webster, Nate 87
Weese, Norris 36
Welch, Herb 54
Wesley, Dante 88
White, James 115
White, Randy 37, 39
White, Reggie 75
Williams, Brian 76–77
Williams, Damien 120–121
Williams, Doug 56–57
Williams, Gregg 101
Wilson, Otis 52, 159
Wilson, Ralph 62
Wilson, Russell 108, 111, 161
Wilson, Stanley 59
Wolfe, Derek 142
Wood, Willie 15, 151
Woodley, David 47
Woodson, Charles 103
Worthy, Xavier 130
Wyche, Sam 59

Y

Yepremian, Garo 27–28, 161, 165
Young, Steve 59, 70–71, 137

Z

Zuerlein, Greg 118

SUPER BOWLS

Super Bowl I: Green Bay Packers vs Kansas City Chiefs 14–15, 25, 151
Super Bowl II: Green Bay Packers vs Oakland Raiders 16–17, 25, 103, 153, 175
Super Bowl III: New York Jets vs Baltimore Colts 18–19, 22
Super Bowl IV: Kansas City Chiefs vs Minnesota Vikings 20–22, 145, 165
Super Bowl V: Baltimore Colts vs Dallas Cowboys 22–23, 28, 153, 155, 159, 165
Super Bowl VI: Dallas Cowboys vs Miami Dolphins 24–25, 27–28
Super Bowl VII: Miami Dolphins vs Washington Redskins 26–28, 141, 165
Super Bowl VIII: Miami Dolphins vs Minnesota Vikings 28–29, 141, 149
Super Bowl IX: Pittsburgh Steelers vs Minnesota Vikings 28, 30–31, 33, 139, 141, 143
Super Bowl X: Pittsburgh Steelers vs Dallas Cowboys 28, 32–33, 39, 139, 147
Super Bowl XI: Oakland Raiders vs Minnesota Vikings 28, 34–35
Super Bowl XII: Dallas Cowboys vs Denver Broncos 28, 36–37, 159
Super Bowl XIII: Pittsburgh Steelers vs Dallas Cowboys 38–39, 140, 160–161, 170
Super Bowl XIV: Pittsburgh Steelers vs Los Angeles Rams 40–41, 51, 81, 137
Super Bowl XV: Oakland Raiders vs Philadelphia Eagles 42–43
Super Bowl XVI: San Francisco 49ers vs Cincinnati Bengals 44–45, 59, 153
Super Bowl XVII: Washington Redskins vs Miami Dolphins 46–47, 149
Super Bowl XVIII: Los Angeles Raiders vs Washington Redskins 48–49, 149
Super Bowl XIX: San Francisco 49ers vs Miami Dolphins 50–51, 152–153, 157
Super Bowl XX: Chicago Bears vs New England Patriots 52–53, 159, 167
Super Bowl XXI: New York Giants vs Denver Broncos 54–55
Super Bowl XXII: Washington Redskins vs Denver Broncos 56–57, 149
Super Bowl XXIII: San Francisco 49ers vs Cincinnati Bengals 58–59, 139, 153, 163
Super Bowl XXIV: San Francisco 49ers vs Denver Broncos 60–61, 136–137
Super Bowl XXV: New York Giants vs Buffalo Bills 62–63, 164–165
Super Bowl XXVI: Washington Redskins vs Buffalo Bills 64–65
Super Bowl XXVII: Dallas Cowboys vs Buffalo Bills 66–67, 141
Super Bowl XXVIII: Dallas Cowboys vs Buffalo Bills 68–69, 141
Super Bowl XXIX: San Francisco 49ers vs San Diego Chargers 70–71
Super Bowl XXX: Dallas Cowboys vs Pittsburgh Steelers 72–73
Super Bowl XXXI: Green Bay Packers vs New England Patriots 74–75
Super Bowl XXXII: Denver Broncos vs Green Bay Packers 76–77, 141
Super Bowl XXXIII: Denver Broncos vs Atlanta Falcons 78–79
Super Bowl XXXIV: St. Louis Rams vs Tennessee Titans 40, 80–81, 137
Super Bowl XXXV: Baltimore Ravens vs New York Giants 82–83, 143
Super Bowl XXXVI: New England Patriots vs St. Louis Rams 51, 84–85, 163, 165
Super Bowl XXXVII: Tampa Bay Buccaneers vs Oakland Raiders 86–87, 158–159
Super Bowl XXXVIII: New England Patriots vs Carolina Panthers 88–89, 161, 165
Super Bowl XXXIX: New England Patriots vs Philadelphia Eagles 90–91, 145, 153, 173
Super Bowl XL: Pittsburgh Steelers vs Seattle Seahawks 92–93, 148–149
Super Bowl XLI: Indianapolis Colts vs Chicago Bears 94–95
Super Bowl XLII: New York Giants vs New England Patriots 9, 96–97, 147
Super Bowl XLIII: Pittsburgh Steelers vs Arizona Cardinals 98–99, 137, 147, 151, 154–155, 161, 168
Super Bowl XLIV: New Orleans Saints vs Indianapolis Colts 100–101, 150–151, 162–163, 171
Super Bowl XLV: Green Bay Packers vs Pittsburgh Steelers 102–103, 172–173
Super Bowl XLVI: New York Giants vs New England Patriots 104–105, 139, 173
Super Bowl XLVII: Baltimore Ravens vs San Francisco 49ers 39, 106–107, 145, 147
Super Bowl XLVIII: Seattle Seahawks vs Denver Broncos 108–109, 173
Super Bowl XLIX: New England Patriots vs Seattle Seahawks 110–111, 139, 151,155, 161
Super Bowl 50: Denver Broncos vs Carolina Panthers 112–113, 142–143
Super Bowl LI: New England Patriots vs Atlanta Falcons 114–115, 137, 147
Super Bowl LII: Philadelphia Eagles vs New England Patriots 116–117, 155, 167
Super Bowl LIII: New England Patriots vs Los Angeles Rams 118–119
Super Bowl LIV: Kansas City Chiefs vs San Francisco 49ers 120–121
Super Bowl LV: Tampa Bay Buccaneers vs Kansas City Chiefs 122–123, 138–139
Super Bowl LVI: Los Angeles Rams vs Cincinnati Bengals 123, 124–125
Super Bowl LVII: Kansas City Chiefs vs Philadelphia Eagles 126–127, 155, 163
Super Bowl LVIII: Kansas City Chiefs vs San Francisco 49ers 128–129, 139
Super Bowl LIX: Philadelphia Eagles vs Kansas City Chiefs 130–131, 143, 145, 151, 155, 171
Super Bowl LX: Seattle Seahawks vs New England Patriots 2–3, 7, 12–13, 132–133

Kicker Adam Vinatieri of the New England Patriots celebrates after kicking the winning 41-yard field goal with 00:04 left at Super Bowl XXXVIII. The New England Patriots won 32–29 against the Carolina Panthers.

ALSO FROM FIREFLY BOOKS

FOOTBALL'S GREATEST STARS
THE 114 BEST PLAYERS OF ALL TIME

4TH EDITION

by George Johnson and Allan Maki

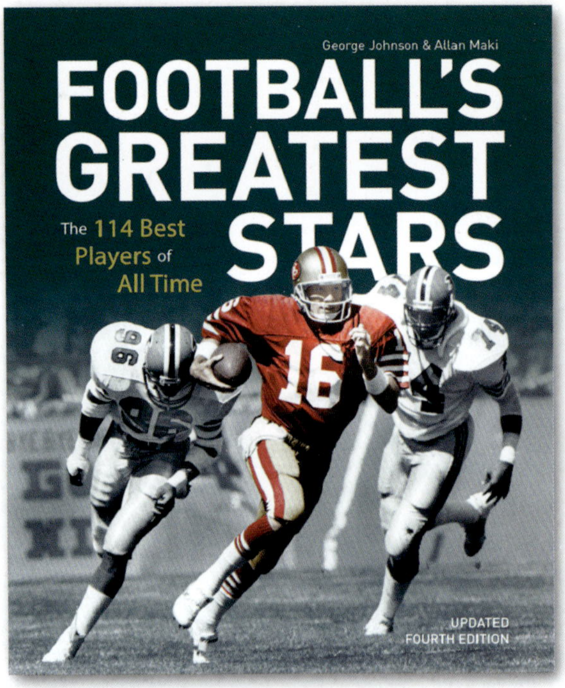

Over a century after the formation of the American Professional Football Conference, the precursor to the National Football League, pro football continues to excite and captivate millions of fans across the globe. At the core of the NFL is its legendary players — the incredible athletes who have thrown, caught, run, tackled and kicked their way into the annals of sports history. *Football's Greatest Stars* presents the best of the best in pro football. From the pioneers, to the current stars, to the all-time legends that occupy the Hall of Fame in Canton, Ohio, they're all here.

This fully updated and expanded edition picks up where *NFL Heroes* left off, featuring 114 riveting stories and over 130 photos of the game's best. *Football's Greatest Stars* is a must-read for any fan of America's favorite sport.

NFL MOMENTS
125 ICONS AND STORIES THAT DEFINE THE NFL

by Allan Maki and George Johnson

Over its 105-year history, the NFL has built franchise empires, created icons, integrated itself into the fabric of American culture and captivated fans around the globe. At the core of the NFL are the stories of the iconic players and leaders who drove the NFL from a modest association struggling to define itself against the college game to the most exciting and profitable sports league in the world. Through snappy prose and historic photographs, *NFL Moments* catalogs the league's larger-than-life characters and their defining stories.

AVAILABLE WHERE BOOKS ARE SOLD.